DOING ACTION RESEARCH
IN YOUR OWN ORGANIZATION

DOING ACTION RESEARCH
IN YOUR OWN ORGANIZATION

David Coghlan
& Teresa Brannick

 4th Edition

Los Angeles | London | New Delhi
Singapore | Washington DC

Los Angeles | London | New Delhi
Singapore | Washington DC

SAGE Publications Ltd
1 Oliver's Yard
55 City Road
London EC1Y 1SP

SAGE Publications Inc.
2455 Teller Road
Thousand Oaks, California 91320

SAGE Publications India Pvt Ltd
B 1/I 1 Mohan Cooperative Industrial Area
Mathura Road
New Delhi 110 044

SAGE Publications Asia-Pacific Pte Ltd
3 Church Street
#10-04 Samsung Hub
Singapore 049483

Editor: Jai Seaman
Assistant editor: Lily Mehrbod
Production editor: Ian Antcliff
Copyeditor: Lisa Cordaro
Proofreader: Jennifer Hinchliffe
Marketing manager: Ben Griffin-Sherwood
Cover design: Francis Kenney
Typeset by: C&M Digitals (P) Ltd, Chennai, India
Printed in Great Britain by Henry Ling Limited at
The Dorset Press, Dorchester, DT1 1HD

Library of Congress Control Number: 2013945863

British Library Cataloguing in Publication data

A catalogue record for this book is available from
the British Library

MIX
Paper from
responsible sources
FSC
www.fsc.org   FSC™ C013985

ISBN 978-1-4462-7256-5
ISBN 978-1-4462-7257-2 (pbk)

Contents

Materials on the Companion Website

 Video content including introductions to chapters and top tips from David Coghlan.

 Further Reading introducing you to a range of resources including journal articles, encyclopedia entries and book chapters. Download author recommended further reading for free.

Visit **www.uk.sagepub.com/coghlanandbrannick** to access material

Video resources

David Coghlan introduces the fourth edition and discusses what it means to do insider action research in your own organisation.

David Coghlan introduces **Chapter 1** and discusses first, second and third person practice

Q&A: David Coghlan explains the action research cycle

Q&A: David Coghlan explains the action research spiral

Q&A: David Coghlan explains how multiple action research cycles operate concurrently using the image of a clock

Q&A: David Coghlan explains the metacycle of action

David Coghlan introduces **Chapter 2** and explores issues such as authenticity and working in the present tense

David Coghlan introduces **Chapter 3** and explains the foundations and philosophy of action research

David Coghlan introduces **Chapter 4** and looks at designing an action research proposal

David Coghlan introduces **Chapter 5** and looks at how to achieve change through your action research project

David Coghlan introduces **Chapter 6** and explores the complex dynamics of working with individuals and groups within your own organization

David Coghlan introduces **Chapter 7** and discusses organisational frameworks

David Coghlan introduces **Chapter 8** and investigates how to assess your research focus whilst researching your own organization

David Coghlan introduces **Chapter 9** and describes the challenges of close engagement in insider action research

David Coghlan introduces **Chapter 10** and discusses politics and ethics in insider action research

David Coghlan introduces **Chapter 11** and provides some tips on how to write up your research

Teresa Brannick (1950–2012)

Teresa Brannick died on 12 December 2012. For many years she had fought the creeping oppression of multiple sclerosis with a steely will and determination. She had a razor sharp mind and was a versatile academic. Her particular interest and skill was in the area of methodology, and she was adept at helping postgraduate students and colleagues confront and work through often complex methodological problems. She was a person of great fun and generosity, and bore her long illness with enormous dignity and courage, never complaining about her pain and discomfort, although they were evident to all. To her, everything scholarly, joyous and life-affirming was important. She was my friend and my colleague for more than thirty-seven years, as is her heartbroken husband, Eddie McIlduff, also my friend and co-author. It is with a heavy heart that I write this edition without her.

David Coghlan

About the Authors

David Coghlan is Adjunct Professor of Business Studies at the School of Business, Trinity College, Dublin, Ireland, and is a Fellow Emeritus of the College. He specializes in organization development and action research, and participates actively in both communities internationally. He has published more than 80 articles and book chapters. His recent co-authored books include *Collaborative Strategic Improvement through Network Action Learning* (Edward Elgar, 2011), *Organization Change and Strategy* (Routledge, 2006) and a co-edited volume (with Tony Dromgoole, Pat Joynt and Peter Sorensen) *Managers Learning in Action* (Routledge, 2004). He is co-editor (with Mary Brydon-Miller) of the *SAGE Encyclopedia of Action Research* (2014) and of the four-volume set, *Fundamentals of Organization Development* (SAGE, 2010). He is a member of the editorial advisory board of several journals, including *Action Research, Journal of Applied Behavioral Science, Action Learning: Research and Practice, Systemic Practice and Action Research* and *OD Practitioner*. Currently he is co-editing (with Rami Shani) a four-volume set, *Action Research in Business and Management* (SAGE, forthcoming 2015).

Teresa Brannick (1950–2012) was a lecturer in the business research programme at the Michael Smurfit Graduate School of Business at University College, Dublin, Ireland. Her undergraduate degree was in mathematics, her master's in sociology and her PhD in marketing research. She was a practising researcher for more than thirty years and published more than thirty research papers in such diverse fields as epidemiology, public policy, industrial relations and marketing. She was the editor-in-chief of *Irish Journal of Management* and a fellow of the Irish Academy of Management. She was co-editor of *Business Research Methods: Theories, Techniques and Sources* (Oak Tree Press, 1997).

Preface

The theory and the practice of insider action research have been afforded increasing attention since the publication of the first edition of this book in 2001. Indeed, any form of insider research has been viewed with suspicion (Brannick and Coghlan, 2007). In our view, the first edition of this book appeared to give voice to a practice that was struggling for legitimacy, and which hitherto had not been framed in a manner that facilitated its place in the action research literature. In the intervening years since 2001, further articulations of theory and accounts of practice have burgeoned through the second and third editions, the special issue of *Action Research* on insider action research (Coghlan and Holian, 2007), and an increasing number of published articles and book chapters, not to mention the number of dissertations in schools of education, healthcare, business and social work that have not found their way into published articles.

In his notion of 'innovation action research', Kaplan (1998) presents an action research cycle of: (a) observing and documenting practice; (b) teaching and speaking about it; (c) writing articles and books; (d) implementing the concept; and (e) moving to advanced implementation. After several years of observing and documenting practice, teaching and speaking about it, writing articles and books, thereby implementing the concept, we see this fourth edition as advanced implementation. The theory and practice of insider action research has advanced, and this fourth edition seeks to mark a further moment in innovation action research.

What is action research? As the name suggests, action research is an approach to research which aims at both taking action and creating knowledge or theory about that action as the action unfolds. The outcomes are both an action and a research outcome, unlike traditional research approaches which aim at creating knowledge only. The first dimension is that action research works through a cyclical process of consciously and deliberately: (a) assessing a situation which is calling for change; (b) planning to take action; (c) taking action; and (d) evaluating the action, leading to further cycles of planning and so on. The second dimension of action research is that it is collaborative, in that the members of the system that is being studied participate actively in the cyclical process. This contrasts with traditional research, where members are objects of the study. As Greenwood expresses it:

Action research is neither a method nor a technique; it is an approach to living in the world that includes the creation of areas for collaborative learning and the design, enactment and evaluation of liberating actions ... it combines action and research, reflection and action in an ongoing cycle of cogenerative knowledge. (2007: 131)

Action research is a generic term that covers many forms of action-oriented research, which may be confusing to any prospective researcher. At the same time, the array of approaches indicates diversity in theory and practice among action researchers, and provides a wide choice for potential action researchers as to what might be appropriate for their research.

We are all insiders of many systems – our families, communities and organizations – and the knowledge that we have of these systems is rich and complex. We act to shape the progress of these systems, for example, through parenting and through enacting professional and managerial roles. Doing research in and on one's own organization means that a member of an organization undertakes an explicit research role in addition to the normal functional role that they hold in the organization. The researcher then has to balance their organizational roles, which they usually hope will continue, with the additional demands of a role of inquiry and research. Insider action researchers need to be aware of how their roles influence how they view their world as well as how they are perceived by others, and to be able to make choices as to when to step into and out of each of the multiple roles that they hold.

There are many issues to be considered for those embarking on research in their own organization, or part thereof. From the perspective of individuals who are seeking to do the research in order to achieve academic certification, there are issues of gaining access and receiving permission, and building and maintaining support from peers and relevant sub-systems within the organization. There are issues of selecting a research question and area for study. In such a case, student-researchers, in effect, take on an additional role to their conventional organizational one: that of active agent of inquiry and change. This multiple role identity both complicates and focuses the research project. There are issues around how to attain some sense of objectivity and move beyond a personal perspective by testing assumptions and interpretations. There are the uses of appropriate frameworks for viewing and understanding the data. There are questions about how to write up such a research project, give feedback to one's superiors and peers, and disseminate the research to the wider community. Handling interpretations or outcomes that would be perceived negatively by the organization is a particularly sensitive issue. They also are likely to have access to external academic supervisors who advise and support them throughout their research project. However, not all insider action researchers are students; they may be internal consultants or managers, in which case there may not be a planned end point for carrying dual roles, or access to advice and support from key external 'critical friends' to help them sustain both doing the work and maintaining a career.

Who does action research in their own organization? A common context for such research is where an individual employee undertakes research as part of an academic programme in order to fulfil requirements for academic certification. In this instance the individual initiates the research agenda and attempts to negotiate a research project which will meet both their own and the organization's needs. This occurs in full-time and part-time programmes, at doctorate, master's, undergraduate and diploma levels, and in business, healthcare, government, education, social work and third-sector organizations. Some research projects may be integrally linked to inquiry into the processes of problem resolution; others may take a broader, more comprehensive and diagnostic perspective. At the same time, typically the selection of a research topic from one's own organization is attached to an expectation or contract that the research will make a useful contribution to the organization.

Action researchers have to deal with emergent processes not as distractions, but as central to the research process. The desire to be involved in or to lead radical change involves high hassle and high vulnerability, which requires a combination of self-reflection with vulnerability, realistic expectations, tolerance, humility, self-giving, self-containment and an ability to learn.

Insider action research is an exciting, demanding and invigorating prospect that contributes considerably to researchers' own learning, and contributes to the development of the systems in which we work and live and with which we have affiliations. It is also daunting, with a high potential for self-destruction, particularly if roles and politics are not managed well. So, what does it take to do insider research? Our learning from our own work and the work of those managers we supervise has enabled us to gain some insight into the attributes, competencies and methodological tools that support effective practice.

Readership

This book is addressed to the reader who is in this dual role of simultaneously holding an organizational functional role that is linked to a career path and ongoing membership of the organization, and a more temporary researcher role for the duration of the research project. While this may imply a distinction between research and ordinary life, we do not intend such a distinction. Our aim is to provide a book that is useful for those who select an action research role in their own organization for a temporary period, and for those in academic institutions who supervise such research.

There are many books that explore the theory and practice of action research (Greenwood and Levin, 2007; Reason and Bradbury, 2008; Shani et al., 2008; Coghlan with Brydon-Miller, 2014). We do not intend to retrace what is well presented in these works, particularly with regard to epistemological issues, the history of action research and detailed formats of research interventions. Indeed, we recommend that this book be used in conjunction with such works as Greenwood and Levin (2007), Reason and Bradbury (2008) and Shani et al. (2008). At the end of each chapter we provide a small number of recommended readings that are aimed to illuminate issues discussed in the chapters. There are also pointers to entries in *The SAGE Encyclopedia of Action Research* (Coghlan with Brydon-Miller, 2014). While the *Encyclopedia* contains a vast array of material on action research, these selected pointers are not intended to be exclusive. We encourage readers to peruse the *Encyclopedia* and follow up entries that interest or intrigue them.

Plan of the book

This edition is divided into three parts and follows a series of questions. We anticipate that these questions are indicative of the ones that you have at different stages of your project, and that they will guide your progress. Part I, Foundations, introduces and explores foundational material on action research. Chapter 1 begins from action and poses the question: 'How do you position your action research initiative?' Chapter 2 is built around the question: 'How do you know in action?' Chapter 3 is grounded in the questions: 'How do you understand what you are doing in your insider action research initiative?' and 'How do you understand how it fits into a rich research tradition?'

Part II, Implementation, deals with issues of putting your action research project into action. The question underpinning Chapter 4 is: 'How might you frame and select an action research project'? Chapter 5 answers the questions: 'How do you design your insider action research project?' and 'How do you implement it?' Chapter 6 explores the questions: 'How do you understand the complex interaction of individuals and teams in organizations and in your action research project?' and 'How do you work with individuals, with a team and across teams in your project?' Chapter 7 opens with the question: 'How do I use frameworks to make sense of what I am seeking to understand?', and explores the use of frameworks in sense-making.

Part III, Issues and Challenges in Researching Your Own Organization, deals with issues particular to doing action research in your own organization. Chapter 8 poses the questions: 'What are the implications of engaging in action research in your own organization?' and 'What are the particular dynamics accompanying insider action research that you need to understand and take into account?' It outlines four different forms that insider research can take, depending on the system's and your own explicit commitment to learning-in-action. Chapter 9 explores the questions: 'How do you build on the closeness that you have to the organization and maintain distance?' and 'How do you balance the potential dilemmas and tugs between your established organizational roles and your researcher role?' Chapter 10 poses the critical questions: 'How do I act ethically in a political environment? and 'How do I survive and thrive in a political environment?' Chapter 11 provides some direction on writing an action research dissertation and publishing. Finally, Chapter 12 draws the book to a close with some general advice about doing action research in your own organization.

David Coghlan
Teresa Brannick
Dublin, Ireland

Acknowledgements

We are grateful to those action research colleagues and friends who have provided valuable support, feedback, ideas and materials for the revision: Vivienne Brady, Mary Brydon-Miller, Mary Casey, Paul Coughlan, Rosalie Holian, Geralyn Hynes and Rami Shani. We thank specifically colleagues who have shared their work with us and gave us permission to reproduce material from their work: David Besancon, Bob Dick, Arthur Freedman, Eddie Grande, Lyle Yorks and Ortrun Zuber-Skerritt. David acknowledges Ed Schein as the mentor and friend who has taught him most about action research as 'humble inquiry'. Hopefully this book enables all of us to inquire humbly into the dynamics of our organizations, and to help them change and understand themselves.

We are very grateful for the feedback from the many groups who used the three previous editions in courses and seminars. We acknowledge the invaluable help and support of the SAGE editorial and production teams, especially Jai Seaman and Ian Antcliff.

Glossary

Actionable knowledge   Knowledge that is usable by practitioners and theoretically robust for scholars

Action learning   An approach to learning through engaging with a group of peers which provides reflective space, support and challenge to work through a problem

Action research   A family of related approaches that integrate theory and action with a goal of addressing important organizational, community and social issues together with those who experience them

Action science   Action research directed towards enabling learning by attending to how people interpret situations and act

Appreciative inquiry   Action research that builds on what is positive as a way of generating rich participation and knowledge

Authenticity   Being attentive to data, intelligent in understanding, reasonable in judging and responsible in taking action

Choice points   Points in an inquiry when choices present themselves and need to be addressed in a conscious and transparent manner

Clinical inquiry   Action research whereby trained helpers work as organizational clinicians to help organizations

Collaborative development action inquiry   Action research that focuses on how stages of ego development influence how we think and act

Collaborative management research   Managers and researchers engaging together in research and action in an organization

Content reflection   Reflecting on what is done or discussed

Cooperative inquiry   Action research involving a group approach where the participants as both co-researchers and co-subjects share an interest in the topic under inquiry

Cycles of action and reflection How action influences reflection, and reflection influences action

Double-loop learning The type of learning that emerges from questioning taken-for-granted assumptions

Epistemology The theory of knowledge

Extended epistemology Describing how in action research there are many ways of knowing that can be used

First-person practice Attending to one's own thinking, valuing, way of learning and behaving

General empirical method A method based on the recognizable and invariant process of human knowing

Inquiry Asking questions and seeking answers – often a less formal or threatening word than 'research'

Insider action research Conducting action research in the organization or community in which one is employed or a member

Interiority The process whereby we process different forms of knowing

Intervention Doing or saying something that alters the status quo

Journalling Keeping a live notebook that captures both the events of the project, and one's own thoughts and feelings about the events and one's own learning-in-action

Ladder of inference A technique for catching inferences and jumping to conclusions without testing the evidence

Learning history Presenting the history of the project in participants' own and often contradicting voices

Meta-cycle A cycle of action and reflection about the cycles of action and reflection

Meta-learning Learning about learning

Methodology The overarching theory of the methods used

Methods Techniques and tools for designing and implementing the research

Mode 2 research A philosophy of research that focuses on action and multidisciplinary teamworking

Ontology Basic belief system or worldview that underpins the whole research project

Organization development An approach to organizational change that is grounded in action research

Participatory action research   Action research that addresses issues of power and powerlessness

Positivism   Philosophy of science that is based on being a detached researcher

Premise reflection   Critiquing taken-for-granted assumptions and perspectives

Process reflection   Reflecting on how things are done

Quality   Meeting the requirements of good-quality action research

Reflexivity   Being attentive to and inquiring into the process as it unfolds

Second-person practice   Face-to-face working with individuals and/or teams or groups

Single-loop learning   The type of learning that emerges from solving everyday problems

Systems thinking   Seeing the whole rather than parts and understanding how elements are interrelated and interdependent

Tacit knowing   Knowing that is implicit and difficult to articulate

Territories of experience   The areas of intentions, planning, actions and outcomes that operate at individual, interpersonal and organizational levels

Third-person practice   Extending first- and second-person learning to an impersonal audience who were not directly involved in the project – this includes dissemination through publishing

1

Foundations

ONE
Introducing Action Research

 See www.uk.sagepub.com/coghlanandbrannick for a short introduction to the chapter from David Coghlan

We begin by focusing on the big picture of your insider action research initiative. As you are poised to embark on this venture, we pose the following questions for your consideration. Out of what experience of your organization are you wishing to change something? What is or has been going on that puzzles you, or what anomalies do you experience that you wish to address? What patterns of deliberate action may support this inquiry and provide the opportunity for insights? With whom will you work so that this initiative will be good for you, worthwhile for your organization and useful for others? In this chapter we present a brief introduction to action research, and then go straight into how it might be enacted. The theoretical discussion of action research and its tenets may be found in Chapter 3.

As a preliminary activity to focus your mind, take a sheet of paper and explore the following questions. Think of a project within your organization on which you are working. What is the context of this project? What is its purpose? What are your hoped-for outcomes? What puzzles or challenges you about it? What do you think needs to change? What obstacles do you anticipate? Where do you fit in, or what role do you have? With whom are you working on this project to complete it successfully? What do you think are the obstacles? What is the potential impact of this project on others? What would you need to do if you wanted to understand this project more deeply and thoroughly than if you were simply focusing on solving a problem, or completing it as a project? If you were invited to give a talk on your project to interested others who have not been directly involved, what might you want to say?

This preliminary activity provides an introductory sense of what action research involves. Now begin reading this chapter and those following it to broaden and deepen your understanding and application of action research in your own organization.

Inquiring in your own organization

As we begin our exploration of doing action research in your own organization, we lay out some foundations about organizations and about studying your own organization, whether action research or not (Costley et al., 2010).

First, we note that organizations are social constructions (Campbell, 2000): they are artefacts created by human beings to serve their ends. They follow processes that are shaped and affected by human purposes, and they do not exist independently of human minds and actions. They are systems of human action in which means and ends are guided by values and intended outcomes. They are, in effect, communities created by meaning with a rich tapestry of cultural rules, roles and interactions (Van Maanen, 1979). There is also the psychodynamic perspective, which understands organizations in terms of unconscious social defences (Hirschhorn, 1988). These perspectives on organizations have implications for rigorous inquiry, as empirical observation and logical reconstruction of organizational activities may not be sufficient to uncover the meanings, whether explicit or tacit, that organizational members hold and have held (Schein, 2010). The action research approach is founded on the notion that organizations may be understood experientially through processes of deliberate change.

Inquiring into your own organization presents challenges that mark it out from studying an organization as an outsider (Evered and Louis, 1981). Schon (2004) [1995] contrasts how researchers can view practice from the high ground, where they can study issues from a distance: for example, because they are not organizational members or because their data are based on pre-constructed surveys or interviews. Or they can be immersed in 'swampy lowlands' where problems are messy, confusing and incapable of a technical solution, because they are either organizational members whose actions influence the reality that they see, or they are outsiders who are contracted to influence what they see. He concludes that unimportant issues may be studied from the high ground according to predetermined standards and rigour, while the critically important ones, such as how to generate whatever changes in practice we wish to see, can be confronted only by being immersed in the 'swampy lowlands'.

Inquiry from the inside involves researchers as natives and actors, immersed in local situations generating contextually embedded knowledge which emerges from experience. Goffman (1959) adopts a dramatic approach and points to a distinction between the 'front region', where performance is public for the benefit of clients or customers, and the 'back region' or backstage, where public access is restricted. Actors can drop their public persona in the privacy of the backstage. Goffman's rich exploration of backstaging provides an important framing of knowing organizations from the inside. Being an insider provides access to the drama of the informal organization with all its paradoxes and problems, Schon's 'swampy lowlands', and what

Evered and Louis (1981) see as 'blooming, buzzing confusion'. Accordingly, we need a method for engaging in such insider inquiry. Evered and Louis (1981) refer to their mode of inquiry for acquiring insider knowledge as 'groping in the dark' into the hidden organizational realities around them, in many directions simultaneously as 'multisensory holistic immersion' and 'messy, iterative groping'.

A brief introduction to action research

In the words of Reason and Bradbury, 'action research is a participatory, democratic process concerned with developing practical knowing in the pursuit of worthwhile human purposes, grounded in a participatory worldview' (2008: 1). This working definition provides a flavour of the broad scope and intent of action research with the ultimate aim of 'the flourishing of individual persons and their communities'. Shani and Pasmore provide a more restricted definition:

> Action research may be defined as an emergent inquiry process in which applied behavioural science knowledge is integrated with existing organizational knowledge and applied to solve real organizational problems. It is simultaneously concerned with bringing about change in organizations, in developing self-help competencies in organizational members and adding to scientific knowledge. Finally, it is an evolving process that is undertaken in a spirit of collaboration and co-inquiry. (2010[1985]: 439)

Given the context of this book, where we expect readers to be working on action research projects in their own organizations, we are working more from Shani and Pasmore's definition than from Reason and Bradbury's.

Shani and Pasmore present a complete theory of the action research process in terms of four factors (Figure 1.1).

1. Context – these factors set the context of the action research project. Individual goals may differ and impact the direction of the project, while shared goals enhance collaboration. Organizational characteristics such as resources, history, formal and informal organizations and the degrees of congruence between them affect the readiness and capability for participating in action research. Environmental factors in the global and local economies provide the larger context in which action research takes place.

Figure 1.1 Complete Theory of Action Research

(Shani and Pasmore, 2010: 253)

2. Quality of relationships – the quality of relationship between members and researchers is paramount. Hence the relationships need to be managed through trust, concern for others, equality of influence, common language, and so on.
3. Quality of the action research process itself – this is grounded in a dual focus on both the inquiry process and the implementation process.
4. Outcomes – the dual outcomes of action research are some level of sustainability (human, social, economic, ecological) and the development of self-help and competencies out of the action and creation of new knowledge from the inquiry.

Several broad characteristics define action research:

• research *in* action, rather than research *about* action;
• a collaborative democratic partnership;
• a sequence of events and an approach to problem-solving.

We will discuss each in turn.

First, action research focuses on research *in* action, rather than research *about* action. The central idea is that action research uses a scientific approach to study the resolution of important social or organizational issues together with those who experience these issues directly. The goal is to make that action more effective while simultaneously building up a body of scientific knowledge. Action research works through a cyclical, four-step process of consciously and deliberately: (a) planning; (b) taking action; (c) evaluating the action; (d) leading to further planning, and so on.

Second, action research is a collaborative, democratic partnership. Members of the system that is being studied participate actively in the cyclical process outlined above. Such participation contrasts with traditional research, where members of the system are subjects or objects of the study. An important qualitative element of action research is how people participate in the choice of research focus, and how they engage in the processes of action and inquiry to co-generate knowledge.

Third, action research is both a sequence of events and an approach to change and to problem-solving. As a sequence of events, it comprises iterative cycles of gathering data collaboratively, jointly analysing the data, jointly planning action, taking joint action and evaluating jointly, leading to further joint data-gathering, and so on. As an approach to change and to problem-solving, it is an application of a rigorous method of fact-finding and experimentation to practical issues requiring action solutions, involving the collaboration and cooperation of the action researchers and members of the organizational system. The desired outcomes of the action research approach are not just solutions to the practical issues, but also important learning from outcomes both intended and unintended, and a contribution to actionable knowledge: that is, knowledge that is useful for practitioners and robust for scholars.

Three audiences, voices or practices

An integrative approach to research incorporates three voices and audiences: first, second and third person (Reason and Torbert, 2001; Reason and Bradbury, 2008). Traditionally, research has focused on third person: researchers doing research on third persons and writing a report for other third persons. In a more complete vision of research as presented by action research and many other transformational inquiry approaches, authentic third-person research integrates first- and second-person voices. Typically, *first-person* research is characterized as a form of inquiry and practice that one does on one's own, and so addresses the individual's ability to foster an inquiring approach to their own life, to act out of awareness and purposefully. First-person research can take researchers 'upstream', where they may attend to and inquire into their basic assumptions, desires, intentions and philosophy of life. In addition, it can take them 'downstream', where they attend to and inquire into their behaviour, ways of relating and their action in the world. *Second-person* inquiry or practice addresses their ability to inquire into and work with others on issues of mutual concern, through face-to-face dialogue, conversation and joint action. Second-person practice poses an important challenge as to who is involved in the research, and how. As action research is integrally collaborative and democratic, the quality of second-person inquiry and action is paramount. *Third-person* inquiry or practice aims at creating communities of inquiry, involving people beyond the direct second-person action. Third person is impersonal and is actualized through dissemination by reporting, publishing and extrapolating from the concrete to the general. As Reason and Torbert (2001) point out, there are plenty of implicit examples of first-, second- and third-person inquiry, but what is required now is explicit integrating of all three persons with action and inquiry. The construct of first-, second- and third-person inquiry is a development of Reason and Marshall's popular notion of three audiences of research:

> All good research is for *me*, for *us*, and *for them*: it speaks to three audiences ... It is *for them* to the extent that it produces some kind of generalizable ideas and outcomes ... It is *for us* to the extent that it responds to concerns for our praxis, is relevant and timely ... [for] those who are struggling with problems in their field of action. It is *for me* to the extent that the process and outcomes respond directly to the individual researcher's being-in-the-world. (1987: 112–113)

In our view, second-person practice is primary. It is through working with others through collaborative processes of engaging in constructing the project, planning action, taking action, evaluating action and framing learning that individual (first person) learning takes place, and it is from that second and first experience and learning that actionable knowledge for a third person audience emerges.

The three approaches, first, second and third person, enacted in and through action, may be understood to underpin the notion of the scholar-practitioner (Wasserman and Kram, 2009; Coghlan, 2013). Scholar-practitioners are not merely practitioners who do research; rather, they integrate scholarship into their practice and generate actionable knowledge. Other terms that capture the same idea are the 'reflective practitioner' (Schon, 1983), the 'practitioner-researcher' (Jarvis, 1999) and the 'manager-researcher' (Coghlan, 2004): that is, those who engage in a science of action (Argyris and Schon, 1974; Torbert and Associates, 2004) and who produce useful research (Mohrman et al., 2011). Traditional research has polarized rigour and relevance, and holds that it is a case of one or other. As Levin (2012) argues, action research has a 'Janus face' – a head which faces in two directions simultaneously – to address relevant issues and problems and to be rigorously scientific is how these issues are investigated and addressed.

As we will develop in this book, the work of scholar-practitioners takes place in the present tense as they endeavour to change their organizations and to generate actionable knowledge. The three interdependent processes described above – learning about oneself through the action, collaborative work with others and the generation of learning that is robust for scholars and useful for practice – may be viewed in terms of Macmurray's reframing of the core of contemporary philosophy when he asserts the primacy of the practical, where the Cartesian 'I think, therefore, I am' is replaced by 'I do, therefore, I am' (1957: 84).

The contrast of researcher roles is between that of a detached observer in positivist science, and of an actor and agent of change in action research. Weisbord (1988) explores the images of taking photographs and making films in relation to organization development. He describes taking photographs as freezing a moment in time and arranging key elements in a conceptual framework. No photograph takes in the whole of reality; it only takes in what is intended to be included in the frame. Photographers decide what is to be in the frame, and they manipulate the setting to include and exclude desirable and undesirable features. In contrast, making films is an engagement in patterns of activity and relationships by multiple actors who are moving and interacting over a period of time and across locations. It is increasingly common to find actors directing their own films. In these cases, actor-directors engage in their acting role in costume, and then return to behind the camera in order to study the take, critique it and make decisions about proceeding to the next take. We find this image of making films and the action researcher as an actor-director pertinent and useful for thinking about doing action research. As Riordan expresses it, action research is:

> [A] kind of approach to studying social reality without separating (while distinguishing) fact from value; [it] require[s] a practitioner of science who is not only an engaged participant, but also incorporates the perspective of the critical and analytical observer, not as a validating instance but as integral to the practice. (1995: 10)

In a seminal article, Chandler and Torbert (2003) explore how first-, second- and third-person voice and practice may be engaged in the past, present and future. Much of what we refer to as qualitative research is focused on the past. Action research builds on the past and takes place in the present, with a view to shaping the future. Action research scholars such as Chris Argyris, Edgar Schein, Bill Torbert, Rami Shani, Judi Marshall and Peter Reason have led the way in exploring how to do first-person and second-person inquiry in the present tense, and how this practice may be rigorous and have quality. Their work permeates this book.

Enacting action research cycles

In its original Lewinian and simplest form, the action research cycle comprises a pre-step and three core activities: planning, action and fact-finding (Lewin, 1997[1946]). The pre-step involves naming the general objective. Planning comprises having an overall plan and a decision regarding what is the first step to take. Action involves taking that first step, and fact-finding involves evaluating the first step, seeing what was learned and creating the basis for correcting the next step. So there is a continuing 'spiral of steps, each of which is composed of a circle of planning, action and fact-finding about the result of the action' (Lewin, 1997[1946]: 146).

These core steps have been articulated differently by different authors, from Stringer's (2013) simple 'look, think, act', to French and Bell's (1999) complex action research organization development framework involving iterative cycles of joint action planning, feedback, further data-gathering, diagnosis and action of an external organization development consultant with a client system.

The action research cycles

For the context of doing action research in your own organization we present an action research cycle comprising a pre-step, context and purpose and four basic steps: constructing, planning action, taking action and evaluating action (Figure 1.2). The

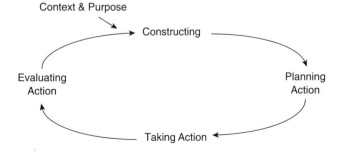

Figure 1.2 The Action Research Cycle

exploration of the action research cycle needs to be understood in terms of the four factors of action research that we presented above: context, quality of relationships, quality of the action research process itself and the outcomes.

Pre-step: context and purpose

The action research cycle unfolds in real time and begins with seeking an understanding of the context of the project. Why is this project necessary or desirable? In terms of assessing the external context, what are the economic, political and social forces driving change? In terms of internal forces, what are the cultural and structural forces driving change? Assessment of these forces identifies their source and potency, and the nature of the demands that they make on the system. Included also is assessment of the degree of choice in how the system responds to the forces for change. Once a sense of the need or desirability for the project is identified, then the most useful focus for attention is the definition of a desired future state. The process of defining the desired future state is critical, as it sets the boundaries for the purpose of the project and helps provide focus and energy for the later stages (these issues are elaborated on in Chapter 5).

Another critical consideration in this pre-step is establishment of collaborative relationships with those who have ownership, or need to have ownership, of the above questions. A central second-person task in this regard is to develop the group or groups with which you will be working on the project. We will pick up these issues later.

Main steps

Constructing

The first step of the action research cycle is a dialogic activity in which the stakeholders of the project engage in *constructing* what the issues are, however provisionally, as a working theme, on the basis of which action will be planned and taken. As this dialogic step involves articulating the practical and theoretical foundations of action, it needs to be done carefully and thoroughly. While this constructing may change in later iterations of the action research cycle, any changes in constructing need to be recorded and articulated clearly, showing how events have led to alternative meanings, and showing the evidence and rationale for the new shared meanings on which further action is to be based. It is important that the constructing step is a collaborative venture: that is, that you as the action researcher engage relevant others in the process of constructing, and are not the expert who decides this apart from others. (In Chapter 4 we focus on how the project may be constructed, and in Chapter 7 we outline some guidelines for using frameworks for understanding organizational phenomena.)

Planning action

Planning action follows from exploration of the context and purpose of the project, and construction of the issue, and is consistent with them. It may be that this action planning focuses on a first step or a series of first steps. In Chapter 5 we will describe how you implement the action research project. Again, we emphasize the importance of collaboration in planning action.

Taking action

At this stage, the plans are implemented and interventions made collaboratively.

Evaluating action

The outcomes of the action, both intended and unintended, are examined with a view to seeing:

- if the original constructing fitted;
- if the actions taken matched the constructing;
- if the action was taken in an appropriate manner; and
- what feeds into the next cycle of constructing, planning and action.

So the cycle continues (Figure 1.3).

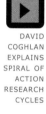

DAVID COGHLAN EXPLAINS SPIRAL OF ACTION RESEARCH CYCLES

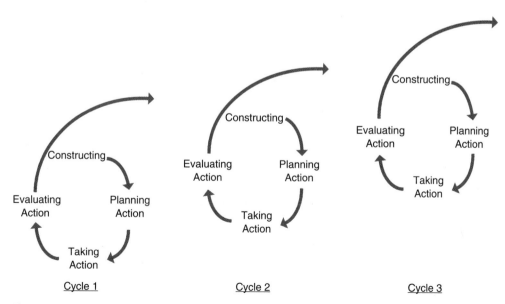

Figure 1.3 Spiral of Action Research Cycles

Figure 1.4   Concurrent Cycles of Action Research

DAVID
COGHLAN
DISCUSSES
THE SYMBOLIC
CLOCK FACE
WITHIN
CONCURRENT
CYCLES

In any action research project there are multiple action research cycles operating concurrently. These cycles typically have different time spans. The image of a clock captures this usefully (Figure 1.4). The hour hand, which takes 12 hours to complete its cycle, may represent the project as a whole. In a large complex project, it may take several years to complete its cycle. The minute hand, which takes an hour to complete its cycle, may represent phases or particular sections of the project. The second hand, which completes its cycle in a minute, may represent specific actions within the project, for example, a specific meeting or interview. As in the clock, where the revolutions of the three hands are concurrent and where the revolutions of the second hand enable the revolutions of the minute hand, and the revolutions of the second and minute hands together enable the completion of the hour hand, the short-term action research cycles contribute to the medium-term cycles, which in turn contribute to the longer-term cycle.

While the action research cycle expresses the core process of integrating action and theory as you inquire in the present tense, it is important to keep it in perspective. For example, Heron (1996) describes two approaches to the use of the cycle. He contrasts one approach, *Apollonian*, whereby the cycles are enacted in a rational, linear and systematic manner, with *Dionysian*, an approach where there is an imaginative, expressive and tacit approach to integrating reflection and action. He cautions against being rigid in adapting the action research cycle formally, and so denying spontaneity and creativity. It is also important not to get too preoccupied in the cycles at the expense of quality of participation.

Meta-learning

In any action research project there are two action research cycles operating in parallel. This is particularly true where the action research is undertaken for academic accreditation. The first cycle is the cycle we have just described of constructing, planning, taking action and evaluating in relation to achievement of the project's aims. Zuber-Skerritt and Perry (2002) call this the *core* action research cycle. The second cycle is a reflection cycle, which is an action research cycle about the action research cycle. Zuber-Skerritt and Perry call this the *thesis* action research cycle. In other words, at the same time as you are engaging in the project or core action research cycles, you need to be constructing, planning, taking action and evaluating how the action research project itself is going, and what you are learning. You need to be continually inquiring into each of the four main steps, asking how these steps are being conducted and how they are consistent with each other, so shaping how the subsequent steps are conducted. As Argyris (2003) argues , this inquiry into the steps of the cycles themselves is central to the development of actionable knowledge. It is the dynamic of this reflection on reflection that incorporates the learning process of the action research cycle, and enables action research to be more than everyday problem-solving. It is learning about learning: that is, meta-learning.

Mezirow (1991) identifies three forms of reflection: content, process and premise. These are useful categories.

1. *Content* reflection is where you think about the issues, what you think is happening, etc.
2. *Process* reflection is where you think about strategies and procedures, and how things are being done.
3. *Premise* reflection is where you critique underlying assumptions and perspectives.

All three forms of reflection are critical. Figure 1.5 presents how content, process and premise reflections are applied to the action research cycle as a meta-cycle of inquiry. The *content* of what is framed, planned, acted on and evaluated is studied and evaluated. The *process* of how constructing is undertaken, how action planning flows from that constructing and is conducted, how actions follow and are

DAVID COGHLAN DESCRIBES THE META-CYCLE OF ACTION RESEARCH

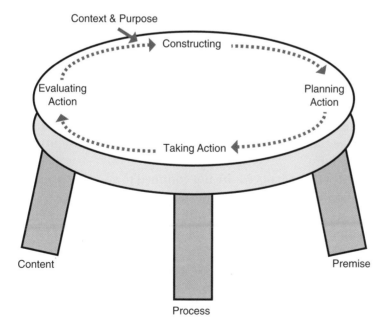

Figure 1.5 Meta-cycle of Action Research

an implementation of the stated plans and how evaluation is conducted, are critical foci for inquiry. *Premise* reflection is inquiry into the unstated and often non-conscious, underlying assumptions which govern attitudes and behaviour, such as that which might be embedded in language. For example, the culture of the organization or sub-culture of the group working on the project has a powerful impact on how issues are viewed and discussed, without members being aware of them (Schein, 2010).

If you are writing a dissertation, then the meta-cycle is the focus of your dissertation. Remember, the action research project and your dissertation project are not identical. They are integrally interlinked, but they are not the same. The project on which you are working may go ahead irrespective of whether or not you are writing a dissertation or seeking to generate actionable knowledge. Your dissertation is an inquiry into the project, hence you need to describe both cycles in a way that demonstrates the quality of rigour of your inquiry.

Mezirow's forms of reflection parallel the four territories of experience commonly used in action research (Fisher et al., 2000; Torbert and Associates, 2004). These four territories operate at the individual, interpersonal and organizational levels.

1. *Intentions* – purpose, goals, aims and vision.
2. *Planning* – plans, strategy, tactics, schemes.
3. *Action* – implementation, performance.
4. *Outcomes* – results, consequences and effects.

Action research aims to develop awareness, understanding and skills across all these territories. You try to understand your intentions, to develop appropriate plans and strategies, to be skilled at carrying them out, to reflect on how well you have carried out the plans and to evaluate their results. In addition, you can inquire about the connections between these phases. For example, you might begin with the outcomes and explore how your actions caused these outcomes; or you may take the inquiry further and look at how your intentions and plans shaped your actions.

The activities of the meta-cycle are not confined to your first-person practice as the individual action researcher. To add another layer of complexity to the learning cycle, the second-person practice with the groups and teams engaged in the action research cycles also attends to the steps of content, process and premise reflection.

Attending to the action research cycle and to the meta-cycle may involve more than simply attending to behaviour. You may draw from techniques in qualitative research approaches through the way in which you formulate the issue, collect and analyse data and report results (Sagor, 2011). Techniques from grounded theory approaches may be useful once the core compatibilities and incompatibilities between the two approaches are recognized (Baskerville and Pries-Heje, 1999).

Quality and rigour in action research

The action research paradigm requires its own quality criteria. Action research should be judged *not* by the criteria of positivist science, but rather within the criteria of its own terms. Reason (2006) points to what he considers to be choice points and questions for quality in action research. As action research is conducted in the present tense, you are always making choices as you reflect on what is happening, wonder what to do next and make choices and decisions.

1. Is the action research explicit in developing a praxis of relational participation? In other words, how well does the action research reflect the cooperation between the action researcher and the members of the organization?
2. Is action research guided by a reflexive concern for practical outcomes? Is the action project governed by constant and iterative reflection as part of the process of organizational change or improvement?
3. Does action research include a plurality of knowing which ensures conceptual-theoretical integrity, extends our ways of knowing and has a methodological appropriateness? Action research is inclusive of practical, propositional, presentational and experiential knowing, and so as a methodology is appropriate to furthering knowledge on different levels.
4. Does action research engage in significant work? The significance of the project is an important quality in action research.
5. Does the action research result in new and enduring infrastructures? In other words, does sustainable change come out of the project?

Reason argues that as an action researcher you need to be aware of these choices and make them clear and transparent to yourself (a first-person process), and to those with whom you are engaging in inquiry (a second-person process), as well as to those to whom you present your research in writing or presentations (a third-person process). The editorial guidelines for the journal *Action Research* invite potential contributors to address these dimensions explicitly in submitting their work to the journal. An integral element of making choices in the present tense is how you make value judgements and decide what is good (or better) to do. This process is the foundation of ethics (which we will discuss further in Chapter 2).

As the action researcher, you need to show the following.

1. How you engaged in the steps of multiple and repetitious action research cycles (how constructing, planning, taking action and evaluating were done), and how these were recorded to reflect that they are a true representation of what was studied.

2. How you challenged and tested your own assumptions and interpretations of what was happening continuously through the project by means of content, process and premise reflection, so that your familiarity with, and closeness to, the issues are exposed to critique.
3. How you accessed different views of what was happening which probably produced both confirming and contradictory interpretations.
4. How your interpretations are grounded in scholarly theory and rigorously applied, and how project outcomes are challenged, supported or disconfirmed in terms of the theories underpinning those interpretations and judgements.

What does a good action research project look like? Eden and Huxham (2006) provide an extensive list of the fifteen characteristics of good action research. The foundational characteristics reflect the intentionality of the researcher to change an organization, that the project has some implications beyond those involved directly in it, and that the project has an explicit aim to elaborate or develop theory as well as to be useful to the organization. Theory must inform the design and development of the actions. Eden and Huxham place great emphasis on enactment of the action research cycles, in which systematic method and orderliness is required in reflecting on the outcomes of each cycle and the design of the subsequent cycles.

In our view a good action research project contains three main elements: a good story, rigorous reflection on that story and an extrapolation of usable knowledge or theory from the reflection on the story. These can be put in terms of three questions: 'What happened?', 'How you do make sense of what happened?' and 'So what?'

What happened?

As action research is about real-time change, its core is the story of what takes place. As mentioned previously, the action research cycle of the general objective pre-step, and the four main steps of constructing, planning, action and fact-finding, describe how the project is conceived, what is intended, the cycles of action and the outcomes, both intended and unintended. The story must be presented in a factual and neutral manner, as if it had been recorded on camera, so that all the actors can agree on what had taken place. In short, the story is based on directly observable behaviour. Therefore, you need to be able to present evidence to support your narrative. Recorded data in journals and organizational documentation are important supporting evidence.

Accordingly, it is critical that fact is clearly distinguished from value, that the basic story does not contain the author's inferences or interpretations, or at least not without such inferences or interpretations being explicitly identified. For example, if an action research story contains an assertion that a certain group was out to wreck the project, the narrative would need to be clear that there was evidence that the group actually was trying to wreck the project, rather than it being an inference of the researcher or any party that saw itself as a victim of that group's action. (We explore the role of making inferences in Chapter 2.)

How you do make sense of what happened?

The critical process with respect to articulating your sense-making is making your tacit knowledge explicit. This involves not only providing an analysis of what you think is going on in the story, but also of how you are making sense of it as the story unfolds. In other words, sense-making is not only a retrospective process, but is also a collaborative process that is concurrent with the story, and in terms of the action research cycle, actually shapes the story – hence the image we used previously of the action researcher as an actor-director. As you report assumptions which you held as the story progressed, you need to show how you tested them, especially if these assumptions were privately held. In terms of our previous example, the researcher needs to test whether or not the group that they think is out to wreck the project, actually intends that.

So what?

The additional issue is how the action research project is contributing theory or usable knowledge. As action research is context-bound in a particular setting and set of events, it needs to have some interest and relevance to the uninvolved reader: the third-person readership. Hence the question 'so what?' is a pertinent and challenging question, or as Friedman puts it, 'if ... then ...' (2001: 168).

Conclusions

We began this chapter by seeing you poised to embark on your insider action research initiative. We have invited you to reflect on your experience of your organization, so as to explore what might change through your deliberate collaborative action involving you and others, and leading to actionable knowledge that would be of use to others who are not directly involved.

David reflects:

> Action research expects us to stop just going through the motions, doing what we've always done because we've done it, doing it the same way because we've always done it that way. Action researchers take a close look at what they are doing and act to make things better than they already are. Taking a closer look is action in and of itself and that research, that knowledge creation – any action taken based on that research – has the potential to transform the work that we do, the working conditions that we sweat under and, most importantly, the people who we are.

Enacting the action research cycle involves not only the pre-step of articulating the context and purpose of the project and the main steps of constructing, planning action, taking action and evaluating, but also reflecting on content, process and premise issues in how the action research cycles are undertaken in the present tense. Both the action research and meta-learning are undertaken by individuals, teams, between teams in the interdepartmental groups and between organizations. The rigour of your inquiry is demonstrated by how you expose these activities to critique, and how your conclusions are supported by your development of theory or usable knowledge. We will now turn to how you as the action researcher can engage in knowing in action.

Recommended reading

Brydon-Miller, M., Greenwood, D. and Maguire, P. (2003) 'Why action research?', *Action Research*, 1 (1): 9–28.

Chandler, D. and Torbert, W.R. (2003) 'Transforming inquiry and action: Interweaving 27 flavors of action research', *Action Research*, 1 (2): 133–152.

Coghlan, D. with Brydon-Miller, M. (2014) *The SAGE Encyclopedia of Action Research*. London: Sage. (See especially 'Cycles of action and reflection', 'Extended epistemology' and 'Symbolic interactionism'.)

Shani, A.B. and Pasmore W.A. (2010[1985]) 'Organization inquiry: Towards a new model of the action research process', in D. Coghlan and A.B. Shani (eds), *Fundamentals of Organization Development*, Vol. 1. London: Sage, pp. 249–260.

Wicks, P.G., Reason, P. and Bradbury, H. (2008) 'Living inquiry: Personal, political and philosophical groundings in action research practice', in P. Reason and H. Bradbury (eds), *The SAGE Handbook of Action Research* (2nd edn). London: Sage, pp. 15–30.

Access a selection of author videos, encyclopaedia entries and recommended reading on this topic at www.uk.sagepub.com/coghlanandbrannick

EXERCISE 1.1

Enacting the action research cycles (from Figure 1.2)

1. Select an issue or problem that you have worked on in your team (or are working on).
2. What is the *context* of this issue? Why is it important? What are the stakes involved?
3. Describe how the issue was *constructed*. How did you decide that an intervention was needed or wanted, what was wrong, what the causes were? How did you deal with different meanings or constructions in the team?

4. What action was *planned*?
5. What happened when the action was *implemented*? What were the outcomes, both intended and unintended?
6. How did the team *review* the outcomes?
7. What was *then* constructed, planned, implemented, etc.?
8. What is the *meta-learning* from this exercise?

   (a) As you look back on this, what insights do you have about the *content* of the issue? Did the initial constructing fit? Had you named the right issue? What have you learned about this issue in your business or organization?

   (b) What insights do you have about process? How did the team work on the issue? What have you learned about how to plan, take action and evaluate?

   (c) Was there any challenge to existing premises of how you thought about things, anything in the event that challenged the team to ask different questions, see the issue in terms of a different category of issue or problem, and so on?

TWO

Knowing in Action

 See www.uk.sagepub.com/coghlanandbrannick for a short introduction to the chapter from David Coghlan

The questions underpinning this chapter direct you to first-person activities as you, the insider action researcher, engage as a scholar-practitioner in first- and second-person inquiry or practice as you enact the action research cycles. How do you know what you know? What methodology is appropriate for inquiring in the 'swampy lowlands' of your own system? How do you inquire in action? How do you attend to what you might be learning as you engage in the issues of your action research project? How might you do research in the present tense? How do you engage in collaborative inquiry and action? As answers to these questions, we outline the familiar and recognizable structure of human knowing, and ground some processes of how you come to know, understand, make judgements and decide to take action.

As an insider action researcher, you are an actor (one who takes action) in the setting of the organization. In contrast with traditional research approaches, you are not neutral but an active intervenor, making and helping things happen. Accordingly, a critical feature of action research in your own organization is how you engage your own thinking and learning processes as you engage in first-, second- and third-person inquiry in the present tense.

At its core, first-person practice means that your own beliefs, values, assumptions, ways of thinking, strategies and behaviour, and so on are afforded a central place of inquiry in your action research practice: as the actor-director, as we portrayed in Chapter 1. It involves attention to how you experience yourself in inquiry and action, what Reason and Torbert (2001) refer to as 'upstream' and 'downstream' inquiry, and Marshall (1999) as 'living life as inquiry'. As Marshall (2001) describes it, self-reflective practice involves enacting inquiry with intent in a manner that is distinct for each person, suggesting that each individual must craft their own practice and attend to its quality through inner and outer arcs of attention, enacting cycles of action and reflection and being both active and receptive.

Knowing-in-action is grounded in the inquiry reflection process. Schon's (1983) notion of the 'reflective practitioner' captures the essentials of knowing-in-action and reflection-in-action. Knowing-in-action is tacit and opens up outcomes that fall within the boundaries of what you have learned to treat as normal. Reflection-in-action occurs when you are in the middle of an action, and you ask questions about what you are doing and what is happening around you. The outcome is immediate, as it leads to an on-the-spot adjustment of your thinking and of your action. As Kahneman (2011) demonstrates, catching how your mind works is an exciting adventure.

Inquiry can be focused outward (e.g. what is going on in the organization, in the team, etc.?) or inward (e.g. what is going on in me?). In Chapter 7 we outline some conceptual frameworks which provide a basis for understanding organizational processes that are utilized for outward-focused inquiry and reflection. Here, we focus on the activities of inward-focused inquiry and reflection of first-person practice. Marshall (1999, 2001) presents individual inquiring in action as 'inquiry as a way of being', and describes this first-person research or practice in terms of: (a) inquiring into the inner and outer arcs of attention; (b) engaging in cycles of action and reflection; and (c) being active and receptive. Lonergan (1992[1957]) and Flanagan (1997) describe the process of grasping and internalizing the process of knowing as 'self-appropriation'.

Knowing and learning

The structure of human knowing is a three-step heuristic process: experience, understanding and judgement (Lonergan, 1992[1957]; Flanagan 1997; Melchin and Picard, 2008) (Table 2.1). First, we attend to our experience. Then we ask questions about our experience and receive an insight (understanding); we follow that up by reflecting and weighing up the evidence to determine whether our insight fits the evidence or not (judgement). Of course, a great deal of our knowing is actually belief, where we accept the work of others, although at times we may need to verify for ourselves. The pattern of the three operations is invariant in that it applies to all settings of cognitional activity, whether solving a crossword clue, addressing an everyday problem or engaging in scientific research.

Table 2.1 Operations of human cognition and doing

Experience	Seeing, hearing, smelling, tasting, touching, remembering, imagining, feeling
Understanding	Inquiring, understanding, formulating what is being understood
Judgement	Marshalling evidence, testing, judging
Decision/action	Deliberating, valuing, deciding, choosing, taking action, behaving

Experiencing

Experience is the empirical level of consciousness and an interaction of inner and outer events, or data of sense and data of consciousness. You can not only see, hear, smell, taste and touch, imagine, remember, feel and think, but you also can experience yourself as seeing, hearing, thinking, feeling, remembering and imagining. As the action researcher you experience a great deal as the project goes through its cycles. Some of your experiences are planned; others are unplanned. Some are what is done to you by others. Some experiences are cognitive: they occur through the intellectual processes of thinking and understanding. Some occur in feelings and emotions: at times you may feel excited, angry, frustrated, sad, lonely, and so on. Other experiences may be experienced in the body: excited energy, embarrassed blushing, tightness in the stomach, headaches, even ulcers. These three domains – cognitive, feelings and body awareness – are where experiencing occurs, and you can learn by attending to these (Gendlin, 1981).

Understanding

Insight is an act of understanding that grasps the intelligible connections between things that previously have appeared disparate. It occurs at the intellectual level of consciousness. Sensory data are what you experience, but do not yet understand. So you ask questions: 'What is this?', 'What does this mean?' Answers to such questions come in the form of insights, which are creative acts of understanding, of grasping and formulating patterns, unities, relationships and explanations in response to questions posed to your experience. The search for understanding is intelligent, focusing on a question or problem. While you might not know yet if a particular current search is intelligent, you anticipate intelligent answers. This act of understanding grasps a pattern in data. There are no recipes, rules or procedures to follow that lead inevitably to insights. The achievement of insight is unpredictable: it can happen quickly or more slowly. For example, if you do crosswords, notice your questions about a clue, the flashes of insight that you get (eventually!), how you check those insights with how they fit with the blank spaces for the letters and the other words that cross it. Then you verify: this must be the answer. Perhaps later when you have completed other parts of the crossword, you find that you were not correct and you have another insight – then you verify that your new insight seems to fit better. If we tell you a joke, you get the unexpected connection at the end and you laugh (hopefully!). If you are watching a detective story on TV, you are furnished with clues throughout and the challenge is to figure out who the villain is with the detective as the story unfolds. You report that it suddenly dawned on you, or that you saw the connection – or it may be that you say 'I just don't get it'. 'Getting it' occurs all the time and in all sorts of situations. Archimedes got it when, while having a bath, he saw how submerging the king's new crown would determine its specific gravity and so inform him of what it was made. You laugh when you get a joke. You get the possible answer to the crossword clue. You understand how you might retrieve the kite stuck in the tree. There are also inverse insights, ones for which there are no intelligible answers or patterns. It is not that you cannot find them, but that you grasp that there are none.

Insight makes the difference between the tantalizing problem and the evident solution. Insofar as it is the act of organizing intelligence, insight is an apprehension of relations and meaning. Every insight goes beyond descriptive experience to an explanatory organization of the experience's possible meaning.

Attending to experience is the first step to knowing. The second step is to stand back from these experiences and inquire into them. What is happening here? What is it that I do not yet understand? What is it that has me feeling angry?

Judgement

While insights are common, they are not always accurate or true. The question then is: 'Does the insight fit the evidence?' This opens up a question for reflection. Is it so? Yes or no? Maybe, I don't know – I need more evidence to be sure. The shift in attention turns to a verification-oriented inquiry for possible accuracy, sureness and certainty of understanding. So you move to a new level of the cognitional process, where you marshal and weigh evidence and assess its sufficiency. You are at the rational level of consciousness. You set the judgement up conditionally; if the conditions have been fulfilled, then it must be true or accurate. There may be conflicting judgements and you may have to weigh the evidence and choose between them. If you do not think that you have sufficient evidence to assert that your insight fits the data, then you can postpone judgement, or make a provisional judgement and correct it later when you have more or other evidence.

Human knowing is not any of these three operations on their own. All knowing involves experience, understanding and judgement (Figure 2.1). The simple operation of knowing whether it is raining or not provides a verifiable example. The experience of feeling drops of water on your skin or seeing splotches on the pavement do not tell you that it is raining, but they evoke the question – so you think that it might be raining (insight). Then you may check that there is not someone watering a window box above your head, and you may look into the near distance and see that there are people putting up umbrellas or scurrying to doorways, and you put all that together to assess the evidence and to confirm your insight that it is indeed raining (judgement).

Each type of question – for understanding, for judgement, for decision – proceeds in sequential order where each question sublates the previous one. By sublating

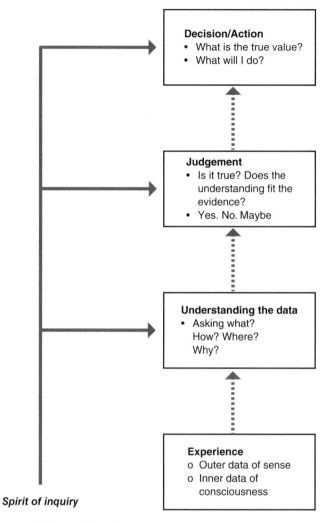

Figure 2.1 Process of Human Knowing

we mean that the core of each activity is maintained and taken further in the next question. Understanding sublates experiencing. Judging sublates understanding. Decision sublates judgement.

Understanding how we know is invariant across the extended epistemology with which action research works. Each of the four ways of knowing, presented by Heron (1996) – experiential, presentational, propositional and practical – involve experience, understanding and judgement, albeit differently in each mode of knowing. For example, an artist establishes insights not by proof or verification, but by skilfully embodying them in colours and shapes, sounds and movements, the unfolding situation and the actions of fiction.

Accordingly, both inner and outer arcs of attention are critical, as the example of knowing that it is it raining confirms. Of course, the factual outcome of whether it is raining or not – where the answer is right or wrong – is not replicated when you try to know the world of human behaviour and social structures, particularly in the 'swampy lowlands' of your organization's backstage. This world is mediated by meaning which constitutes human living. You may learn to construct your respective world by giving meaning to data that continuously impinge on you from within yourself as well as from without. Meaning goes beyond experiencing, as what is meant is not only experienced but also is something you seek to understand and affirm. There is the task of seeking to understand the many meanings that constitute organizations and social structures in language, symbols and actions (Campbell, 2000; Gergen and Gergen, 2008; Bushe and Marshak, 2009). Accordingly, you may question how taken-for-granted values, behaviour and assumptions are actually socially constructed and embedded in meaning. You may also question how power influences the meanings that others put on events (Marshall and Reason, 2007). There is also the meaning of the world you make through your enactment of the four territories of experience: intentions, plans, actions and outcomes (Torbert and Associates, 2004). So, in terms of conscious intentionality, we enact operations of intending, planning, acting and reviewing within ourselves as first-person practice, with others as second-person practice, and to influence a broader impersonal audience as third-person practice.

However, as we know, it is not that simple. Of course, there are such things as stupidity, obtuseness, confusion, divergent views, lack of attention and a general lack of intelligence. Understanding may not spontaneously flow from experience. Many insights may be wrong. Your interpretations of data may be superficial, inaccurate or biased. Your judgements may be flawed. Being careless about these operations have their consequences. If you are careless about being attentive, then your understanding is flawed. If you are careless about your understanding, then your judgements are untrustworthy. You can gain insight into these negative manifestations of knowing by the same threefold process of knowing of experience, understanding and judgement.

Valuing, deciding and taking action

You are not merely a knower; you also weigh options, make decisions and take action. Decision and action are at the responsible level of consciousness, and explain the first-person process underpinning ethics. There are two types of judgement: judgement of fact (e.g. 'it is raining'), and judgement of value (e.g. 'that it is raining is not a good thing, as I want to cut the grass'). In his dense and exciting first-person exploration of value, Dworkin (2011) presents the case that the one big

thing in life is value. Value constitutes what truth is, what life means, what moral-
ity requires and what justice demands. He explores how value proposes a way to
live, based on two foundational principles: self-respect and authenticity.

Valuing is a spontaneous process that you engage in very early in life, long before
you can talk about it. You are always valuing. You use words such as 'good' and
'bad' about a wide range of issues. You like this, you don't like that. You choose
one item over another. You choose to take this action rather than an alternative.

Not all judgements of value lead to a sense of responsibility or an obligation
to act. You may affirm that an object is good without needing to do anything.
However, besides thinking about reality, you may want to change it. You may experience a situation and judge it to be unjust, so you may decide not to leave it at that
but to say or do something. You have the ability to ask what you might do before
deciding what you will do. You may ask questions such as: 'Will I?', 'Is it better or
worse?', 'Is it worth my while?' These questions are clearly normative, and capture
the most fundamental and moral drive to live in a responsible way (Dunne, 2010).

The process of judging value and deciding is a similar process to that of knowing.
You experience a situation. Using sensitivity, imagination and intelligence, you
may seek to answer the question in order to understand what possible courses of
action there might be. At this level you may ask what courses of action are open to
you, and you may review the options, weigh choices and decide. You may reflect
on the possible value judgements as to what is the best option; you may decide to
follow through the best value judgement and take responsibility for consistency
between your knowing and doing.

When we use the term 'good', we ask: what do we mean by 'good'? Why is something good? What is good about it? Can we use a term such as 'truly good'? A simple
answer is that the good is what is intended by the judgement of value which extends
beyond the merely satisfying. While we will return to the topic of ethics later, what
we are doing here is grounding the valuing process in the assumption that what
is considered 'good' is considered by a person. When you hear two people arguing
about the 'objective' worth of something, you may realize that you cannot talk about
the objective worth of things without talking about human people, their value judgements and the kinds of moral bias that may be distorting those judgements. Once
you have understood what goes on when people make choices, you can build collaboration more intelligently and realistically in the process of doing good in the world.

We are taking a position countering the notion that objective value must be
somehow a concept that is 'out there'. Such a notion is based on the mistaken
assumption that knowing is taking a look at something that is 'out there'. By
understanding what we do when we say that option A is better than option B, we
may realize that all things valuable are valued through responsible consciousness,
and that true values are learned by people being responsible – thus our emphasis
on the activities of knowing.

To conclude this section, these four processes operate as a cycle where experiencing, understanding, judging and deciding or acting set up another cycle of experiencing, and so on. Learning becomes a continuous cycle through life. You need to develop skills at each activity: to be able to experience directly, stand back and ask questions, conceptualize answers to your questions, and take risks and experiment in similar or new situations. The insider action research process makes particular demands on how you experience, understand, judge, value, decide and act.

General empirical method

The operations of experience, understanding, judgement and decision and action form a general empirical method which requires:

- attention to observable data;
- envisaging possible explanations of that data;
- preferring as probable or certain the explanations which provide the best account for the data; and
- deliberating and choosing between alternative actions and taking action.

These require the dispositions to perform the operations of attentiveness, intelligence, reasonableness and responsibility (Table 2.2).

A method is not the same as a recipe, which delivers another instance of the same product. The key to method is the relationship between questioning and answering: it is a framework for collaborative creativity that deals with different kinds of questions, each with its own objective. So questions for understanding of specific data (What is happening here?) have a different focus from questions for reflection (Does this fit?) or questions of responsibility (What might I do?). The general empirical method of being attentive, intelligent, reasonable and responsible is a normative heuristic pattern of related and recurrent operations that yield ongoing and cumulative results. It is operative in natural science, the human sciences, spirituality and the practical world of the everyday. As it is grounded not in any thesis or grand theory, but in the recognizable activities of human inquiry and action, it crosses technical philosophical boundaries and is applicable to inquiring from critical, constructive and constructionist perspectives. It is also the ground for first-person authenticity, which we now explore.

Table 2.2 General empirical method in action research

Empirical level	Attentiveness
Intellectual level	Intelligence
Rational level	Reasonableness
Responsible level	Responsibility

Authenticity

There is no guarantee that you will be attentive, intelligent, reasonable or responsible all the time. You can be inattentive and miss or ignore data. You can distort data. You can fly from insight by turning a blind eye, refusing to ask questions, ignoring awkward or disconfirming questions and not facing unresolved feelings. While the desire to know manifests itself in attentive questioning, so there are fears which block and divert this questioning: censoring, repressing, controlling symbols of feeling and imagining, selecting what you choose to question. You can be unreasonable in your judgements, settling for what is comfortable rather than for what the questions evoke. You can resist the evidence and try to escape responsibility. Sometimes, you might do these in ignorance; at other times you probably know that you are being strong-headed, obstinate or fearful. This is not a peculiar aberration but a frequent occurrence, and you are likely to be resourceful and inventive in how you flee from attentiveness, intelligence, reasonableness and responsibility.

Hence, authenticity is characterized by four process imperatives: be attentive (to the data); be intelligent (in inquiry); be reasonable (in making judgements); and be responsible (in making decisions and taking action) (Coghlan, 2008). They address *process* issues in that they point to how you are engaging in inquiry and action, and are *imperative* in that they point to what 'ought' to be. You experience data, so you ought to be open to experience – hence the imperative: be attentive. Avoiding issues, closing your eyes to reality, turning a blind eye, burying your head in the sand, refusing to inquire into a matter, and so on diminish your authenticity. You ask questions and seek answers, so you ought to question, wonder and seek to understand – accordingly, the imperative is: be intelligent. Refusing to question or wonder, uncritically or sheepishly following the party line, suppressing curiosity, and so on, destroy authenticity. You wonder if your ideas are correct, so you ought to have sound reasons for what you hold and base your judgements on evidence – so the imperative is: be reasonable. Suppressing discussion or dissent, lying about facts, obscuring evidence and so on destroy authenticity. You discern what you ought to do, so you ought to be sensitive to value and choose what you

AUTHENTICITY
AS FIRST
PERSON
PRACTICE

Table 2.3 Authenticity

Operations	Activities	Process imperatives
Experience	Attending, sensing, imagining	Be attentive
Understanding	Inquiring, understanding	Be intelligent
Judgement	Reflecting, weighing evidence, judging	Be reasonable
Decision	Deliberating, deciding, acting	Be responsible

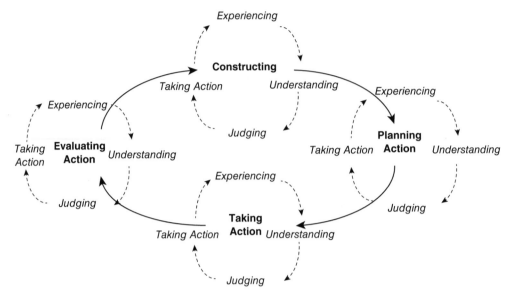

Figure 2.2 The General Empirical Method in Action Research Projects

believe to be right – therefore, the imperative is: be responsible. Cheating, destroying resources, being unjust and so on destroy authenticity (Table 2.3).

Because the *core* action research project and the *thesis* research project are not identical, you need to engage your own learning-in-action as you participate in the action research cycles (Figure 2.2) so you are experiencing what it is like to engage in constructing, planning, action, taking action and evaluating, inquiring and seeking insight and understanding into the enactment of the cycles, judging what is appropriate and then taking action on the basis of your judgement.

Action science and collaborative developmental action inquiry as first-person practice

In the earlier editions, in Chapter 3 where we introduced some of the modalities of action research, we provided a brief introduction to action science and collaborative developmental action inquiry. In this edition we have moved from that perspective and are incorporating these approaches as core first-person practices, adopting Friedman and Rogers' argument that these are not distinct methods, but sets of 'value-based and practical tools that can be integrated into and enhance many forms of action research' (2008: 252). These approaches complement the general empirical method, as they direct you to attend to how you know.

ACTION
SCIENCE

Action science is associated with the work of Chris Argyris (1993, et al., 1985; Friedman and Rogers, 2008). Argyris places an emphasi tive processes of individuals' 'theories-in-use', which he describes in I (strategies of control, self-protection, defensiveness and covering up ment), and Model II (strategies eliciting valid information, free choice and commitment). Collaborative developmental action inquiry is associated with the work of Bill Torbert (Fisher et al., 2000; Torbert and Associates, 2004; Torbert and Taylor, 2008). Torbert extends the notion of action science to include the developmental dynamic of learning to inquiry-in-action, emphasizing that as we progress through adulthood we may intentionally develop new 'action-logics' through the stages of our development. Collaborative developmental theory offers an understanding of our transformation through a series of developmental stages, so that we gain insight into our own action logic as we take action.

Action science and collaborative developmental action inquiry provide more focused approaches to attending to individual knowing-in-action. In action science, you focus on how your actions tend to produce defensiveness and undesired outcomes: the opposite of what you intend (Argyris, 2004). This happens because you may hold assumptions which govern your behaviour, and may make private inferences and attributions about the motives and thought processes of others which you typically do not test. Accordingly, the core of action science is learning how to identify the assumptions which govern behaviour and to develop skills at testing assumptions and inferences, while at the same time exposing your own privately held theories to public testing. Through collaborative developmental action inquiry you may learn to grasp how your ability to learn-in-action is integrally linked to the stages of your ego development (Torbert and Associates, 2004).

I take ACTIONS based on
my beliefs

I adopt BELIEFS about the person &
the situation

I draw CONCLUSIONS

I make ASSUMPTIONS based on
the meanings added

I add MEANINGS (cultural and personal)

I select DATA from what I observe

I OBSERVE data and experiences

Figure 2.3 The Ladder of Inference

(Argyris, Putnam and Smith, 1985; Ross, 1994)

Techniques from action science, such as the ladder of inference, the right/left hand column and treating facts as hypotheses, provide valuable tools for testing consistency between the process imperatives. The ladder of inference plots how meanings and assumptions are attributed to selected observable data and experiences, and conclusions and beliefs are adopted on which actions are based (Argyris et al., 1985; Ross, 1994) (Figure 2.3). For example, at a team meeting you make a proposal for action. One of your colleagues, Joe, does not say anything. You think he looks as if he is sulking, and you conclude that he is sulking because his proposal has not been considered. Accordingly, you decide that Joe will not be on your side, and that you cannot rely on him for support: subsequently you do not inform him of meetings as the project progresses. What has happened here is that you observed an event, i.e. all that is going on in the room. You selected part of that event (Joe not speaking), and added your own interpretations and meaning, i.e. that Joe is sulking, which you did not share or test. Then your own subsequent actions of excluding Joe from further meetings were based on the beliefs and assumptions deduced from your private interpretation. In terms of the image of a ladder, you have ascended the steps of inference from the bottom rung of what is directly observable behaviour, to the upper rungs of acting on privately-held, untested inferences. As Fisher and Sharp (1999) express it: data are at the bottom rung, reasoning is in the middle rung and conclusions are at the top rung. Differentiating between these three elements is central to the process of learning-in-action. The ladder of inference helps us retrace our steps from what we have seen and heard (directly observable behaviour), to the way we think about them (reasoning) and the conclusions we draw (inferences and attributions). The general empirical method enables us to separate these three operations of human knowing, and to examine how we are engaging authentically in each operation (Figure 2.4).

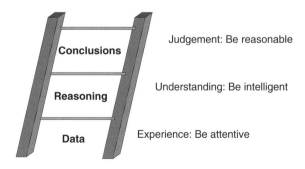

Figure 2.4   Ladder of Inference and General Empirical Method

Argyris' (2004) (Argyris et al., 1985) technique of right hand/left hand column provides a useful technique for you to uncover your own privately-held inferences and
attributions in second-person practice. He illustrates how, in a conversation, there
are privately-held thoughts about the situation in the minds of the two participants
which are not shared or tested, and which shape the flow of the conversation. These
private thoughts are inferences and attributions, and they foster defensiveness and
inhibit inquiry in action (see Exercise C at the end of this chapter).

Another useful construct to support knowing-in-action is the notion of cognitive
distortions, whereby you may become aware of how you might be prone to distorting reality, particularly when under pressure (Coghlan and Rashford, 1990). You
may distort reality when you engage in such activities as:

- over-generalization;
- 'all-or-nothing' thinking;
- mental filtering;
- jumping to conclusions;
- emotional reasoning;
- fortune-telling; and
- other similar ways of misperceiving what is happening.

Distortions such as these impair your ability to engage in inquiry in action. The
general empirical method enables you to review what it is that you actually know
(i.e. have experienced, understood and tested through judgement), rather than
jumping to a conclusion based on emotional reasoning or an inference.

Emotions as well as thoughts are part of the knowing process. You need to be
able to recognize and acknowledge the role that feelings play in the formation of
judgement and in taking action. *Focusing* (Gendlin, 1981; Cornell, 1996) provides a
valuable method of listening to experiences within the body, by noticing how you
feel and having a conversation with that feeling in a friendly way. It is a process of
listening to your body in a gentle, accepting way, and hearing the messages that
your inner self is sending through your body.

In terms of the general empirical method you are seeking to be intelligent and
reasonable about what you are attending to, so you inquire of yourself what you
are doing and what is going on in your head, such as: 'What is the evidence of my
understanding?', 'Do I know something, or am I inferring it?', 'How have I come to
understand in the way that I have, and not in another?', 'How do I know that my
understanding fits the data?' Argyris poses similar questions in a more focused way.
What are your espoused theories and your theories-in-use, and can you express
them in such a way that you cannot squirm out of them? How can you become
more aware of your skilled incompetence: that is, how your reasoning functions
to protect yourself, and how you become blind to your blindness? How do you
cover up inconsistent messages that you produce, deny producing them, and make

that denial undiscussable? How is the undiscussability of what is undiscussable itself undiscussable? On what evidence are you forming a judgement about what is going on and what you choose to do? Is your insight an inference or attribution? How might you test it?

Developing first-person skills through journalling

Journal-keeping is a significant mechanism for developing first-person skills. You note your observations and experiences in a journal and, over time, learn to differentiate between different experiences and ways of dealing with them. Journal-keeping helps you to reflect on experiences, to see how you think about them and to anticipate future experiences before you undertake them (Moon, 1999; Boud, 2001; Raelin, 2008). It enables you to integrate information and experiences which, when understood, help you to understand your reasoning processes and consequent behaviour, and so anticipate experiences before embarking on them. Keeping a journal regularly imposes a discipline and captures your experience of key events close to when they happen, before the passage of time changes your perception of them. McNiff et al. (2009) describe some of the useful functions that a journal or research diary can have.

- A systematic and regularly kept record of events, dates and people.
- An interpretative, self-evaluative account of the researcher's personal experiences, thoughts and feelings, with a view to trying to understand their own actions.
- A useful way of dumping painful experiences.
- A reflective account where the researcher can tease out interpretations.
- An analytic tool where data can be examined and analysed.

Journals may be set to a particular structure. One obvious structure is to follow the one provided in this chapter through the general empirical method. You can keep track of your experiences, the questions that arise out of those experiences, the insights you receive, how you weigh evidence in order to verify your understanding, how you make decisions and what actions you take. Kolb's (1984) experiential learning cycle is another useful structure whereby experience, reflection, conceptualization and experimentation form useful headings. These formats work well. You may learn to attend to the details of a situation, and with practice can isolate critical incidents which have affected your cognitive and emotional processes and your judgement as to what to say or do. You develop skills of awareness and attentiveness. You may be challenged in your use of theory, and may learn to use theory in a practical manner. Moreover, you may learn to experience learning as a continuous life task, as you apply your learning to future situations.

Another useful framework for journal-keeping is Schein's (1999, 2013) ORJI model. ORJI (Observation, Reaction, Judgement, Intervention) focuses on what goes on inside your head and how it affects your covert behaviour. You observe (O); react emotionally to what you have observed (R); analyse, process and make judgements based on observations and feelings (J); and intervene in order to make something happen (I). Schein pays particular attention to the movement from observation to judgement, because he believes that frequently the individual does not pay attention to the reaction stage. In his view, the individual typically denies feelings, short-circuiting them, and moves straight to judgement and action. You may react to an event by saying to yourself – 'That's stupid' – a judgement. What you have probably done is to miss an emotional reaction of feeling threatened by the event. You may not have recognized or acknowledged that feeling of being threatened, yet it is present and governing your judgement. By learning to iden-tify and attend to feelings as initial reactions and influencing judgements, you may learn to deal with them and choose whether or not to act on them. Denial of feelings frequently means acting on them without adverting to the fact that you are acting on them. Acknowledgement of feelings to yourself and the subsequent judgement as to the origins and validity of those feelings are critical to learning and change. A journal may be structured around the four ORJI activities.

Schein's ORJI model adds a sophistication to Kolb's experiential learning cycle in two ways (Coghlan, 1993). First, it focuses on a neglected area, namely the sponta-neous reaction (which is typically bypassed) to an incident. It provides a framework whereby you may learn to recognize feelings and distinguish them from cognitive processes. Second, it inserts a structured reflection process that works back from action to judgement to reaction to observation. When your view of a situation is not confirmed by how events develop, you may question the original judgement. When you find that the judgement is based on an emotional reaction, then you can question the source of that reaction. With practice, you may learn to become more aware of emotional reactions so as to be able to recognize them as they arise, rather than in retrospect.

Second-person skills

The core skills underpinning action research are relational: that is, we need to be skilled at engaging with others. When we engage in second-person work, we need to be able to build relationships with others, listen well and have a range of ways of interacting with them so that collaborative inquiry and joint action can take place. This involves attending to building participation in the early stages of a project (Wicks and Reason, 2009) and throughout (Arieli et al., 2009).

INITIATING
ACTION
RESEARCH

Schein (1993) explores two ways of talking together. First, there is the traditional discussion mode where the emphasis is on advocacy, competing and convincing. Here, the dialectic of exploring opposites predominates through debate. Second, there is the mode of dialogue which is marked by suspending one's own presuppositions and engaging in internal listening, accepting differences and building mutual trust. This involves revealing feelings, building common ground, challenging one's own assumptions and learning to think and feel that the whole group may build new and shared assumptions. In Schein's view, if new organizational responses are needed to change cultural assumptions or to learn across sub-cultural boundaries, the second mode of dialogue will be most important. This is because organizational learning involves going beyond the cultural status quo. In the dialogue form, the general empirical method operates as the basis for inquiry. Members of dialogue groups may inquire into the insights of others and work to develop shared understanding, judgements and planned actions. As Scharmer (2001) explores, such conversations need to be reflective and require participants to take a higher viewpoint, seeking insights into the whole situation rather than the constituent parts, and into the forms of conversation required in order that learning may take place.

The starting point for second-person practice is to examine your own dispositions. In describing the characteristic of the helping relationship, Carl Rogers (1958) invites those in the helping role to face certain questions about their own dispositions. These dispositions relate to the ability to:

- build trust;
- allow oneself to experience positive feelings towards the other;
- be strong enough in oneself to allow freedom to the other;
- be able to enter the subjective world of the other and see things as they see them;
- be free from external evaluation; and
- allow the other person to be in the process of becoming (Rogers, 1958).

At the same time, you need to be politically astute and ethical in your engagement in your second-person work (as we will discuss in Chapter 10).

Second-person research involves core skills in engaging with others in the inquiry process. In his articulation of the dynamics of helping, Schein (1999, 2009, 2013) describes several types of inquiry. His first category is *pure inquiry*. This is where you prompt elicitation of the story of what is taking place, and listen carefully and neutrally. You may ask: 'What is going on?', 'Tell me what happened'. His second type of inquiry is *diagnostic inquiry*, in which you begin to manage the process of how content is analysed by the other by exploring emotional processes, reasoning and actions. So you may ask, 'How do you feel about this?', 'Why do you think this happened?', 'What did you do?', What are you going to do?,' and so on. His third type of inquiry is *confrontive inquiry*. This is where, by sharing your own ideas, you challenge the other to think from a new perspective. These ideas may refer to process and content. Examples of confrontive questions would be:

'Have you thought about doing this...?', 'Have you considered that [X] might be a solution?'

Schein's typology may be reframed in terms of the general empirical method: working with others to attend to their experience, to have insights into that experience, to make judgements as to whether the insights fit the evidence, and then to take action (Coghlan, 2009). Observation of people in systems and subsequent conversations between you and your co-researchers seek to bring out experience (through pure inquiry), test insights, form judgements about that experience (through diagnostic inquiry) and then make decisions and take action (through confrontive inquiry). Through these conversations, constructed meanings may be uncovered and tested and action planned, taken and reviewed.

TOWARDS A PHILOSOPHY OF CLINICAL INQUIRY/ RESEARCH

Because you are part of the situation as an insider-researcher, you may not always act as an external facilitator or consultant might: that is, as the sole enabler of emergent information and action. Of necessity you have a view of things as they are and what needs to change, and will be expected to share and argue that view. Accordingly, a critical skill for you as the insider action researcher is to be able to combine advocacy with inquiry: to present your own inferences, attributions, opinions and viewpoints as open to testing and critique (Argyris et al., 1985; Ross and Roberts, 1994). This involves illustrating inferences with relatively directly observable data, and making reasoning explicit and publicly testable in the service of learning.

Argyris et al. (1985) provide seven rules for hypothesis testing.

1. Combine advocacy with inquiry.
2. Illustrate your inferences with directly observable data.
3. Make your reasoning explicit and publicly test for agreement at each inferential step.
4. Actively seek disconfirming data and alternative explanations.
5. Affirm the making of mistakes in the service of learning.
6. Actively inquire into your own impact in the learning context.
7. Design ongoing experiments to test competing views. (1985: 258–261)

Fisher et al. (2000) and Torbert (Torbert and Associates, 2004) suggest four 'parts of speech' as useful to the action inquiry role.

1. *Framing* – explicitly stating the purpose of speaking for the present occasion: what dilemma you are trying to resolve, sharing assumptions about the situation.
2. *Advocating* – explicitly stating the goal to be achieved, asserting and option, perception, feeling or proposal for action.
3. *Illustrating* – telling a bit of the concrete story that makes the advocacy concrete and orients the others more clearly.
4. *Inquiring* – questioning others to understand their perspectives and views.

Putnam (1991) asks if there are recipes which might be useful in helping others explore their reasoning processes. He suggests that questions such as 'What prevents you from … ?' and 'What have I said or done that leads you to believe that … ?' facilitate a focus on directly observable behaviour rather than on attribution, inference or privately-held meanings. They are not one-liners; rather, they are interventions to open up conversation so as to explore insights and meaning – particularly those that are being privately held. These interventions may occur in one-to-one or group situations.

Conclusions

In this chapter we have placed the focus on you as the action researcher, as you inquire in the 'swampy lowlands' of your own organization. When you engage in the action research cycles of constructing, planning action, taking action and evaluating action with others, and try to understand and shape what is going on, you are engaging in your own knowing, acting and learning activities of experiencing, understanding, judging, valuing, deciding and taking action (as seen in Figure 2.5). The general empirical method provides a normative pattern of related and recurrent operations that yield ongoing and cumulative results. It envisages

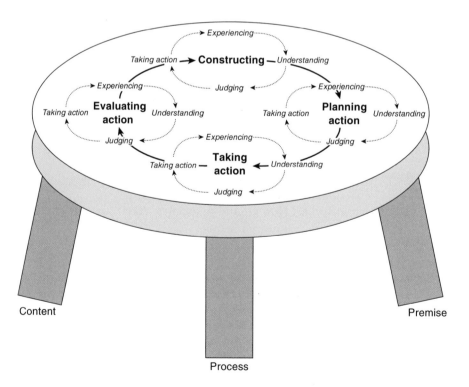

Figure 2.5 The complex dynamics of action research

all data, both of sense and data of consciousness. It enables you to inquire into how you think, construct meaning and verify your understanding, as you receive insights as to what is going on in any situation and seek to take appropriate action.

The underlying assumption is that you as the researcher are an agent in the generation of data. Brydon-Miller (2008a) suggests that prior to entering into a research setting we critically examine ourselves as researchers. Drawing on the image of dance training, she suggests that we need to find our centre, that is, our core values, and then engage with others – hence our focus on first person in this chapter. As Buchanan and Boddy (1992) remind us, the desire to be involved or to lead radical change involves high hassle and high vulnerability, so you need a combination of skills in self-reflection with vulnerability, realistic expectations, tolerance, humility, self-giving, self-containment and an ability to learn (Bell, 1998). When you inquire into what is going on, when you show people your train of thought and put forward hypotheses to be tested, you are generating data. Accordingly, some of your core first-person skills are in the areas of self-awareness and sensitivity to what you think and feel within yourself, and to what you observe going on around you, supported by the conceptual analytic frameworks on which you base your observations and interpretations. In this respect your knowledge base in the field of organization behaviour and change, on which you frame your observations, is central.

Recommended reading

Coghlan, D. (2008) 'Authenticity as first person practice: An exploration based on Bernard Lonergan', *Action Research*, 6 (3): 339–343.

Coghlan, D. (2009) 'Toward a philosophy of clinical inquiry/research', *Journal of Applied Behavioral Science*, 45 (1): 106–121.

Coghlan, D. with Brydon-Miller, M. (2014) *The SAGE Encyclopedia of Action Research*. London: Sage. (See especially, 'Action science', 'Advocacy and inquiry', 'Collaborative developmental action inquiry', 'First person action research', 'Living life as inquiry', 'Second person action research', 'Third person action research'.)

Friedman, V. and Rogers, T. (2008) 'Action science: Linking causal action and meaning making in action research', in P. Reason and H. Bradbury (eds), *The SAGE Handbook of Action Research* (2nd edn). London: Sage, pp. 252–265.

McArdle, K. (2008) 'Getting in, getting on, getting out: On working with second-person inquiry groups', in P. Reason and H. Bradbury (eds), *The SAGE Handbook of Action Research* (2nd edn). London: Sage, pp. 602–614.

Torbert, W.R. and Taylor, S. (2008) 'Action inquiry: Interweaving multiple qualities of attention for timely action', in P. Reason and H. Bradbury (eds), *The SAGE Handbook of Action Research* (2nd edn). London: SAGE, pp. 239–251.

Wicks, P.G. and Reason, P. (2009) 'Initiating action research: Challenges and paradoxes of opening communicative space', *Action Research*, 7 (3): 243–262.

Access a selection of author videos, encyclopaedia entries and recommended reading on this topic at www.uk.sagepub.com/coghlanandbrannick

EXERCISE 2.1

First-person knowing in action

The following exercises are aimed at stimulating your own skills in learning-in-action. There is an extensive literature that is aimed at helping people learn to develop skills in awareness, attentiveness and mindfulness through, for example, Tai Chi, Yoga, Gestalt, Focusing and the meditation practices in all religious traditions. These are most useful. In this context we build on these and seek to provide tools for you to develop skills in a more focused area: namely, insider action research. Fisher et al. (2000) provide very useful attention and reflective exercises that you may practice to develop your skills in learning-in-action in the workplace. For illustrations of teaching reflective practice, see Taylor et al. (2008).

Exercise A. General empirical method

1. Take any puzzle with which you are confronted – crossword clue, Sudoku, jigsaw, arithmetic teaser, how to get the kite down from the tree, how to prevent the water from leaking, how to help your class learn differential calculus, etc.
2. Attend to your experience of movement, from puzzlement or confusion to understanding through insight your search for an intelligible solution, and the flash of insight (the 'aha!' moment) that you receive.
3. Attend to how you verify and test your insight, and how you may go through many iterations of trial and error and of testing alternative insights.

Keep doing this exercise in as many of your everyday activities as is feasible or appropriate, so that you learn to appropriate how you know.

Exercise B. The ladder of inference

Take Figure 2.4 and apply it to an incident in your project. Retrace your steps from what you saw and heard during the incident.

1. What evidence did you select from all that was going on around you?
2. What inferences did you draw and did not test?
3. What conclusions did you draw?
4. What actions did you take or did not take?
5. Now review the whole process, and receive what insights come about as to how you may have moved from data to reasoning to conclusions.

Exercise C. Double-column

1. Take a blank sheet of paper and write down the progress of a conversation that you are having with another person, with whom you are working on your project.
2. Then, on another page or column, write down what you have been thinking privately about what is being said in the conversation, and what you have *not* said.
3. Notice how you make inferences and attributions privately in your own head out of what is rather hazy evidence, and how you act on them by what you say in response.

EXERCISE 2.2

Keeping a journal

Exercise A. Kolb's Cycle

This is based on Kolb's (1984) experiential learning cycle (McMullan and Cahoon, 1979; Coghlan, 1993).

1. *Concrete experience*: describe a concrete event which has taken place in the work situation: what happened, who said or did what, what you felt, said or did; what happened next, what the consequences were. Stick to a single event bounded by time. Be clinically neutral in the description – like a news bulletin.
2. *Reflection*: now, looking back with hindsight, what are your feelings, reactions, observation and judgements on this event? Perhaps now you notice that this has happened before or often. Maybe you are disappointed, angry or pleased with your own reactions at the time? How do you view your reactions and/or behaviour? What were the triggers that provoked your reaction?
3. *Conceptualization*: relate relevant concepts to the experience described and formulate tentative conclusions, generalizations or hypotheses.
4. *Experimentation*: suggest action implications for applying, testing or extending what you have reflected on, with a view to setting some behavioural goals for similar future situations. These are not general resolutions, but specific and concrete actions coming directly from your experience, reflection and conceptualization.

(Continued)

(Continued)

Exercise B. ORJI

This is based on Schein's (1999, 2013) ORJI (Coghlan, 1993).

1. Take a situation or event where your own behaviour resulted in an unpredicted outcome.
2. What did I actually observe? Can I describe it?
3. How did I react? What feelings were aroused in me?
4. What was my judgement about what happened? What thoughts or evaluations did the event trigger?
5. What did I do about it? How did I intervene? (Remember: doing nothing or remaining silent is also an intervention.)

EXERCISE 2.3

Developing inquiry skills

1. In your learning group or with colleagues, form a triad and adapt roles A, B and C.
2. A presents an issue that they are dealing with in their action research project.
3. B inquires into the issue, using Schein's intervention typology.
4. C observes, and then facilitates reflection on the process using Schein's intervention typology.
5. Change roles and repeat.
6. Change roles and repeat.

This exercise also may be done using Argyris' seven rules for hypothesis testing, or Torbert's four forms of speech. McGill and Brockbank (2004) provide other useful techniques for developing skills in working in action learning sets.

THREE
Understanding Action Research

 See www.uk.sagepub.com/coghlanandbrannick for a short introduction to the chapter from David Coghlan

Now that you have a sense of the action and learning-in-action processes as you engage in your project, we step back and consider some of the theoretical issues in action research. The guiding questions underpinning this chapter are: 'How do I understand what I am doing in my insider action research initiative?' and 'How do I understand how it fits into a rich research tradition?'

We begin by noting that understanding of the nature of research is changing. As Gibbons et al. (1994) have argued, it is time for a mode of research (which they call Mode 2 research) that is transdisciplinary, heterogeneous, socially accountable, reflexive and produced in the context of application. Mode 2 is contrasted with Mode 1 which captures the normal meaning of the term 'science', whose aim is to produce universal knowledge and build and test theory within a disciplinary field, and where the role of the researcher is that of an observer whose relationship to the setting is detached and neutral. Mode 2 or 'the new production of knowledge' as articulated by Gibbons and colleagues is a network activity and, therefore, research needs to follow and move away from a model whereby it is embedded currently in the expertise of isolated individuals operating from a 'top-down' expert model (Gustavsen, 2003). MacLean et al. (2002) make the point that action-oriented research, such as action research, has the potential to meet the criteria of Mode 2 research (Shani et al., 2012).

Action research has been traditionally defined as an approach to research that is based on a collaborative problem-solving relationship between researcher and client, which aims both to solve a problem and to generate new knowledge. Reason and Bradbury say that it is 'a family of practices of living inquiry ... it is not so much a methodology as an orientation to inquiry' (2008: 1). Accordingly, what is noticeable is that there is a wide diversity not only in practice, but in the discourse on action research practice. In this chapter we present some foundational perspectives on this diversity, in order to help you establish some grounds for what you are doing in your insider action research project (for a flavour of discussions on this variety, consult such sources as Cassell and Johnson, 2006; Docherty et al., 2006; Greenwood and Levin, 2007; *International Journal of Action Research* 3(1–2); Reason and Bradbury, 2008).

Action research as practical knowing

In what is referred to as an extended epistemology, action research distinguishes four kinds of knowing, reflecting different ways in which we deal with and act within the world (Heron, 1996; Reason and Torbert, 2001; Reason and Bradbury, 2008):

1. *experiential knowing* – the knowledge arising as we encounter the realities around us;
2. *presentational knowing* – the knowledge expressed in our giving form to this experiential knowing through language, images, music, painting and the like;
3. *propositional knowing* – the knowledge distilling our experiential and presentational knowing into theories, statements and propositions; and
4. *practical knowing* – the knowledge that brings the other three forms of knowing to full fruition by *doing* appropriate things skilfully and competently.

The form of knowledge that action research aims to produce is practical knowing – the knowing that shapes the quality of your moment-to-moment action.

What we know and how we know in day-to-day living is the realm of practical knowing, or 'common sense knowing' as Lonergan (1992[1957]) terms it. Its interests and concerns are human living, the successful performance of daily tasks and discovering immediate solutions that will work. It differs from scientific knowing in that it is particular and practical, and draws on resources of language, support of tone and volume, eloquence and facial expression, pauses, questions, omissions, and so on. One of its particular characteristics is that it varies from place to place and from situation to situation. What is familiar in one place may be unfamiliar in another. What works in one setting may not work in another. What we know needs to be differentiated for each situation. Understanding actions in the everyday requires inquiry into the constructions of meaning that individuals make about themselves, their situation and the world, and how their actions may be driven by assumptions and compulsions as well as by values. In a similar vein, large systems and groups hold their own shared meanings which direct their actions: such meanings are likely to be hidden and taken for granted (Schein, 2010). Accordingly, practical knowing is always incomplete and can be completed only by attending to figuring out what is needed in the situations that one is in at a given time. No two situations are identical. This is why we reason, reflect and judge in a practical pattern of knowing in order to move from one setting to another, grasping what modifications are needed and deciding how to act.

In summary, a contrast of scientific and practical knowing points to differences in how practical knowing has a concern for the practical and the particular, while science has theoretical aspirations and seeks to make universal abstract statements (De Vos, 1987). Practical knowing is content with only what it needs for the moment, while scientific knowing tries to be exhaustive and seeks to know everything and state accurately and completely all it knows. Practical knowing is typically spontaneous, while science is methodical. Practical knowing uses language with a range of meanings, while science develops technical jargon. Practical knowing remains in the world of things-related-to-us, while scientific knowing wants to relate things to each other (Lonergan, 1992[1957]). As we explored in Chapter 2, engaging in the cycles of action and reflection in practical knowing involves researching in the present tense, as we try to understand and make a judgement about what is going on in a given situation and decide what to say or do.

Practical knowing has been neglected by scholars. In the seventeenth century philosophers turned to problems of the objectivity of knowing: this marked a shift from knowing in a descriptive mode to knowing in an explanatory mode, where things were no longer presented in relation to the knowing subject but were related to one another in recurring patterns. A tendency to relate any method of thinking to the subject was criticized as being subjective and invalid, and limited to surface appearances, contrasted with scientific patterns of knowing which emphasize the objectivity and separation of the knower (subjective) from the known (objective). This view continues to be held, particularly in the academy and by those who hold a particular view of the nature of science. Descriptions of action research that focus only on the action, and do not include the understanding that comes from insight into action and which can contribute to the action, miss the point about the link between theory and practice. The adage that there is nothing as practical as a good theory, captures the essential link between theory and practice that underpins action research (Lewin, 1997 [1943,1944]).

The foundations of action research

Action research has many origins and roots: in the work of Kurt Lewin, one of the founding fathers of social psychology (Burnes and Cooke, 2012), Paulo Freire's work on consciousness-raising (Chevalier and Buckles, 2013), critical and pragmatic philosophy (Johansson and Lindhult, 2008), various schools of liberation thought, notably Marxist and feminist (Brydon-Miller et al., 2003) and Aristotelian philosophy (Eikeland, 2006a, 2008). We are building particularly on how action research developed largely from the work of Kurt Lewin and his associates, and involves a collaborative, cyclical process of constructing a change situation or a problem, planning, gathering data, taking action and then fact-finding about the results of that action in order to plan and take further action (Lewin, 1997[1946], 1999[1948];

Dickens and Watkins, 1999; Coghlan and Jacobs, 2005; Bargal, 2006, 2012; Neilsen, 2006; Burnes, 2007; Burnes and Cooke, 2012). The key idea is that action research uses a scientific approach to study the resolution of important social or organizational issues together with those who experience these issues directly.

Argyris (1993) summarizes the four core themes of Lewin's work. First, Lewin integrated theory with practice by framing social science as the study of problems of real life, and connected all problems to theory. Second, he designed research by framing the whole and then differentiating the parts. Third, he produced constructs which could be used to generalize and understand the individual case, particularly through the researcher as intervenor, and his notion that one could understand something only when one tried to change it. Fourth, he was concerned with placing social science at the service of democracy, thereby changing the role of those being studied from subjects to clients, so that help, if effective, could improve quality of life and lead to more valid knowledge. Marrow, Lewin's biographer, states:

> Theory was always an intrinsic part of Lewin's search for understanding, but theory often evolved and became refined as the data unfolded, rather than being systematically detailed in advance. Lewin was led by both data and theory, each feeding the other, each guiding the research process. (Marrow, 1969: 128)

Argyris et al. (1985) summarize Lewin's concept of action research.

1. It involves change experiments on real problems in social systems. It focuses on a particular problem and seeks to provide assistance to the client system.

2. It, like social management more generally, involves iterative cycles of identifying a problem, planning, acting and evaluating.

3. The intended change in an action research project typically involves re-education, a term that refers to changing patterns of thinking and action that are currently well-established in individuals and groups. A change intended by change agents is typically at the level of norms and values expressed in action. Effective re-education depends on participation by clients in diagnosis, fact-finding and free choice to engage in new kinds of action.

4. It challenges the status quo from a participative perspective, which is congruent with the requirements of effective re-education.

5. It is intended to contribute simultaneously to basic knowledge in social science and to social action in everyday life. High standards for developing theory and empirically testing propositions organized by theory are not to be sacrificed nor the relation to practice be lost. (1985: 8–9)

After Lewin's untimely death in 1947, action research became integral to the growth of the theory and practice of organization development (French and Bell, 1999;

McArdle and Reason, 2008; Burnes and Cooke, 2012; Coghlan, 2012a; Weisbord, 2012), and significant for organizational research (Gummesson, 2000; Eden and Huxham, 2006) such as in commercial organizations (Adler et al., 2004; Bradbury et al., 2008; Coughlan and Coghlan, 2009), education (Pine, 2008; Somekh, 2006), community work (Stringer, 2013), health and social care (Parkin, 2009; Koshy et al., 2011) and nursing (Williamson and Bellman, 2012).

ACTION RESEARCH AT WORK

Lippitt (1979) distinguishes three different meanings that have been denoted by the term action research, which reflect different roles played by the researcher. First, diagnostic research is conducted concerning some ongoing aspect of an action process. In this form of research the researcher gathers the data and presents it to those who are in a position to take some action. The research originates from the researcher's interests and is useful to the organization, partly as a pay-off for allowing access. In Lippitt's view this does not constitute action research. Second, action research is connoted by a procedure of collecting data from participants of a system and providing feedback about the findings of the data as an intervention to influence – presumably in a helpful way – the ongoing action process of the system. In this model the researcher may be acting either as a data-gatherer solely, or in a helping role to the members of the system. Third, action research is defined as a procedure in which the participants of a social system are involved in a data collection process about themselves, and utilize the data that they have generated to review the facts about themselves in order to take some form of remedial or developmental action. In this model, the researcher and the researched are working in collaboration. In Lippitt's view, this is the purest form of action research.

Cooperrider and Srivastva (1987) criticize how action research has developed to be viewed as a form of problem-solving. They challenge what they see as underlying assumptions about the nature of action research, which are based on utilitarian and technical views of organizations as 'problems' to be 'solved'. As an alternative, they propose appreciative inquiry as a form of action research that focuses on building on what is already successful rather than what is deficient, and which enables the emergence of generative thinking and solutions (Bushe, 2012).

For Gummesson, action research is 'the most demanding and far-reaching method of doing case study research' (2000: 16). He integrates the characteristics of action research from several case studies, and focuses on it from a management perspective.

Action researchers take action

They are not merely observing something happening; they are actively working at making it happen.

Action research always involves two goals

These are: to solve a problem and to contribute to science. As we pointed out earlier, action research is about research-in-action, and does not postulate a distinction between theory and action. Hence, the challenge for action researchers is to engage in both making the action happen and to stand back from the action and reflect on it as it happens, in order to contribute theory to the body of knowledge.

Action research is interactive

Action research requires cooperation between the researchers and the client personnel, and continuous adjustment to new information and new events. In action research the members of the client system are co-researchers, as the action researcher is working with them on their issue so that it may be resolved or improved for their system, and a contribution made to the body of knowledge. As action research is a series of unfolding and unpredictable events, the actors need to work together and be able to adapt to the contingencies of the unfolding story.

Action research aims to develop holistic understanding

The aim is to achieve this during a project, as well as recognizing complexity. As organizations are dynamic socio-technical systems, action researchers need to have a broad view of how the system works and to be able to move between formal structural, technical and informal people sub-systems. Working with organizational systems requires an ability to work with dynamic complexity, which describes how a system is complex, not due to a lot of detail (i.e. detail complexity), but due to multiple causes and effects over time (Senge, 1990). Action research is fundamentally about change.

Action research is applicable to the understanding, planning and implementation of change in groups, organizations and communities. As action research is fundamentally about change, knowledge of and skill in the dynamics of organizational change are necessary (we develop this point in Chapter 5).

Action research requires an understanding of the ethical framework

This is about understanding the values and norms within which the research is used in a particular context. In action research ethics involves authentic relationships between the action researcher and the members of the client system as to how they understand the process and take significant action. Typically, the values and norms that flow from such ethical principles focus on how the action researcher works with the members of the organization (we will develop this point in Chapter 10).

Action research can include all types of data-gathering methods

Action research does not preclude the use of data-gathering methods from traditional research. Qualitative and quantitative tools such as interviews and surveys are commonly used. What is important in action research is that the planning and use of these tools is well thought out with the members of the organization, and clearly integrated into the action research process (we return to this point in Chapter 7).

Action research requires a breadth of preunderstanding

This preunderstanding is of the corporate or organizational environment, the conditions of business or service delivery, the structure and dynamics of operating systems and the theoretical underpinnings of such systems. Preunderstanding refers to the knowledge that the action researcher brings to the research project. Such a need for preunderstanding signals that an action research approach is inappropriate for researchers who, for example, think that all they have to do to develop grounded theory is just to go out into the field.

Action research should be conducted in real time

However, retrospective action research is also acceptable. While action research is a live case study being written as it unfolds, it also can take the form of a traditional case study written in retrospect, when the written case is used as an intervention into the organization in the present. In such a situation the case performs the function of a 'learning history', and is used as an intervention to promote reflection and learning in the organization (Kleiner and Roth, 1997).

The action research paradigm requires its own quality criteria

In Chapter 1 we introduced the notion of quality in action research and we will return to it in Chapter 12.

Notwithstanding business consultancy language, Gummesson's characteristics apply to the action researcher in any organization. The research project unfolds as the cycles of planning, data-gathering, taking action, reviewing and further planning and action are enacted.

The philosophy of action research

In earlier editions we located action research within general traditions of research philosophies, such as subjectivist and objectivist ontologies and epistemologies. Action research has a solid grounding in many philosophical approaches: Aristotelian praxis (Eikeland, 2008), pragmatic philosophy (Pasmore, 2001; Greenwood and Levin, 2007; Bradbury, 2008), Habermasian communicative action (Shani et al., 2004), phenomenology (Ladkin, 2005), critical theory (Kemmis, 2001), constructivism (Lincoln, 2001), social contructionism (Gergen and Gergen, 2008) and in the philosophy of Wittgenstein (Shotter, 2003).

The ongoing debate has been about arguing whether or not or how action research may be called 'scientific'. While some writers have articulated the ontological and epistemological foundations of action research, and contrasted them with those of the scientific method associated with positivistic philosophy (Susman and Evered, 1978; Riordan, 1995; Schon, 2004[1995]; Reason and Torbert, 2001; Eikeland, 2007; Greenwood and Levin, 2007), others have emphasized the compatibility between the two approaches (Aguinis, 1993; Stephens et al., 2009).

There is a problem about the use of the term 'science'. Susman and Evered describe action research as 'a kind of science with a different epistemology that produces a different kind of knowledge' (1978: 601). Argyris et al. refer to 'a science of practice' (1985: 4), and Torbert to 'a kind of scientific inquiry conducted in everyday life' (1991: 220). Such uses are extending the usual connotations associated with the term 'science'. Cassell and Johnson (2006) explore five alternative perspectives based on different conceptions of 'science' underpinning action research praxis: experimental action research practices, inductive action research practices, participatory action research, participatory action research practices and deconstructive action research practices. They conclude that while the problem is that 'science' is defined typically in terms of a particular form of knowledge articulated by positivist norms, a review of the philosophy of science shows that any expression of ontological and epistemological stance is contentious. Accordingly, in their view, 'there is no incontestable scheme of ontological and epistemological standards which may be deployed to govern action research' (2006: 806). Lonergan (1992: 233) proposes that the use of the term 'science' be restricted to knowledge content in principles and laws that are verified universally. He suggests that 'scholarship' be employed to connote learning that consists in common sense thought and other social science.

Action research challenges traditional science in several action-oriented ways. We have emphasized already Macmurray's (1957) assertion of the primacy of the practical and of the self as agent. Action researchers work on the epistemological assumption that the purpose of academic research and discourse is not just to describe, understand and explain the world, but also to change it (Reason and Torbert, 2001). One issue is more than the form of the knowledge produced or the methodology employed to gather data or evidence, but who decides the research agenda in the first place, and who benefits directly from it. Sharing the power of knowledge production with the researched subverts the usual practice of knowledge and policy development as being the primary domain of researchers and policymakers. Action researchers need to attend to these issues, and to be politically astute in manoeuvring between the political posturing of groups within an organization or community in a manner that is congruent with action research values, without being politically naïve.

At the core of the debate appears to be modernism's adherence to the split between the knower and the known, where the position on knowing is a matter of a subject 'in here' looking at or reflecting on an object 'out there' (Coghlan, 2010a). For the empirical philosophers, inner perception was conceived by the analogy of taking a look at something outside of ourselves, and so consciousness was held to be a faculty of inner perception. For Kant, for anything to be an object of knowledge, first it had to be the object of sense perception. Modernist social science embedded itself in this perceptualist standpoint on human cognition, which found expression in behaviourism and positivism. Modern philosophy, under the influence of positivism, avoided the issue of the subject in their acts of consciousness, and so the subject became neglected and excluded from management and organizational research. Where perceptualism failed is in its lack of attention to the world mediated by meaning, and to the active role of human consciousness in constructing that world. The postmodern and phenomenological perspective critiqued this focus on immediacy and objectivity, bringing the focus to bear on meaning and value and how this world is constructed through human consciousness and language (Ladkin, 2005; Shotter, 2007). Action research goes beyond the 'linguistic turn', and now argues that it is time for the 'action turn', whereby 'inquiry contributes directly to the flourishing of human persons, their communities and the ecosystems of which they are part' (Reason and Torbert, 2001: 6).

Interiority

There are philosophical implications that provide a means of relating the general empirical method to the challenges of understanding action research from both inside and outside the action research community. Understanding consciousness as a quality in the operations of human knowing, rather than a form of perception, is at the heart of the general empirical method. As Coghlan (2010b) explores, the general empirical method encourages us to attend to how we understand, and how new experiences and insights change our understanding. Through grasping that insights are not simply more sophisticated sense perceptions, the general empirical method challenges assumptions that inquiry is a matter of getting outside of a self 'in here' to integrating an existing world of things 'out there'. It also dispels the distinction that some make between research that discovers and research that verifies. Discovering (seeking understanding) and verifying (making a judgement about what one has discovered through insight) are both activities in the knowing process. As we have explored, all knowing involves both activities.

As a frame to build linkages between propositional and practical knowing, we propose the notion of *interiority*, by drawing on the general empirical method introduced in Chapter 2, which enables action researchers to move between the realms of theory and practical knowing, valuing both while recognizing the different contributions that each makes (Coghlan, 2010b). The challenge is to turn from the outer world of practical knowing and theory to appropriation of oneself as a knower, i.e. one's own interiority. Interiority involves shifting from *what* we know to *how* we know, a process of intellectual self-awareness. Interiority analysis involves using one's knowledge of how the mind works to critique an intellectual search for truth in any area. The turn to interiority is not just cognition, but an appropriation of self and one's mind. Interiority is the means by which we can turn from the outer world of practical knowing and theory, with the ability to recognize their competence and meet the demands of both, without confusing them. It is the means by which we can wax poetically about the sunset in the realm of practical and aesthetic knowing, while at the same time being aware that in the realm of scientific theory, the sun does not set.

Interiority leads to a critical realist approach. It is realist in that through judgement you can affirm what is real, critique your insights and affirm which ones best fit the evidence. Burgoyne (2011) argues that the critical realist position holds a position between the excesses of positivism and constructionism. In his view, positivism sees the world as a deterministic machine that can be understood and controlled with enough experimentation, while extreme constructionism sees the world as nothing but a shifting sea of cultural meaning. Interiority goes beyond practical knowing and theory, not by negating them or leaving them behind, but by appreciating them and recognizing their limitations. Questions of science can be settled by appealing to observable data. However, in the world of interiority, data are not sensible or observable, but belong to the private world of intentional consciousness (as we discussed in Chapter 2 when we explored the process of valuing).

Reflection is a process of interiority and is normally explained as a process of stepping back from experience to question it, and to have insights and understanding with a view to planning further action (Kolb, 1984; Boud et al., 1985; Moon, 1999; Raelin, 2008). It is the critical link between the concrete experience, the judgement and taking new action. As Raelin (2008) discusses, it is the key to learning, as it enables you to develop an ability to uncover and make explicit to yourself what you have planned, discovered and achieved in practice. He also argues that reflection must be brought into the open so that it goes beyond your privately-held assumptions, and helps you to see how your knowledge is constructed. In action research, reflection is the activity which integrates action and research. As we discussed in Chapter 1, reflection on content, process and premise is critical to both the action research cycle and meta-learning.

Interiority calls for a self-knowledge of how we see, think, judge, imagine, remember, criticize, evaluate, conclude, etc. Understanding the activity of human understanding is the main characteristic of interiority. By using the general empirical method we can attend to data, ask the relevant questions and think a matter through. We can know when we have reached reasonable conclusions and can take responsibility for them. We can reflect and discover our mistakes. We can inquire into the sources of our misunderstandings, biases, inferences, prejudices, fears, anxieties and false judgements, how we subvert the inquiry process by ignoring awkward questions, not attending to all the data or jumping to conclusions (Argyris et al., 1985; Coghlan, 2008).

Argyris (2004) commented that scholarship typically focuses on espoused theory and cannot address theory-in-use. Research cannot address how we create the theory that we describe. The general empirical method provides a frame and method for doing this, and for providing the basis of a science or scholarship of action. Interiority enables us to attend to the different realms of meaning that coexist in a given situation, thereby giving us insight into how we are thinking and how we hold theory and practice together.

Meynell (1999) argues that interiority, whereby we work to attain truth and value through the general empirical method of trying to be attentive, intelligent, reasonable and responsible, may be envisaged as the 'new Enlightenment' – a synthesis of modern and postmodern thought. We can be attentive to our feelings and mental acts as well as to the sense experiences that are the staple of the empiricists. We can come to reasonable judgements as we probe what and why questions, and affirm definitely or provisionally as appropriate an understanding that fits the evidence. We can come to reasonable judgements about what is good or bad, true or false, and act responsibly following such judgements. We can decide how attentive we want to be, whether our understanding is intelligent or biased, our judgements are reasonable and how responsible we are for our actions. As there are always further questions, more evidence to attend to and more bias to be overcome, our judgements of fact and value will change accordingly. As we explored in Chapter 2, the core challenge is to be authentic, because the alternative is self-destruction.

Modalities of action research

The term 'action research' is a generic one, and is used to refer to a family of what might seem to be a bewildering array of activities and methods. At its core, action research is a research approach which focuses on simultaneous action and research in a collaborative manner. Within this approach are multiple modalities, each of which has its own distinctive emphasis (Raelin, 2009; Coghlan 2010a, 2011). Some action research modalities have developed from sociology and focus on how communities as sociopolitical systems enact social change. These approaches have a focus outside of the organizational context and tend to address structural emancipatory issues, relating to, for example, education, social exclusion and power and control (Chevalier and Buckles, 2013). This tradition of action research is associated particularly with the southern hemisphere. Other action research approaches, particularly in the northern hemisphere, have their origins in applied behavioural science and have developed in the organizational context (Coch and French, 1948; Foster, 1972; French and Bell, 1999; Adler et al., 2004; Coghlan 2012a). Parallel to this approach is one that focuses on relationships, both in the workplace and between social partners in regional development (Fricke and Totterdill, 2004). The central process for building relationships is democratic dialogue. This book is addressed primarily to those working within organizational settings, and as such is part of the northern hemisphere tradition of action research.

Each modality within action research is based on a generative insight which describes the foundational understanding that has led to the particular framing of each modality by the person or group that created that modality. These generative insights, in turn, generate further insights and methods of working within each modality (Coghlan, 2010a). Here we provide an introduction to some of the more prominent modalities: organization development, action learning, appreciative inquiry, clinical inquiry/research, cooperative inquiry and learning history. Each of these modalities is based on generative insights that give it its own distinctive character and emphasis. Through focusing on generative insights and how the general empirical method may be applied, we hope that you will receive your own insight into these action modalities and, thereby, discover for yourself how to engage with them.

Organization development through action research

Action research is one of the distinctive features of organization development and one of its core origins (Schein, 2010[1989]; Pasmore, 2001; Bradbury et al., 2008; Coghlan, 2012a; Klev and Levin, 2012). As a collaborative, interventionist form of research it is grounded in its Lewinian roots in the scholarship of practice (Coghlan and Jacobs, 2005; Bushe and Marshak, 2009; Burnes and Cooke, 2012; Coghlan, 2012a). As we noted previously, its generative insight may be found in Lewin's (1997[1946], 1999[1948]) own insight that it was not enough to try to explain things; one also had to try to change them. This insight led to the development of action research and the powerful notion that human systems could be understood and changed only if one involved the members of the system in the inquiry process itself. So the tradition of involving the members of an organization in the change process, which is the hallmark of organization development, originated in a scientific premise that this is the way to get better data and to effect change. Action research was based on two assumptions which are the cornerstones of organization development. One is that involving the clients or learners in their own learning not only produces better learning, but more valid data about how the system really works. The other is that one only understands a system when one tries to change it, as changing human systems often involves variables which cannot be controlled by traditional research methods. Action research used in organization development is based on collaboration between the behavioural scientist-researcher and the client, where they collaborate on intervening in the organization (the action), and in exploring issues and generating data on the development of the organization (the research activity). They develop action plans to address the issues and implement them. Together they evaluate the outcomes of the actions, both intended and unintended. This evaluation then may lead to further cycles of examining issues, planning action, taking action and evaluation. Cyclical-sequential phases may be identified that capture the movements of collaboration through planning and action to evaluation and knowledge generation. These activities may serve also to generate new behavioural science knowledge, which is fed into the depository of information for other behavioural scientists as general laws, types of issues or the process of consultant–client collaboration, thus addressing issues beyond the specific case.

Participatory action research

Participatory action research typically has a focus outside of the organizational context, and involves egalitarian participation by a community to transform some aspects of its situation or structures. Its generative insight is how power and powerlessness excludes groups from decision-making, and so participatory action research moves to empower people to construct and use their own knowledge (Lykes and Mallona, 2008; Rahman, 2008; Chevalier and Buckles, 2013). Many of the liberation or emancipatory action research approaches are variations on participatory action research. However, in this book we are not focusing on this context.

Action learning

Action learning is an approach to the development of people in organizations which takes the task as the vehicle for learning. It reverses the traditional learning process where one learns something first and then applies it. In action learning the generative insight is found in Revans' two statements: 'There can be no learning without action and no (sober and deliberate) action without learning' (2008: 83), and 'Those unable to change themselves cannot change what goes on around them' (2008: 85). Central to action learning is a distinction between puzzles and problems. On the one hand, *puzzles* are those difficulties for which a correct solution exists and which are amenable to specialist and expert advice. On the other hand, *problems* are difficulties where no single solution can possibly exist because different people advocate different courses of action in accordance with their own value systems, past experience and intended outcomes.

Action learning is formulated around Revans' (2008) learning formula:

$$L = P + Q$$

where L stands for learning, P for programmed learning (i.e. current knowledge in use, what is already known, in books, etc.) and Q for questioning insight.

This formula embeds the general empirical method through its focus on Q as questioning insight into experience (Coghlan, 2012b). Revans (1982) describes three processes central to action learning, which he refers to as a 'praxeology of action'.

1. *System Alpha* – a process of inquiry into the issue under consideration: its history, manifestation, what has prevented it from being resolved and what has been previously attempted.
2. *System Beta* – action learning is science in progress through rigorous exploration of resolution of the issue through action and reflection.
3. *System Gamma* – action learning is characterized by a quality of group interaction which enables individual critical reflection and, ultimately, the learning. This is the essence of action learning.

These three processes emphasize how action learning involves engagement with real issues rather than with fabrications, and is both scientifically rigorous in confronting the issue and critically subjective through managers learning-in-action. Participating managers take responsibility for and control of their own learning, so there is minimal use of experts (Revans, 2008; Pedler, 2011). Implementation of the praxeology of Systems Alpha, Beta and Gamma provides a process through which the learner, in the company of peers in an action learning group, engages in critical inquiry into experience, gains insights and takes risks in taking action on the problem, which sets up further experiences for reflection – and so the process continues (Pedler and Burgoyne, 2008; Coghlan and Rigg, 2012). While action learning has flourished in the context of management education, its practice as an approach to research is embryonic. There is an emerging literature that explores how its theory and processes form the basis of an action-oriented research (Coughlan and Coghlan, 2011).

Appreciative inquiry

Appreciative inquiry has emerged from the work of Cooperrider, and aims at large system change through an appreciative focus on what already works in a system, rather than what is deficient (Reed, 2007; Ludema and Fry, 2008). It is built on the generative insight of inquiry as positive: that is, if people focus on what is valuable in what they do and try to work on how this may be built on, then it leverages the generative capacity of metaphors and conversation to facilitate transformational action (Ludema and Fry, 2008; Bushe, 2012).

There are two cycles that appreciative inquiry utilize: the 'Four Ds' (Discovery, Dream, Design, Delivery), and the 'Four Is' (Initiate, Inquire, Imagine, Innovate). These enable researchers and practitioners to move from experience to selected action, and to attend to and receive insights into understanding the power of positive questioning. Accordingly, each step of the cycles involves experience, understanding and judgement. For example, the *discovery* step involves inquiry into the experience of what works well, insight into how and why it is successful, affirmation by judgement and then creation of the *dream* to build on it. So the general empirical method continues in the other steps of the cycles.

Clinical inquiry research

In writing about an organization development approach to organizational research, Schein (1987, 1995, 2008) introduces the notion of the 'clinical' approach to research. For Schein, clinical refers to those trained helpers (such as clinical and counselling psychologists, social workers, organization development consultants) who work professionally with human systems. These trained helpers act as organizational clinicians in that they:

- emphasize in-depth observation of learning and change processes;
- emphasize the effects of interventions;
- operate from models of what it is to function as a healthy system, and focus on pathologies, puzzles and anomalies that illustrate deviations from healthy functioning; and
- build theory and empirical knowledge through developing concepts that capture the real dynamics of systems (Schein, 1997).

At the heart of clinical inquiry is the generative insight that when researchers gain access to organizations at the organization's invitation, in order to be helpful and intervene to enable change to occur, that is the most fruitful way of understanding and changing organizations (Schein, 1987, 1995, 2008).

The general empirical method underpins the practice of clinical inquiry research as clinical researchers help clients to attend to their experience, have insights into that experience, make judgements as to whether the insights fit the evidence, and then take action (Coghlan, 2009). As Coghlan (2009) argues, clinical inquiry research makes demands on clinical researchers to apply the general empirical method to themselves as well as to their clients by being attentive to data, intelligent in understanding, reasonable in making judgements and responsible in making interventions with their clients. In this book, while we describe clinical inquiry as a distinct modality, we also are drawing on it to provide core second-person skills (as we have done in Chapter 2).

Cooperative inquiry

One of the forms that action research takes is cooperative inquiry (Reason, 1988, 1999; Heron, 1996; Heron and Reason, 2008). Heron and Reason define cooperative inquiry 'as a form of second person action research in which all participants work together in an inquiry group as co-researchers and co-subjects' (2008: 366). Reason (1999) sets out the process of cooperative inquiry in the following stages.

1. The group talks about the group's interests and concerns, agrees on the focus of the inquiry and develops together a set of questions or proposals that its members wish to explore.
2. The group applies actions in the everyday work of the members, who initiate the actions and observe and record the outcomes of their own and each other's behaviour.
3. The group members as co-researchers become fully immersed in their experience. They may deepen into the experience, or they may be led away from the original ideas and proposals into new fields, unpredicted action and creative insights.
4. After an agreed period engaged in phases two and three, the co-researchers reassemble to consider their original questions in light of their experience.

The generative insight for *understanding* cooperative inquiry is how each person is a *co-subject* in the experience phases by participating in the activities being researched, and a *co-researcher* in the reflection phases by participating in generating ideas, designing and managing the project and drawing conclusions.

The general empirical method operates in cooperative inquiry as participants' experience is brought to the group and exposed to questioning. Group members inquire into how individuals construct the meanings of these experiences. Further questions are asked. As the group explores its members' experiences, further insights are generated and meanings are articulated. So there are continuing cycles of experiences being shared, questions asked, insights generated, meanings articulated and tested in action, leading to further insights, tested, understood and acted on. An important element of cooperative inquiry is that it works with the different ways of knowing, so experience and insights may be expressed in different forms. In Chapter 8 we present a case example where Meehan used cooperative inquiry in his own organization.

Learning history

A learning history is a document composed by participants in a change effort, with the help of external consultants who act as 'learning historians' (Kleiner and Roth, 1997; Roth and Kleiner, 1998; Roth and Bradbury, 2008). 'The goal of a learning history is to increase participation in a dialogic reflection on past action for creating desired future practices' (Bradbury and Mainmelis, 2001: 342). It presents the experiences and understandings, in their own words, of those who have gone through and/or been affected by the change in order to help the organization move forward. The learning history is an action research process by being an intervention into the organization. This happens when action research documentation is made available to organizational stakeholders as 'a written narrative of a company's recent set of critical episodes' (Kleiner and Roth, 1997: 173) with the purpose of facilitating learning.

Rather than presenting the univocal voice of a single author or group of researchers, the learning history presents concurrent, multiple and often divergent voices in an organizational story. Presenting the jointly-told tale is enabled by the format, whereby columns of narrative text are juxtaposed with the interpretative voice of participants (often disagreeing) and the voice of the learning historian. The generative insight underpinning the learning history is that by capturing what groups have learned and presenting it through the jointly-told tale, readers may learn about organizational change. Readers are encouraged to attend to the questions that arise from their engagement with the text, as they choose which column to read first and how they might switch back and forth from participants' narrative and learning historians' comments to the insights that they receive from reading multiple voices and perspectives. Kleiner and Roth (1997) present a framework for how this might be done. The narrative is read by significant stakeholders who contribute to the story from their perspective in a special right-hand column on the page. Those social scientists and learning historians who study the narrative use a left-hand column for their reflection and analysis as the basis for further discussion in the organization.

The general empirical method is enacted through both conversations and written texts. Hearing and reading these multiple voices and perspectives within the process of a learning history enable insight into the insights of others, and through conversation the possibilities for new shared insights to emerge, on which judgements may be reached and actions planned and taken.

Collaborative management research

Collaborative management research is defined by Shani et al. as follows:

[A]n effort by one or more parties, at least one of which is a member of an organization and at least one of whom is an external researcher, to work together in learning about how the behaviour of managers, management methods or organizational arrangements affect outcomes in the system or systems under study, using methods that are scientifically based and intended to reduce the likelihood of drawing false conclusions from the data collected, with the intent of improving performance of the system and adding to the broader body of knowledge in the field of management. (Shani et al., 2008: 20)

Shani et al. (2008, 2012) understand that collaborative management research is unique and different from action research, in that it seeks to add value to the action research approaches discussed in this chapter through the way in which practitioners and researchers engage in a joint undertaking, where each partner takes some responsibility for the others partners' learning and knowledge.

There are other expressions of action that stress some particular emphases. *Intervention research in management* and *qualimetrics intervention research* are terms that express the form that some action research takes in France in the way that researchers work with companies (Hatchuel and David, 2008; Savall and Zardet, 2011). *Interactive research* is a term that is used in the Nordic countries. This action research approach emphasizes the relationships between participants as among equals, as well as a high degree of participation. It stresses the joint learning that goes on between participants and researchers throughout the entire research process (Nielsen and Svensson, 2006).

Reflective practice

Reflective practice refers to how individuals engage in critical reflection on their own action. It is associated with the work of Schon (1983). Reflective practice may be viewed as a specific dimension of action research, i.e. first-person inquiry. By and large, published accounts of reflective practice focus only on the individual, and generally do not consider any organizational dynamics or outcomes related to the individual's action. Schon (1983) reflects on four ways that reflective practitioners might engage in 'reflective research'.

1. *Frame analysis* – when practitioners become aware of their 'frames' and consider alternatives.
2. *Repertoire-building research* – accumulating and describing examples of reflection in action.
3. *Research on fundamental methods of inquiry and overarching theories* – by examining episodes of practice in an action science.
4. *Research on the process of reflection in action* – studying processes whereby practitioners learn to reflect in action.

Evaluative inquiry

Closely related to action research is the process of evaluative inquiry, which is a reformulation of traditional evaluation practices through an emphasis on using the process of inquiry to generate organizational learning (Preskill and Torres,

1999). Many of the processes within action research, such as collaborative inquiry, reflection, joint planning and taking action, are utilized as interventions to shape how projects are evaluated in order to stimulate organizational learning.

For the neophyte reader, these multiple modalities may be confusing. In our view, it is important to emphasize that these different methodologies are not mutually exclusive. They are sets of general principles and devices that emerged from generative insights, and which can be adapted to different research issues and contexts. Each has its own emphasis and can be appropriately used in conjunction with other approaches. What is important is that you, as the action researcher, be helped to seek the method appropriate to your inquiry and situation.

Conclusions

In this chapter we have stepped back from the action dynamic of action research in order to explore its nature, and to assist you to ground your work in its rich and deep tradition. We have outlined its foundations as based on a collaborative action relationship between researcher and members of an organization or community which, although inquiring in the present tense as action is designed and unfolds, aims both to address an issue or solve a problem, and co-generate actionable knowledge. Regretfully, action research often has become a glib term for involving clients in research and has lost its role as a powerful conceptual tool for uncovering truth on which action can be taken. Action research is a form of scholarship in the field of practical knowing that differs from the model of experimental physics, but is genuinely scientific in the emphasis on careful observation and study of the effects of behaviour on human systems as their members manage change.

Rather than discussing complex nuances of research philosophy we have selected to remain focused on the recognizable and verifiable processes of human knowing in the general empirical method. This is so that whatever philosophical tradition or action research modality you choose to embed your research, formally you can be grounded in the authenticity of the general empirical method. No one can take that away from you.

Recommended reading

Cassell, C. and Johnson, P. (2006) 'Action research: Explaining the diversity', *Human Relations*, 59 (6): 783–814.

Coghlan, D. with Brydon-Miller, M. (2014) *The SAGE Encyclopedia of Action Research*. London: Sage. (See especially: 'Critical theory', 'John Dewey', 'Kurt Lewin', 'Philosophy of science', 'Phenomenology', 'Postmodernism', 'Pragmatism', 'Ludwig Wittgenstein'.)

Friedman, V.J. and Rogers, T. (2009) 'There's nothing so theoretical as good action research', *Action Research*, 7 (1): 31–47.

Heron, J. and Reason, P. (2008) 'Extending epistemology with a co-operative inquiry', in P. Reason and H. Bradbury (eds), *The SAGE Handbook of Action Research* (2nd edn). London: Sage, pp. 367–380.

Levin, M. (2012) 'Academic integrity in action research', *Action Research*, 10 (2): 133–149.

Ludema, J. and Fry, R. (2008) 'The practice of appreciative inquiry', in P. Reason and H. Bradbury (eds), *The SAGE Handbook of Action Research* (2nd edn). London: Sage, pp. 280–296.

Pedler, M. and Burgoyne, J. (2008) 'Action learning', in P. Reason and H. Bradbury (eds), *The SAGE Handbook of Action Research* (2nd edn). London: Sage, pp. 319–332.

Roth, G. and Bradbury, H. (2008) 'Learning history: An action research in support of actionable learning', in P. Reason and H. Bradbury (eds), *The SAGE Handbook of Action Research* (2nd edn). London: Sage, pp. 350–365.

Schein, E.H. (2008) 'Clinical inquiry/research', in P. Reason and H. Bradbury (eds), *The SAGE Handbook of Action Research* (2nd edn). London: Sage, pp. 267–279.

Access a selection of author videos, encyclopaedia entries and recommended reading on this topic at www.uk.sagepub.com/coghlanandbrannick

EXERCISE 3.1

Finding Your Philosophical Roots

From your reading of the key sources and underlying philosophies that underpin and inform action research, write a reflective note for yourself that captures how you wish to position your own work philosophically.

EXERCISE 3.2

Selecting a Modality

From your understanding of your insider action research project as you are currently framing it, write a reflective note for yourself on how the generative insights that underpin the action research modalities might inform its design and what strengths they would bring to it.

2

Implementation

FOUR

Constructing and Selecting Your Insider Project

 See www.uk.sagepub.com/coghlanandbrannick for a short introduction to the chapter from David Coghlan

The question underpinning this chapter is: 'How might you construct and select an action research project?' When you construct an issue you are naming it, and by naming it you are focusing on how you might set up its analysis and set the criteria for evaluation. Constructing is a heuristic process, by which we mean that the definition of an issue already includes elements of the solution. You may reconstruct it later, whereby you question an existing construction of the issue and possibly discard it in favour of a different one. Then, new frames of reference need to be created to reconstruct the issues in such a way that supports your endeavour.

Constructing the action research project

Constructing an issue can be a complex process. It may be that what is attractive to you as an insider action research project is a practical operational issue: for example, there is a recurring problem or a developmental opportunity that your management or superiors would like researched, and a solution found. Bartunek et al. (2000) present an example of where the project was identified as one of improving relationships between the bank and a client. Clearly, such a research project can meet criteria of being useful, particularly to management, achievable in the research timeframe and manageable for the researcher.

As the action research progresses, it also may turn out that this apparent operational problem is more complex than it appears, requiring key people to alter their mandates and ways of thinking. Bartunek et al. (2000) demonstrate how in a manufacturing plant, the development of an integrated manufacturing system involved radical changes in how the company did business.

The complexity of issue identification and selection illustrates that the search for an appropriate issue to study is difficult. How do you get a sense of the array of possible issues which may be addressed? By using the term 'array' we are acknowledging the existence of a wide and diverse set of issues in an organization which all vie for action research attention. Of course, this is not to say that all issues are immediately apparent to you: some may be blatantly obvious while others may go unnoticed, unless attempts are made to uncover organizational members' perceptions of key issues. Not every issue will volunteer itself automatically for resolution. It is human perception that makes the difference, thus leading us to conclude that organizational actors' interpretations are pivotal in this whole process.

While acknowledging the existence of a wide and diverse array of issues, it is important to understand that once selected for attention, any issue may be embedded in a set of related issues (Beckhard and Harris, 1987). You are confronted then with choices concerning boundaries, and are obliged to choose between what can be achieved within the time specified for your research, and the available resources.

Thinking in terms of issues rather than problems or opportunities that warrant attention is vital, as language and labels are of the utmost importance at the outset (Dutton et al., 1983; Cooperrider and Srivastva, 1987). For example, constructing proposed research initiatives in the context of addressing problems or opportunities carries some inherent risks. Constructing an issue as a problem may influence who gets involved in problem resolution. It may be that organizational members embrace problems with a sense of loss, wondering about the organization's ability to reach a satisfactory resolution and often preferring to remain somewhat detached and uncommitted. The action research project may be challenging traditional procedures and ways of thinking.

Moreover, using the word 'problem', as distinct from 'opportunity', may lead to convergent thinking (Dutton et al., 1983). The mental effort expended on problem resolution may restrict the range of alternatives considered, blinding organizational members to the possible existence of novel solutions. In a similar vein, use of the label 'opportunity' may lead to divergent thinking, as this label has a greater sense of gain associated with it. Organizational members may feel a sense of excitement about tackling a significant opportunity which may have the potential for creativity. Bushe (2012) makes a strong case that constructing the issue in positive terms is a powerful act of generativity: it has a rich potential to generate both participative action and rich theory.

Finally, language and labels are important as they have the potential to influence risk-taking behaviour (Dutton et al., 1983). It may be that thinking in terms of opportunities cultivates a risk-taking culture, while thinking in terms of problems cultivates a risk-averse culture. If you think with an opportunity mindset, then you are less likely to embark on a witch-hunt, looking for someone to blame, as there is nothing for which to blame them; while the mindset associated with problems embraces the notion of finding a scapegoat. It seems obvious from the above that there is merit in thinking in terms of issues, without any attempt to sub-classify such issues in the first instance.

> Williander and Styhre (2006) report on how Williander designed a collaborative research proposal to serve as an intervention to develop an individual experience among corporate engineers, product planners and other stakeholders. A later project stage would focus on the dissemination of that individual experience in order to develop an organizational capability at Volvo, regarding how to capitalize on the common good. It was assumed that an intervention research approach might positively affect the time required for the company to change and build capability, since it might avoid using a trial-and-error approach, span the area from individual via organizational to institutional change, and benefit from the multidisciplinary research setting and rigour of the research methodology.

What becomes important, then, is to uncover the issues which are viewed by organizational members as key issues warranting attention at any point in time. In those key issues, which involve complex organizational change, many may fall into the category of operational problem-solving initially. As already noted, not all issues are blatantly obvious, and therefore it is important for you as the researcher to get a sense of both the obvious and less obvious. It may be that the obvious is but an outward manifestation of a deeper issue that organizational members are not so willing to embrace publicly. Identification of these deeper issues may point to a need for inquiry into the fundamental assumptions that are causing a problem to recur. What if the obvious only seems that way, due to being ill-informed on the nature of the issue at hand? Could it be that the obvious has become so because it embraces the language of dissent, and reflects the preoccupations of organizational members with consequences without ever reflecting on root causes?

> Williander and Styhre (2006) reflect that when the research proposal was brought to Volvo's senior management and approved, there was no budget reserved for it. Even though the insider action researcher received strong support for his project, at least in the form of lip service, there was no money available that could be released to finance it in the current fiscal year.

As insider action researcher you need to go with the story as it evolves. As the initial questions and data demonstrate that they are inadequate to address the issues, you work at keeping inquiry active. You are continually testing whether consensus exists concerning the array of issues which could be addressed. Such an array may be constructed, having considered organizational members' perceptions of key issues. It may embrace a healthy diversity of thinking among organizational members, or alternatively it may point to significant pockets of conflict in certain issue domains. Change triggers discussion, debate and arguments between people who champion competing ideas and proposals. Such discussion provides useful data, and is desirable in order to expose different ideas to public scrutiny and examination.

Regardless of what the array of issues reflects, it is impossible to construct research without leaving one's own familiar world and entering into the world of others through open and honest dialogue. Of necessity, this means that you need to be willing to explore key concepts and themes, and to attempt to construct others' perceptions concerning the range of issues. It involves understanding why organizational members frame such issues in the first instance, while simultaneously capturing causal relationships.

No issue in an organization is context-free. Uncovering issues necessitates establishing not only multiple versions of 'the real facts', but also understanding the role that history and experience have to play in organizational members' perceptions of these facts. In a similar manner, any given issue may be embedded in a system of political behaviour that is critical to understand if issue resolution is ever to be negotiated.

> In his inquiry into how he, as chief executive of a charity organization, would inquire into how he might improve governance practice and improvement, Moore (2007) found parallels between his experience of undertaking insider action research and the biblical image of the original sin committed by Adam and Eve when they ate the forbidden fruit from the tree of knowledge. Accordingly, he traces his experience in these allegorical terms: feeling that he was in the Garden of Eden at the start of his research, and finding forbidden fruits as he descended into the details of the norms of the organization through his questioning. He describes his 'sin' as bringing to light and starting to taste his underlying assumptions, which challenged the dominant views and values that held sway in the organization's board. Then, he found that he had exposed perceptions that he had not previously encountered, and was faced with an inherent conflict between his role as an insider and researcher, an experience to which he refers as realizing that he was 'naked'. He concludes that having eaten of the 'Tree of Knowledge', he found the tension of trying to occupy the worlds of both knowledge and innocence unbearable, and he resigned.

It is worth reading Moore's article in full to get the richer picture of his understanding of his insider action research experience.

Questions for reflection and discussion

- How do you relate to Moore's image of the Garden of Eden for his insider action research project?
- How might an image help frame an action research initiative? What insights might flow from such an image?
- Is there any image emerging for you for your insider action research project?

The process of identifying issues may be characterized as fluid, dynamic and emergent (Dutton et al., 1983). It is fluid in the sense that it is difficult to establish precise boundaries, and when such boundaries are established, often they are subject to change. It is dynamic in the sense that the core focus is subject to continuous revision as understanding deepens. It is emergent in the sense that issues appear over time. These key characteristics point to a process which is characterized further by the unfolding nature of interpretation and reinterpretation, making extensive use of organizational members' judgements and revision of judgements based on insights gained from new and existing data, stimuli and perceptions.

Of immediate importance then, to you, is the need to gather and organize these data, stimuli and perceptions of yourself and others. The subsequent sense-making process points to the need for you to have good organizational and analytical capabilities. Krim (1988) kept a journal of his reflections and observations, and used his academic supervisors to test them in a safe environment.

In the context of deriving meaning, it is useful at this juncture in the research process to frame issues in broad categories, without attempting to attach a single dominant interpretation to any issue. The existence of multiple interpretations concerning an issue must not be eliminated. Capturing multiple and diverse interpretations adds to a deeper, richer picture of the issue at hand, and holds the key to more effective resolution for the long term.

There is an inherent danger in the process of attempting to simplify an issue by reducing ambiguity at an early stage. Such endeavours are manifested by ignoring some interpretations of an issue, and attempting to attach a single dominant interpretation with a view to aiding resolution. Such a process may seem quite rational to the researcher, who may be eager to get on with the task at hand. Rationality plays a role in the analysis stage, but you cannot assume that rational analysis will lead to resolution. Resolution often involves a process of negotiation, embracing a sense of give and take, where political interests warrant careful management. Neglecting political influences is a recipe for inaction, as any proposed course of action may be planned to death and eventually be stillborn. You need to be sensitive to the possible ethical issues and consequences of constructing, as you may be exposing colleagues to risk in how you interpret the project.

Attaching a dominant interpretation to an issue is not necessarily bad, as long as you remain cognisant of the fact that other interpretations exist, and are willing to test such interpretations as the need arises. It is equally important to understand the basis for such dominance. Does the interpretation reflect a shared mind at all or almost all organizational levels, or does it reflect the shared mind of a particular group, such as management or trade unions? The extent to which a dominant interpretation of an event or issue is shared or otherwise by organizational members is important for you as the researcher, as it implies that different strategies must be employed to aid issue resolution. Where a dominant interpretation is widely shared, you are more likely to gain a greater degree of commitment to the resolution process, with lower levels of political activity – at least at the early stages. Where the interpretation reflects the mind of a specific group, you need to be cognisant of the fact that other groups may not share that interpretation, and may choose never to share it for political reasons. Friedman (2001) presents projects initiated by individuals on a continuum, with technical issues at one extreme and non-technical at the other. In his view, technical operational issues are easier to have support for, while non-technical issues are harder to influence and embedded in organizational defensive routines.

Finally, it is important when categorizing issues, that each issue is framed in the context of its implicit and explicit assumptions, any known causal relationships and any predictive judgements concerning the speed of issue resolution (Dutton et al., 1983). Making assumptions explicit aids the resolution process, as organizational members develop a shared understanding of the issue being addressed in terms of its history, scope and possible outcomes. Establishing causal relationships helps to place an issue in context by grounding it in organizational reality, while simultaneously establishing how organizational members attribute certain outcomes to root causes. Outlining predictive judgements attaches a sense of urgency or otherwise to the issue at hand.

Angela, working in a professional public health service, sought to devote her insider action research project to the problem of client waiting lists, and to work with her colleagues on reducing the time that clients had to wait for an appointment and treatment. With such a clear framing of the initiative on what was accepted as a pressing problem, Angela received widespread support from her colleagues and management. She recruited her colleagues to engage in a cooperative inquiry process to explore the problem of the waiting lists, and to engage in action research to resolve it as best they could. As the cooperative group met over several weeks, Angela found that the group was showing a high dependence on her: for example, waiting for her to chair meetings and to keep the initiative alive and moving forward. While she had insights that this was a normal pattern to be expected in a developing group (Wheelan, 2012), her generative insight was that this whole process of jointly exploring a shared concern was radically new for her colleagues. Discussion of the problem of waiting lists led to discussions on priorities and the values underpinning the service, and it was apparent that this group had never engaged in such conversations. In short, this was a professional organization in which each member had an individual caseload, and there was no tradition of its members meeting as a group to explore core values, priorities and strategies. It was this agenda that began to dominate the group meetings. Accordingly, as Angela was confined to a particular schedule in which to deliver her master's dissertation, and it was clear that the topic of waiting lists would not now be addressed adequately within that timeframe, she reframed her dissertation topic to focus more on how individual professionals formed a more cohesive group. The issue of waiting lists remained a concern for the service and would be addressed consequently at a later date, but would not be the subject of Angela's dissertation.

Questions for reflection and discussion

- How does Angela's reframing of her dissertation topic make sense?
- How are you currently framing your insider action research initiative? Might that change? What might make it change? How do you keep your options open?

Selecting the research project

Having identified a range of issues, you are confronted with selecting an issue or issues for immediate attention in the context of a specific research agenda. Before making a final selection, you are well advised to reflect on each issue identified from personal and organizational perspectives, with a view to establishing:

1. the degree to which it offers an opportunity to experiment with existing and/or newly-acquired knowledge;
2. the degree to which it offers opportunities for personal growth and learning;
3. the degree to which issue resolution offers the possibility to increase your profile within the organization;
4. the balance between personal gain and organizational gain in the event of successful resolution; and
5. the degree to which the issue may be resolved within known resource and time constraints.

Bjorkman and Sundgren (2005) reflect on their respective insider action research projects and note that obtaining management attention, creating interest among colleagues, creating and maintaining legitimacy and allocating time and financial resources are key strategies. They draw their shared experience together and suggest four features of framing and selecting an insider action research initiative:

1. finding 'red and hot' issues for the organization;
2. positioning the relational platform;
3. using the inside;
4. using and diffusing results.

Questions for reflection and discussion

- Do you know of any 'red and hot' issues for your organization that you might be, and are, in a position to take up?
- How might you position your 'relational platform'?
- What are your strengths as an insider to take on this project, and how might you use them?

Writing an insider action research proposal

The dissertation proposal is your statement of intent. It should demonstrate that:

- you know what you are getting yourself into (through showing familiarity with both the organizational setting and some relevant literature);
- what you intend to do is worthwhile; and
- you have a potential contribution to knowledge to make – for example, for a specific audience, the school's research application committee, your doctoral committee or some similar body.

There are four areas that your insider action research proposal needs to address: context, action, research and the insider process.

Context

This refers to the social and academic context of the research. There are three context areas:

1. broad general context at the global and national levels;
2. local organizational or discipline context – what is going on in your organization; and
3. your specific topic area.

Social context is very important in action research, therefore you need to describe your own organization or community. This would include details of the organization, community or group; what it does; some historical background; what its concerns are; what the issues that you are engaging with mean; and what is intended and hoped for out of the action research project. This description contains not only a presentation of the facts of the organization in its setting, but also an introductory literature on the setting. For example, participants undertaking action research in the Master's programme in Health Service Policy and Management at Trinity College Dublin typically have a chapter describing general developments in the Irish health system, locating their action research in national strategy, and then in developments in their particular discipline or service.

Action

This covers the basic thrust of the action that you intend to take or lead. The headings in the 'Process of Planned Change' section in Chapter 5 provide an important construct in this regard. What is the action? What is the rationale for this action? Why is it worth doing? What is the desired future? What is the present situation? What is the plan to move from here to there? What is the time schedule? With whom will you collaborate? Where do you, as the researcher, fit into the action? What are the ethical challenges?

Research

This describes the focus of inquiry in action. What is the rationale for researching this action? What is the contribution to knowledge that this research intends to make? How do you intend to inquire into the action? How do you ensure quality and rigour in your action research?

The insider process

This brings the focus specifically on insider inquiry. How do you do action research in the 'swampy lowlands' of your own organization? How will you manage preunderstanding, role duality and organizational politics? (These topics are discussed in Chapters 8, 9 and 10.) How will you engage others? What are the ethical issues (particularly if you have to apply for ethical approval from a review board; see the discussion in Chapter 10)?

As you are formulating your proposal there a couple of things worth keeping in mind. These help you to remain grounded in the action research approach. Action research is a different form of research than traditional research as it begins with what we do not know and seeks to find out what we don't know. Traditional research tends to begin from what we know. What we do not know that we do now know is a particular outcome of action research.

As we discussed in Chapter 1, there are two action research projects running concurrently, what Zuber-Skerritt and Perry (2002) call the *core* action research project, and the *thesis* action research project. Now we are focusing on writing the *thesis* action research proposal, which is the inquiry-in-action into how the 'core' action research project will be designed, implemented and evaluated, how you intend to enact your role in it and how you intend to reflect on it.

Developing the action research

As you embark on your project, you are moving from preliminary construction of the issue to developing a deep, broad understanding of the issue and its context. You will begin to identify pressures in the system (and in the larger context) that affect the situation. You will be learning to identify key individuals and groups whose support is required to bring about change. Who has knowledge and understanding? Whose support is critical to developing and conducting the action research and its outcomes? As you enact cycles of action and reflection, you will discover new information. New opportunities, obstacles and constraints will emerge.

In parallel, you will need to be working on building collaborative relationships: contracting, building rapport, negotiating roles and levels of involvement. If you have pre-existing patterns of relationships, the challenges of role duality may have an impact.

> As part of her insider action research project for her master's degree, Margaret was engaging her own team in a collaborative inquiry process on how to improve their occupational therapy service. A particular challenge for her was that her team, particularly in the initial stages, saw themselves as helping her on her action research project. Accordingly, they were deferential to her with regard to what they would explore at the meetings, and at one point cancelled a meeting because she would not be present – as in the words of one of the members, 'There would be no point if you're not there'. Margaret had to put a great deal of effort into getting the group to own the project of service improvement themselves, and so to engage in collaborative inquiry. She did this by rotating the chairing and note-taking role.

Questions for reflection and discussion

- Does this story evoke any resonances with your project?
- How would you deal with the dilemma of dependence?

Conclusions

Constructing and selecting an action research project is a complex project in itself. What appears clear at the outset may lose its apparent clarity as the project unfolds. How you construct and subsequently reconstruct your understanding of the project may hold important learning for you. The critical issue for you is to be able to construct and select a project from a position of being close to the issue. The acts of constructing and selecting your action research project are action research learning cycles in themselves. In other words, you do your initial constructing, reflect on how that construction fits or not, articulate some understanding of why that construction fits or does not fit, then take action accordingly and so test that situation. Similarly, you make your initial selection, test it and adapt according to the data generated by the constructing and selection processes.

Recommended reading

Arieli, D., Friedman, V.J. and Agbaria, K. (2009) 'The paradox of participation in action research', *Action Research*, 7 (3): 263–190.

Coghlan, D. with Brydon-Miller, M. (2014) *The SAGE Encyclopedia of Action Research*. London: Sage. (See especially 'Appreciative inquiry' and 'Research methodology'.)

Access a selection of author videos, encyclopaedia entries and recommended reading on this topic at www.uk.sagepub.com/coghlanandbrannick

EXERCISE 4.1

Questions for constructing and selecting

As you look at your organization or the section in which you work, consider the following.

1. What questions arise out of your experience which you would like to search for answers?
2. What might be the answers to these questions?
3. What do you think might be the underlying causes of the situation why you have these questions?
4. What alternative answers might exist?
5. Where do you fit into the situation as defined by the question?
6. What would other members of the organization think of you working on this issue?
7. What support will you have?
8. What opposition will you encounter?
9. Where are the sensitive issues?
10. What are the constraints?
11. Who needs to be involved? Whose support do you enlist?
12. Where would be a good place to begin?
13. How will you engage in uncovering the data?

EXERCISE 4.2

Writing a thesis proposal

1. Context

What are the current issues and trends in your area of focus?

(a) The broad external and internal context of the environment in which your organization is located. For example: what is going on, the strategy policy documents, etc.
(b) The local organizational or discipline context. How is your organization situated in relation to the broader context? What is going on in your hospital, school, business or service?
(c) Your particular topic issue. Where does that fit into the above two contexts? What will your work contribute in these contexts?

(Continued)

(Continued)

2. Action

What is the action? What is the rationale for this action? Why is it worth doing? What is the desired future? What is the present situation? What is the plan to move from here to there? What is the time schedule? Where do you, as the researcher, fit into the action? What are the ethical challenges, both within the project itself and in seeking approval from an ethics review board?

3. Research

What is the rationale for researching this action? What is the contribution to knowledge that this research intends to make? Why should anyone not directly involved be interested in this? How do you intend to inquire into the action? How do you ensure quality and rigour in your action research?

4. Insider action research

How do you do action research in your own organization? How will you manage preunderstanding, role duality and organizational politics? How do you plan to learn in action? What quality processes will you build into your initiative? What are the particular ethical challenges that you will face?

FIVE

Designing and Implementing your Action Research Project

 See www.uk.sagepub.com/coghlanandbrannick for a short introduction to the chapter from David Coghlan

The questions underpinning this chapter are: 'How do you design your insider action research project?' and 'How do you implement it?' In this chapter we explore how you may design and implement an action research project in a system, whether in an organization, be it a company, hospital, school or unit or department or service within your organization. The action research process in your own organization follows the general empirical method and action research cycle introduced in Chapter 1. This involves:

1. constructing the initiative and desired outcomes with relevant stakeholders, and systematically generating and collecting research data about an ongoing system relative to some objective or need;
2. engaging with others in reviewing the data generated and collected;
3. conducting a collaborative analysis of the data;
4. planning and taking collaborative action based on shared inquiry; and
5. jointly evaluating the results of that action, leading to further planning.

So the cycle is repeated.

Underpinning these activities is the first-person activity of building 'creative confidence' (Kelley and Kelley, 2012). Kelley and Kelley explore the notion of creativity as something to be practised, rather than a talent with which you are born. In the context of designing your action research project, we think it useful to refer you to their work on creative confidence and, in particular, getting in touch with what might inhibit you from confidently designing your project, such as fear of the unknown, of being judged, taking the first step or losing control. Here, attending to your own first-person processes and conversations with significant others may enable you to approach the design of your project in an open, flexible and creative manner.

Our starting point for the topic of designing your action research as a change project is to remind you that we are working from the organization development approach to change that is grounded in action research and essentially dialogical (Schein, 2010[1989]; Bushe and Marshak, 2009; Burnes and Cooke, 2012; Coghlan, 2012a; Klev and Levin, 2012). Accordingly, designing a change project in an organization development manner involves building participation and commitment to the project, and working with colleagues and others to understand why change is needed, developing a shared vision of its outcome, and co-constructing and implementing both the change itself and the accompanying learning and knowledge generation.

There are many ways of clustering the wide types of change that may take place in organizations (Coghlan and Shani, 2013). Here, we draw on Mitki et al.'s (2000) clustering of change programmes as limited, focused and holistic.

- *Limited change programmes* are aimed at addressing a specific problem, such as team-building or communication improvement. It is likely that such projects might be appropriate outlets for insider action research for a Master's in Business Administration (MBA) or other master's students.
- *Focused change programmes* identify a few key aspects such as time, quality and customer value, then use these by design as levers for changing the organization system-wide. This type is also likely to be attractive for insider action research for MBA and other master's programmes.
- *Holistic change programmes* are aimed by design to simultaneously address all (or most) aspects of the organization.

The key question that you need to ask at the outset is what type of change is at stake in your insider action research initiative. As indicated previously, limited and focused change programmes fit well with limited-term master's dissertation contexts, where you have a specific focus for your research that needs to be completed in a year or thereabouts. Holistic change, of its nature, takes more time and is likely to be the focus for a doctorate.

Buono and Kerber (2008) describe three approaches to change.

1. *Directed change* is where there are tightly defined goals – the leadership directs and commands.
2. *Planned change* is where there is a clear goal and vision of the future – the leadership devises a road map to reach it, and influences how it is reached.
3. *Guided changing* is where the direction is loosely defined – the leadership points the way and keeps watch over the process. This approach to change fits with much of what is written about as the 'new science' of leadership, and draws on constructivism and postmodernism as a foundation for dialogue and conversation about change referred to by Bushe and Marshak (2009) as 'dialogic organization development'.

Again, you need to consider your approach to change in your insider action research project. If you are the agent of a tightly-controlled, directed change approach, then you may find that it conflicts with action research values of participation. The planned change approach provides a very useful format for most insider action research projects, and the process for such an approach is presented in the next paragraph. Scope for the guided changing approach is more likely to be linked to action research at doctoral level, where there is collaborative engagement in multiple cycles of action and reflection over several years.

The process of planned change

Taking planned change as the most likely approach for insider action research, especially at master's level, the question then is: 'How do you go about implementing the action research cycle in a planned way, in a large system?' While actor-directors go with the story in their film-making, they also create and follow a script. The process whereby the action research agenda is identified and worked through has been well articulated by Richard Beckhard (Beckhard and Harris, 1987; Beckhard and Pritchard, 1992; Nadler, 1998; Coghlan and Rashford, 2006; Pasmore, 2011). Beckhard's framework has four phases (Figure 5.1):

1. determining the need for change;
2. defining the future state;
3. assessing the present in terms of the future to determine the work to be done; and
4. managing the transition.

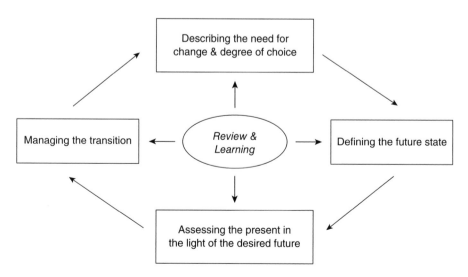

Figure 5.1 The Process of Change

As we will discuss in Chapters 9 and 10, doing action research in your own organization is intensely political and involves you in concurrent and sometimes conflicting roles. We think that it is important to remind you that managing the political system at every step is more important than any rigid adherence to an idealized picture of how these steps might work.

Determining the need for change

The preferred starting place is to inquire into the context for change in the organization, unit or sub-unit. It may seem obvious that naming the need for change and its causes is essential. The forces for change may be coming from the external environment, such as global market demands, developing customer needs, and so on. They may be coming from the internal environment, such as budget overruns, low morale among staff, excessive dysfunctional political intergroup rivalry, and so on. Understanding these forces identifies their source and potency, and the nature of the demands that they are making on the system. These forces for change have to be assessed so that major change forces are distinguished from the minor ones. You engage in this inquiry in collaboration with colleagues, superiors and relevant others so that you have agreement and permission to pursue what is accepted as a valuable project (hopefully what Bjorkman and Sundgren call a 'red and hot' issue).

Another key element in evaluating the need for change is the degree of choice about whether to change or not. This is often an overlooked question. Choices are not absolute. While there may be no control over the forces demanding change, i.e. a budget reduction, there is likely to be a great deal of control over how to respond to those forces. In that case there is likely to be a good deal of scope as to what changes, how and in what timescale the change can take place. The action research cycle enables shared inquiry into how these forces for change are having an impact, and what choices exist to confront them. The outcome of determining the need for change is to ask a further question, which is whether first- or second-order change is required. By first-order change we mean an improvement in what the organization does, or how it does it. By second-order or third-order change we mean a system-wide change in the nature of the core assumptions and ways of thinking and acting. The choice of whether to follow a first- or second-order change process may be determined as much by organizational politics as by the issues under consideration. How the key organizational actors interpret the forces for change, and how they form their subsequent judgement as to what choices they have, are important political dynamics. The more collaboration there is at this stage, the stronger your relational platform is to proceed.

Defining the future state

Once a sense of the need for change has been established, the most useful focus for attention is to define a desired future state. This process is essentially that of articulating what the organization, unit or sub-unit would look like after change has taken place. This process is critical: it helps provide focus and energy because it describes desires for the future in a positive light. Conversely, an initial focus on the problematic or imperfect present may overemphasize negative experiences and generate pessimism. Working at building consensus on a desired future is an important way of harnessing the political elements of the system.

Assessing the present in terms of the future to determine the work to be done

When the desired future state is articulated, you then attend to the present reality and ask: 'What is it in the present that needs changing in order to move to the desired future state?' Because the present is being assessed in light of the desired future, it is assessing what needs changing, and what does not. It may judge that for the change to take place effectively, a change in current structures, attitudes, roles, policies or activities may be needed. As any change problem is a cluster of possible changes, it may need to group particular problems under common headings, i.e. human resource management policies and practices, service delivery, information management, reward systems, organizational structure and design, and so on. Then it describes the problem more specifically and asks: 'Which of these requires priority attention? If A is changed, will a solution to B fall easily into place? What needs to be done first?' This step is about taking a clear, comprehensive and accurate view of the current state of the organization, involving an organizational inquiry which names:

- the priorities within the constellation of change problems;
- the relevant sub-systems where change is required;
- an assessment of readiness and capability for the contemplated change.

Another element in describing the present is to describe the relevant parts of the organization that will be involved in the change. This description points to the critical people needed for the change to take place. This is an explicit consideration of the political system, and where you draw on your skills as a 'political entrepreneur'. Examples of who needs to be involved might include specific managers, informal leaders, information technology (IT) specialists, and so on. Their readiness and capability for change must be explored. *Readiness* points to their motivation and willingness to change, while *capability* refers to whether they are able, psychologically and otherwise, to change. There are some key questions to ask yourself and others. Who do you need to have on your side for this project to succeed? Your insider-backstage knowledge gives you a sense of who might fall into general categories, such as those who will create obstacles, those who may be passive about the project, those who will help and those who will make it happen. Your question might be: 'What will you do to move certain people from one category to another?' Here you need to remain grounded in your action research values, and be sensitive to the ethical and political issues in both the design of the change process, and the involvement required for the project to succeed.

Managing the transition

This step is what is generally perceived as being the actual change process, although as we have seen, preparation for change is equally essential. The critical task is to move from the present to the future and manage the intervening period of transition. This transition state between the present and future is typically a difficult time because the past is found to be defective and no longer tenable, and the new state has not yet come into being. So, in essence, the transition state is somewhat particular, as the old has gone and the new has not been realized yet, and so needs to be seen and managed as such.

There are two aspects to managing this transition state. One is having a strategic and operational plan that simply defines the goals, activities, structures, projects and experiments that will help achieve the desired state. As no amount of change can take place without commitment, the second aspect is a commitment plan. The commitment plan focuses on who in the organization must be committed to the change, if it is to take place. As we discussed in the previous section, from your insider knowledge you have a sense of particular individuals whose support is a prerequisite for the change, and a critical mass whose commitment is necessary to provide the energy and support for the change to occur. The political dynamics of building commitment involves finding areas of agreement and compromise among conflicting views, and negotiating cooperation (Fisher and Ury, 2012; Ury, 1991).

It is at the managing transition stage that you are likely to make most use of a group that works with you as the core project team. While you are the one doing the dissertation, this group is an organizational project group which contains both technical competence and hierarchical status to manage the project. Hence there is a need for you to be able to build and maintain the team (Wheelan, 2012).

Planned change through action research

Beckhard's change process developed out of his action research approach (Beckhard, 1997), and involves continuous interaction between constructing, planning, action and review in order to move a change through a system. Action research has a large degree of messiness and unpredictability about it, in that it is research in real-life action. As the story unfolds, unforeseen events are likely to occur. Environmental events may create a crisis in the organization, fellow key actors may change, and so on. In terms of the image presented in Chapter 1, as the insider action researcher and actor-director you are both creating and acting a script.

Figure 5.2 describes the process and provides the structure for shared inquiry into the planned and unanticipated events that occur through the implementation, so as to create the conditions and opportunity for learning and for the change to be sustainable. The aim is to move from the current state to the desired state. Having consolidated the context and purpose of the project, the task is to execute the project realistically. This involves moving through multiple iterative cycles of action and reflection, some of which, as we described in Chapter 1 in terms of a clock, are concurrent, have different time spans and different levels of complexity. Each cycle involves the activities of constructing, planning action, taking action and evaluating action. The general empirical method is central to

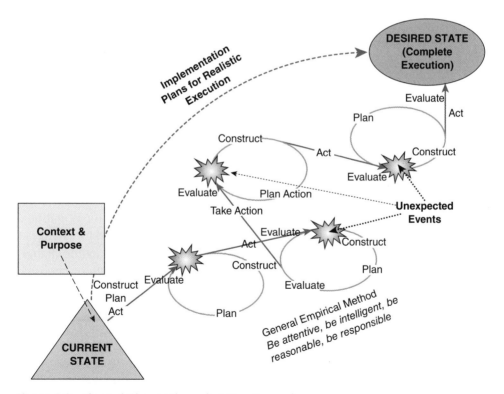

Figure 5.2 Planned Change through Action Research

(From the work of Arthur Freedman with gratitude)

the entire process. Being attentive, intelligent, reasonable and responsible to both the action as it unfolds and the theory as it emerges maintains the core process of action research. Exercise 5.2, one of the central exercises of the book, captures this twin focus: it is an exercise that you might do on many occasions throughout your project.

A good deal of reflection is reflection *on* action: it is a retrospective look at what has happened, as Darling and Parry (2000) illustrate in their application of 'after action review' to the US American military, of how post-mortems can move from being a review of the past to a living practice that anticipates issues and generates emergent learning *in* action. Figure 5.2 and Exercise 5.2 facilitate such reflection.

The critical dimension to action research is how review or evaluation is undertaken and managed. Review is essentially reflection on experience, and in any such reflection the critical questions are asked not to evoke guilt or blame, but to generate learning as to what is taking place and needs to be adjusted. If review is undertaken in this spirit, then the likelihood of individual or team defensiveness can be lessened and learning can take place. As we explored in Chapter 2, learning comes out of reviewing the process and examining emergent questions about content, process and premise.

Pasmore (2011) offers a complementary four-phase framework for examining factors that threaten change intervention success, and which may generate reflection on creating more positive outcomes from your insider change endeavour:

1. understanding the need for change;
2. framing the change;
3. undertaking the change; and
4. sustaining the change.

With regard to understanding the need for change, Pasmore points to failure to heed objective signals indicating the need for change, different judgements about urgency and scope, lack of deep commitment to changes undertaken for aspirational reasons, and ambivalence arising from conversations about the need for change as common reasons why change efforts fail. Under the heading of framing the change, Pasmore points to failure ensuing from lack of authentic participation, choosing the wrong intervention, ignoring the need for readiness, and failure to ensure alignment and commitment across the various levels of leadership. With regard to undertaking the change he identifies emergent issues, unanticipated side-effects, irrational emotional and political responses and resistance, and lack of leadership as critical factors leading to failure. Finally, he notes that losing focus, shifting priorities, turnover of key champions, passive-aggressive resistance, resource starvation, exhaustion and unpredicted shift in the external context as reasons why change is not sustained. These are issues that you may need to keep your eye on, although some of them may not be within your control. It is important to know what the research on organizational change offers, and at least not to fall into the traps that the literature has identified.

Deane (2004) was the chief executive of an ad hoc government agency, 'Oldorg', whose role was to set, monitor and certify standards for vocational education and training programmes provided within the public further education sector. Under new government legislation, 'Oldorg' was replaced by a new agency, 'Neworg', established in 2001, which subsumed the existing functions of Oldorg and considerably extended its remit. Deane undertook an action learning project to explore how learning could support change in an organization. It involved designing and implementing a learning programme for staff of Oldorg at a time of great uncertainty for the organization, and in a context of vigorous internal and external debate surrounding introduction of the new legislation.

Deane reports how she adopted Beckhard and Harris' (1987) framework for implementing in Oldorg. A vision of the future had been formulated by examining the given and possible dimensions of the change arising from the legislation. There also had been an analysis of the present state and an identification of key change issues, focusing in particular on the cultural aspects. What was needed was to complete the process by managing the transition to the changed state: this called for a high level of openness to change across the whole organization. In effect, it called for a dynamic and continuous learning process at both the individual and organizational levels, in order to cope with the rate of change in the external environment. While in the past Oldorg had worked through change by learning in a largely intuitive and informal way, Deane now proposed to adopt a more systematic approach. This would link closely the themes of learning and change, first, to effect change through learning, and second, to discover how change could act as a catalyst for learning. Deane recognized that it was her responsibility to prepare the organization for the future, to predict and plan for change, influence the change process and protect and preserve what was important to the organization in the new situation. She was aware that this presented a great challenge to her leadership: a great deal depended on managing the process effectively, both within and outside the organization.

Having identified the major reasons why change was necessary, Deane moved towards answering the second question: 'What needs to change?' She saw how the new organizations would have to develop new relationships with stakeholders, serve new customers, adopt new processes and new technologies, and provide new products and services to a bigger market. She reports that she found the notion of a 'constellation' of change issues, with a complex set of interrelationships between them, particularly helpful. Allied to the notion that it is almost impossible to change only one thing, this concept helped her to frame a change agenda for Oldorg. Focusing mainly on the cultural aspects of change for which, it was suggested by the earlier analysis, the organization's readiness was low, the action learning project then sought an answer to the final question: 'How can we change?'

Drawing on her reading on organizational learning and the learning organization, a learning programme was designed and implemented. Put simply, the purpose of the programme was to ensure that all staff members were given the opportunity to participate in focused learning activities to help them prepare for the changes ahead.

The programme comprised a number of learning modes targeted at producing spe-cific learning outcomes for individuals and the organization as a whole. Political, technical and culture change issues were explored by means of a learning audit, project teams, action learning groups, staff seminars, future focus groups and train-ing. In terms of culture, the openness of communication and information-sharing enabled a high level of ownership of the change. In technical terms, participation in training and new skill development led to new technical systems to prepare for the post-legislation organization. In political terms, the future focus group's submission was accepted and contributed to the development of the process.

Deane reflects on the whole action learning process in first-, second- and third-person terms. For herself, applying the principles of general management to her-self and the public sector, and being challenged by the action learning setting, was the important learning for her. In second-person terms, the organization learned to change and was well adapted to meet the challenges of the new organization. In third-person terms, there was a major impact for the clients of the new organiza-tion, in that they would be able to gain credits for action research undertaken in a work context or elsewhere. The new organization would have a flexible assessment approach to meet the needs of learners. You may wish to read Deane's account to gain a fuller picture of her project.

Questions for reflection and discussion

- How does Deane follow the Beckhard and Harris framework for planned change?
- Are there insights I am receiving from this case that I may bring to my own project?

A critical question in designing and implementing your insider action research project is how you can build survival and sustainability into your project, so that it does not evaporate like the morning dew when the project is over and the energy has died down. In our day, where management and change fads are prevalent, this is a pertinent question. Here, we draw on the notion of learning mechanisms as a way of exploring how you might embed what may emerge from your insider action research project.

Learning mechanisms

Contemporary organizational learning literature is focusing on how organiza-tions develop organizational learning mechanisms (Lipshitz et al., 2007). These mechanisms typically refer to planned organizational structures and processes that encourage dynamic learning, particularly to enhance organizational capa-bilities. The mechanisms can apply at the individual, group, organizational or inter-organizational levels, and can aim to initiate, facilitate, monitor and reward learning.

Shani and Docherty (2003, 2008; Docherty and Shani, 2008) present three types of learning mechanism: cognitive, structural and procedural.

Cognitive learning mechanisms

These provide language, symbols, theories, values and concepts for thinking about and understanding learning issues. For example, single-loop and double-loop learning concepts can help to identify a starting point and evaluate a change of state resulting from an action (Argyris and Schon, 1996). Critical to attending to learning is to grasp how the mind works in questioning experience, processing and weighing data and forming judgements (Coghlan, 2010a). Conscious application of the learning perspective represents a language and concepts with which to frame, think about and reflect on an ambition that requires relationships and procedural steps to realize (the focus of the following mechanisms).

Structural mechanisms

These comprise organizational, physical and technical infrastructures, such as action learning sets (Marquardt, 2004; Pedler, 2008), parallel learning structures (Bushe and Shani, 1991), quality teams, continuous improvement taskforces, inter-organizational supply chain groups (Coughlan and Coghlan, 2011), feedback channels, databases, intranets, document sharing systems and the physical layout of the workspace.

Procedural mechanisms

These are the institutionalized procedures that promote and support learning, suc' as learning meetings and action learning programmes (Marquardt, 2004; Pe' 2011). Recognition and recording of interactions among key functionaries tates this capturing and application of the learning achieved.

From an insider action research perspective the three learning mech? any variation or tapestry of them, reflect the three core processes ' research that we discussed in Chapter 1. Cognitive learning mec' with the first-person process of how you think. Central to actio' ing how the operations of human knowing and doing – exper' ing, judging, deciding and taking action – provide a gene whereby you develop to know your knowing. By this we me' into experience, have insights into that experience, and these insights fit the evidence. Thus, both you as an insi' your fellow organizational members can learn to have ' ments, because you have been attentive to how you

The cognitive mechanism is not only a naming of issues, but also an attention to how issues are named and confirmed. Structural learning mechanisms go beyond individual knowing to engaging in the second-person processes of collaborative inquiry and shared action. As we have been emphasizing, what is paramount in creating co-generated knowledge is the quality of conversation whereby experiences are shared, collective insights are generated and shared judgements formed, which lead to joint action. Procedural learning mechanisms engage with the third-person processes of how learning is sustained and extended beyond you as the insider action researcher and the immediate group that worked on the project. This is where it might be said that you as an insider action researcher make yourself redundant, as the system now has structures in place to continue and develop the sustainability of its insights.

The notion of sustainable development suggests that organizations need to be open to alternative learning mechanisms. They have choices as they determine the direction, scope and structural learning mechanisms. They may draw on existing capabilities and build their own learning mechanisms, or build a new mechanism that seems to have worked elsewhere, or choose any combination of the above. As such, a unique tapestry of learning mechanisms is likely to evolve in each insider action research effort. The critical issue is not so much which choices are made, or what specific tapestry of learning mechanisms are designed, as the learning process followed in making choices.

Roth et al. (2007) present their account of insider action research in terms of building learning capabilities. They construct a model of new organizational capabilities in the biopharma firm, AstraZeneca, drawing on business strategy, insider action research and learning mechanisms. They note that when experimenting with different ways of creating learning between project teams, they created an arena for reflection and dialogue about operational practices and team behaviours. This intervention became more focused on creating learning within and between teams in a systematic manner. The concept of learning was developed across the organization, supported by a knowledge facilitation method and a team of facilitators. This structure became the preferred way of approaching team learning, and became an organizational capability. You may wish to read Roth et al. to gain a fuller picture of their project.

Questions for reflection and discussion

What learning mechanisms were set up in this insider action research project?
What learning mechanisms could be adopted in my setting?

...utioned earlier against limiting action research to a logical and clinical pro-
...here individuals and groups move through the action research steps in a
... – albeit politically aware – manner. However, such approaches are not

exclusive. It is not uncommon for researchers to utilize storytelling, drama or photography as a core process of their data generation.

> Evans (1997) studied her own practice as a deputy head of a large secondary school in the UK. Within a hierarchically organized institution, she worked with teachers collaboratively, enabling the creation of a learning community through a dialogue in which they took ownership of their own development, established value positions and supported one another. She created case studies out of her experiences in the school and presented them as stories to the group. For example, she composed one story titled, 'Just Tell Me What to Do' out of her own experience. The other teachers were able to relate to the story, as it reflected school culture. This and other stories enabled the teachers to reframe their perspectives and explore new perspectives together.

Questions for reflection and discussion

- What insights do you have into the possible effect of Evans' approach in her school?
- Are there ways in which it would be useful for you to employ techniques such as storytelling, drama and art to give voice to the participants in your project?

Data generation as intervention

In action research data comes through engagement with others in the action research cycles. Therefore, it is important to know that acts which are intended to collect data are themselves interventions. So asking an individual a question or observing them at work is not simply collecting data, but also *generating* learning data for both you as the researcher and the individual concerned. In short, you are not neutral: every action – even the very intention and presence of research – is an intervention, and has political implication across the system. Accordingly, it is more appropriate to speak of data *generation* than data-gathering.

For you as the insider action researcher, data generation comes through active involvement in the day-to-day organizational processes relating to the action research project. As the researcher in your own organization, you are an inconspicuous observer, as your presence is taken for granted. Your observations are made as a member of the organization in day-to-day interactions with colleagues and others. Not only are data generated through participation in and observation of teams at work, problems being solved, decisions being made, and so on, but also through the interventions that are made to advance the project. Some of these observations and interventions are made in formal settings, such as meetings and interviews; while many are made in informal settings, such as over coffee, lunch and other recreational settings.

You will need to document your reflections for all these occasions. Apart from your journalling activities, which typically take place in private, there will be situations at meetings where you want to take notes or jot down reflections. Of course, this is a sensitive process, as appearing to take notes may create suspicion. A useful rule of thumb is to adopt what others are doing. If at a meeting most people take notes, then it is okay for you to take notes. If no one is taking notes, then do not take notes. In that case, try to jot down your reflections afterwards, as soon as possible, while events are fresh in your memory.

When you observe the dynamics of groups at work – for example, communication patterns, leadership behaviour, use of power, group roles, norms, elements of culture, problem-solving and decision-making, relations with other groups – you are provided with the basis for inquiry into the underlying assumptions and their effects on the work and life of these groups (Schein, 1999). As you are dealing with directly observable phenomena in the organizations with which you are working, the critical issue for you is how to inquire into what you are observing and, at the same time, to be helpful to the system. For example, at a team meeting, you may notice all sorts of behaviour which you suspect is affecting how the team goes about its work: people not listening to each other, wandering off the agenda, and so on. If you make an intervention into these areas you are aiming to focus on what is useful for the advancement of the action research project, rather than what you have observed. Without this discipline you may reflect on what you have observed, but the observation may not be owned by the participants in the system because it does not meet their needs as experienced, or it appears to be showing how clever you are in observing these things. For you, observation and inquiry into how the systemic relationship between the individual, team, interdepartmental group and organization operates is critical to the complex nature of organizational problem-solving and issue resolution (Coghlan and Rashford, 2006).

You may consider using some form of survey instrument (Nadler, 1977). An action research approach suggests that data-gathering tools need to be designed to fit both the organizational setting and the purpose of the research. While surveying employees by questionnaire as to their views on some aspects of their work or the organization tends to be seen merely as a method of collecting information, it is more important to see how it is an intervention. The reception of a questionnaire by employees may generate questioning, suspicion, anxiety or enthusiasm – all of which are real data for you. If you ignore this, you may be missing a key element of how the organizational issues exist and do not get resolved, and indeed what opportunities or obstacles lie ahead in the research process.

In a similar vein, interviewing in action research is not simply a tool for collecting data. As we have pointed out, asking someone a question or a series of questions is a data-generating intervention. Interviewing in action research tends to be open-ended and unstructured, focusing on what the interviewee has to say rather than confirming any hypothesis that the action researcher might have. In Chapter 2 we presented a typology of interview techniques, pure inquiry, diagnostic inquiry and confrontive inquiry (Schein, 1999, 2009, 2013). As we emphasized in that chapter, combining inquiry with advocacy is a critical skill for you as an insider action researcher.

It is unhelpful, if not inaccurate, to refer to groups in your insider action research project as 'focus groups'. Focus groups are consultation without responsibility, where members of the public are invited to contribute their views anonymously on a subject, and then return to their lives without having any further engagement with that subject. If you hold meetings to elicit views in the organization, these are not focus groups, as the participants are members of the organization and you are intervening in their thinking and creating expectations. Instead, call these groups 'consultation groups' or some other term that captures the interventionist nature of your interaction with them.

While a distinction is made between the study of formal documentation (what Gummesson calls 'desk research') and interviews, Gummesson (2000) makes the point that these are artificial distinctions, as the researcher is faced with a continuous flow of data. Secondary data are both numeric and textual, and were developed for some purpose other than helping to solve the action research question in hand. You need to evaluate this data on the basis of their relevance to the research question, their availability and accuracy. In order to have confidence in the worth, validity and reliability of the data, you need to consider the following questions for each archival source.

1. Who collected the data?
2. When was it collected?
3. What was collected?
4. Why was it collected?

Studying relevant documentation can be an important part of organizational research. Access to documentation is integrally linked to level of access in order to engage in research. Reports, memoranda, minutes of meetings, and so on may be highly confidential, and access to them may depend on the degree to which an organization's management is willing to grant access to the inside researcher.

The role of technology

Technology has transformed the world of communication. Within organizations, communication through email, websites and intranets has become the norm. Virtual team meetings transcend boundaries of time and space. Increasingly, IT is becoming the standard method for communication between people and organizations; in addition, technology is shaping the development of action research processes (Koch, 2007; Dymek, 2008).

The roles that IT can play in your action research process are manifold. You can use technology to gather information, process it and present conclusions. You can use it to communicate with your co-researchers, colleagues and clients on a one-to-one basis, hold virtual group meetings and communicate with large numbers of people. In regard to this latter use of IT, an important challenge for you as the action researcher is to attend to the quality of participation that occurs through the technology. As Schein (2003) points out, the absence of 'functional familiarity' – the experience that we build up of working with individuals in a face-to-face manner, where we know how to read their responses, body language and general way of interacting – can become a severe limitation on collaborative processes.

How do you know when to stop?

As mentioned previously, action research projects which act as dissertations typically have an in-built time schedule. Especially within single year or two-year master's programmes, you are expected to do your action research project within a designated time period, in order to meet the requirements of the programme in which you are enrolled. Accordingly, you should take your submission deadline, the amount of time that you are going to give yourself to write up the dissertation, and work back to where your organizational story will end. In many respects, the decision you make as to when your story will end is arbitrary, but it is important to set a date after which whatever takes place will not be included in your story – however exciting and relevant it may be.

When completion deadlines have more flexibility, your decision to stop is still arbitrary, and may depend on your judgement as to the extent that your project has yielded sufficient learning.

Conclusions

In this chapter we have explored how you might go about designing and implementing your action research project. We have shown that, after determining the need for it, it is useful to work at articulating a desired future before getting into the details of what to do and how to build commitment to the action. Accordingly, you need to keep in mind that everything you do is an intervention, and you need to be sensitive to the impact that asking questions and observing may have on your fellow participants. You need to manage the politics of the situation at all times. As we noted at the outset, having creative confidence is central, as it facilitates you to be open and flexible in your design and implementation.

Recommended reading

Coghlan, D. with Brydon-Miller, M. (2014) *The SAGE Encyclopedia of Action Research*. London: Sage. (See especially: 'Asset mapping', 'Cognitive mapping', 'Collaborative data analysis', 'Cycles of action and reflection', 'Data analysis', 'Design research', 'Evaluation methodologies', 'Facilitation', 'Interviews', 'Quantitative methods'.)

Docherty, P. and Shani, A.B. (2008) 'Learning mechanisms as means and ends in collaborative management research', in A.B. Shani, S.A. Mohrman, W.A. Pasmore, B. Stymne and N. Adler (eds), *Handbook of Collaborative Management Research*. Thousand Oaks, CA: Sage, pp. 567–582.

Dymek, C. (2008) 'IT and action sensemaking: Making sense of new technology', in P. Reason and H. Bradbury (eds), *The SAGE Handbook of Action Research* (2nd edn). London: Sage, pp. 573–588.

Mead, G. (2008) 'Muddling through: Facing the challenges of managing a large-scale action research project', in P. Reason and H. Bradbury (eds), *The SAGE Handbook of Action Research* (2nd edn). London: Sage, pp. 589–601.

Access a selection of author videos, encyclopaedia entries and recommended reading on this topic at www.uk.sagepub.com/coghlanandbrannick

EXERCISE 5.1

The process of implementation (for group discussion)

Step 1: Determining the need for change.

What are the external forces driving change? What are the internal forces driving change? How powerful are these forces? What choices do we have?

Step 2: If things keep going the way that they are without significant intervention:

What will be the predicted outcome? What is our alternative desired outcome?

Step 3: What is it in the present that we need to change in order to get to our desired future – what is done, how work is done, structures, attitudes, culture?

Step 4: What are the main avenues that will get us from here to there?

What are the particular projects within those avenues? Long, medium, short-term? How do we involve the organization in this project? Where

(Continued)

(Continued)

do we begin? What actions do we take to effect maximum effect, medium or minimum effect? How will we manage the transition? How do we build commitment? Who is or is not ready for, or capable of, change? How will we manage resistance? Who will let it happen, help it happen, make it happen? Do we need additional help – consultants, facilitators?

Step 5:   What review procedures do we need to establish?

How do we articulate and share what we are learning?

EXERCISE 5.2

Reflection for praxis

(This exercise is the work of Bob Dick. We are grateful to Bob for permission to reproduce it.)

Reflection before the action

The 'a' questions lead to practice. The b' question lead to theory.

1a. What do I think are the salient features of the situation I face?
1b. Why do I think that these are the salient features? What evidence do I have for this insight?
2a. If I am correct, what outcomes do I believe are desirable?
2b. Why do I think that these outcomes are desirable in this situation?
3a. If I am correct about the situation and the desirability of the outcomes, what actions do I think will give me the outcomes?
3b. Why do I think that these actions will deliver these outcomes in this situation?

Reflection after the action

0a. Did I get the outcomes that I wanted? Or more realistically, what were the outcomes that I got, and how well do these accord with those I sought?
0b. To the extent that I got them, do I still want them? Why, or why not?
0c. To the extent that I didn't get them, why not?
These questions return in more detail to the earlier planning questions.
1a. In what ways, if any, was I mistaken about the situation?
1b. If so, which of my assumptions about the situation misled me?

1c. What have I learned? What different conclusions will I reach about similar situations in the future?

2a. In what ways, if any, was I mistaken about the outcomes or their desirability?

2b. If so, which of my reasons for favouring these outcomes misled me?

2c. What have I learned? What outcomes will I try to pursue when next I am in such a situation?

(Notice that 3a takes a different tack.)

3a. Did I succeed in carrying out the planned actions? If not, what prevented or discouraged me? What have I learned about myself, my skills, my attitudes, and so on?

3b. If I did carry out my actions, in what ways (if any) was I mistaken about the effect that they would have? Which of my assumptions about the actions misled me?

3c. What have I learned? What actions will I try next time I am pursuing similar outcomes in a similar situation?

SIX
Interlevel Dynamics in Insider Action Research

 See www.uk.sagepub.com/coghlanandbrannick for a short introduction to the chapter from David Coghlan

The questions underpinning this chapter are both theoretical and practical. How do you understand the complex interaction of individuals and teams in the 'swampy lowlands' of your organization and in your action research project? How do you work with individuals, a team and across teams in your project?

Levels of analysis are commonly used as frameworks for researching, understanding and intervening in organizational systems (Harrison, 2005). Levels of analysis typically refer to the identification of issues at units of complexity, such as the individual, group, intergroup and organization. They are an important dimension in action research as traditionally they are seen as targets for research: that is, action research focusing on the workings of a team. This chapter extends the traditional focus of levels of analysis as the target for research to the notion of levels of aggregation or interlevel dynamics, and how interlevel dynamics are important in doing action research in your own organization (Coghlan, 2002). Interlevel dynamics illuminate first-, second- and third-person practice.

Levels of complexity – individual, group, intergroup, organizational – are used frequently as frameworks for understanding organizational processes. Several essential points need to be made about the concept and usage of the term *levels*. First, the notion of levels must be distinguished from that of *echelon* (Rousseau, 1985). Echelon refers to position in a chain of command in an organization, such as worker, supervisor, manager, group manager and chief executive. However, the less common use of organizational levels as a construct in organizational behaviour describes levels of complexity.

Coghlan and Rashford (2006) present levels in terms of how people participate in organizations, and link them to provide a useful tool for the manager, consultant and teacher of organizational behaviour. They distinguish four levels of behaviour in organizations: individual, face-to-face team, interdepartmental group and organizational. The first level is the *matching* relationship that the individual has with the organization, and the organization with the individual. For the individual, this involves utilizing of membership and participating in the organization in order to meet personal life goals; while for management the core issue is to have a person committed to the goals, values and culture of the organization so as to perform more effectively. The more complex approach to participation exists in establishing *effective working relationships in a face-to-face team*. An even more complex involvement exists in terms of the interdepartmental group type of interface, where teams must be *coordinated* in order to achieve complex tasks and maintain a balance of power among competing political interest groups. Finally, the most complex, from the viewpoint of the individual, is the relationship of the total organization to its external environment, in which other organizations are individual competitors for scarce resources to produce similar products or services. The key task for any organization is its ability to *adapt* to environmental forces driving for change.

Viewing organizations through levels of analysis is only one part of the picture. The other part refers to how levels are related to each other. In an organization, there is an essential interlevel element in that each level (individual, group/team, interdepartmental group, organization) has a dynamic relationship with each of the others (Coghlan and Rashford, 2006). This relationship is grounded in systems dynamics, whereby the relationship that each level has with each of the others is systemic, with feedback loops forming a complex pattern of relationships (McCaughan and Palmer, 1994; Williams and Hummelbrunner, 2011). For example, dysfunctions at any level can lead to dysfunctions at any of the others. An individual's level of disaffection may be expressed in dysfunctional behaviour in the team and affect its ability to function effectively, which in turn reinforces the individual's disaffection. If a team is not functioning effectively, it can limit the interdepartmental group's effectiveness, which may depend on the quality and timeliness of information, resources and partially completed work from that team. If the interdepartmental group's multiple activities are not coordinated, the organization's ability to compete effectively may be affected. In systemic terms, each level affects each of the others. Viewing organizational levels as simply 'levels of analysis', without taking interlevel dynamics into consideration, misses the point about the systemic relationship that the individual has with the team, the team with the individual, the team with other teams, the organization with its environment and each with each other.

When you are working at each or any of the above levels, typically you will find that you are challenged to include the other levels in your understanding and intervention. For example, you may be working with a team on an aspect of your action research project. In the process of this work, it emerges that some of the individual members are experiencing dissatisfaction with their relationship with the organization, and do not provide optimal contribution to the team's endeavours. Or it may be that the flow of information from other teams is having a negative effect on the work of the team with which you are working. In these instances, you are challenged to move beyond the team level intervention in which you are engaged to consider the dynamics at the other levels which are having an impact on the team.

Organizational levels are important dynamics in organizational politics. Organizational political behaviour may be individual, team and interdepartmental group. Individuals may engage in covert political behaviour in order to advance their own standing in the organization. Teams may engage in overt or covert political behaviour to gain advantage over other teams in order to obtain more resources.

Interlevel dynamics of change

Organization change typically means that individual employees have to change. Individuals may be required to change what they do or how they do it. It may be required of them to change their attitudes towards their work or some particular aspect of it. A consequence of this may be that an individual's relationship to the changed or changing organization may be altered, either positively or negatively. If not well managed, an organizational change can result in individuals feeling alienated. A change agenda in an organization typically affects the work of teams. Teams may set new goals and targets; they may have to work differently. As resources are reallocated, and technology and advanced information systems alter access to the flow of information, teams are required to communicate more effectively across functions and departments. So we can see that organization change comprises individual change, team change and interdepartmental group change.

What happens at one level has an impact on each of the others. So, for example, in a healthcare context, a recession may lead to a government's reduction of its budget allocation to a hospital. This affects the hospital's resource allocation across its departments and services, leading to a change in the work of teams, who may have fewer members and an increased workload, and result in individuals becoming stressed and alienated from their professional work. If a team is working well, that contributes positively to the motivation and participation of the individual members; the reverse is also true. The work of one team affects the work of others. So each level is systemically linked to each of the others, and events at one level are both the cause and effect of events at other levels.

There are critical interlevel dynamics in the process of organizational change that we described in the previous chapter. The change process has to begin somewhere, and typically it begins with an individual, although not exclusively at the top. For the change agenda to progress, that individual has to take it to a team, and that team needs to adopt the need for change. When a management team adopts the need for change and begins to act, it has then to win over other teams in the system. Each of these movements – from individual to team to other teams – is an iterative process. In other words, when the team adopts an individual's position, that adoption reinforces the individual. When other teams adopt a particular team's position, this reinforces that team; and, of course, when customers adopt a new product or service, that reinforces the organization.

The process of designing the vision of the future involves interlevel dynamics. If the vision comes from the chief executive, then there are interlevel dynamics from that individual to the senior management group, and then to other teams, and on to the organization. So the iteration of issue presentation, reaction and response ebbs and flows from individual to individual, team to team and so on. Interlevel dynamics are pivotal to the processes of the transition state, as individuals and teams address the implications and implementation of the change agenda. As the change agenda affects the work of individuals in what they do and how they do it, individual commitment is essential. As the change agenda affects the work of the permanent teams and typically requires the creation of new teams and work in temporary committees or project groups, team dynamics are critical to the change process. In a similar vein, the change agenda involves the interface of multiple teams with respect to information sharing, problem identification and resolution, resource allocation and collective bargaining, and inter-team dynamics can enable or hinder successful management of the change process.

Interlevel dynamics of strategy

Interlevel dynamics abound in the strategy process, and are important processes with which you may work as an insider action researcher. The complex process of generating strategic thinking and acting evolves through five strategic foci (Coghlan and Rashford, 2006):

1. framing the corporate picture;
2. naming the corporate words;
3. doing the corporate analysis;
4. choosing and implementing corporate actions; and
5. evaluating corporate outcomes.

Framing the corporate picture

This deals with the key individuals and the history of the organization as it comes to affect strategy formulation and implementation. The contents of this focus are on the core mission and its statement of the organization, as well as the characteristics of the key players. If the corporate picture comes from the senior manager, then they work to get the senior management group to accept it, and then to the interdepartmental group and ultimately to the organization: stakeholders, shareholders and customers. A new corporate picture forces the senior management group to set new priorities and allocate work to the divisions and departments in a different way. Interdepartmental issues centre on the new allocation of resources and information flow required in carrying out the new corporate picture.

Naming the corporate words

This deals with those operations or functions which have become the lead operations or functions over time. They are most often referred to as 'driving forces', and become the articulation or lived out mission statement of the organization. There are interlevel dynamics in choosing the corporate words, as functional areas compete for priority and status. For example, those who are not in engineering or marketing, where one or other is defined as the prime function, may feel undervalued and peripheral in terms of their contribution to the organization.

Doing corporate analysis

This deals with obtaining critical information and preparation of this data into a comprehensive scenario or modelling of alternatives for the organization. The analytic process acknowledges the appropriate connectedness of this focus to the previous focus of the mission in framing the corporate picture, and to the subsequent focus of choosing and implementing corporate actions which, of necessity, will follow. There are cultural issues in how an organization engages in analysis. Each functional area has to examine its own analysis and process its own functionality, as well as how the interdepartmental group's function affects others and its output. Each functional area is a sub-culture that exists in an organization, where functional groups have developed their own traditions, language and basic assumptions which provide a self-contained sub-system. So, each functional level is offering its view of the whole from the perspective of its own sub-culture in interdepartmental group activity. How these analyses or 'views' interrelate or are accepted is critical, as most often in integrating multiple functions the cross-links between functions are the sources of trouble.

Choosing and implementing corporate actions

This deals with the selection and structured implementation of a strategic plan of action with its concurrent implementation plans. In choosing and implementing corporate actions, the role of the final decision-maker resides with the chief executive officer (CEO). CEOs interface with a senior management group: when this interface is prolonged, and the differences between alternatives are ambiguous at best, the CEO can get trapped into deciding along the lines of their own past career experience.

Evaluating corporate outcomes

This deals with acceptance of the choice of criteria in the appropriate review and evaluation of the resulting state of the organization. The process aspect of evaluating corporate outcomes looks at the appropriate and fair evaluation of outcomes. Evaluation of these corporate outcomes most often resides with the senior management group and CEO.

Evaluation of both outside and inside reviews provides the grist for the inter-level interaction between the senior management group and CEO. This discussion focuses on the nuances of how the data are formed into information. The senior management group views the data from its interdepartmental perspective, as it represents that perspective on the senior management group, while the CEO looks at the data most often from the total organization's viewpoint, or even an outside viewpoint.

The five foci capture the core processes of any human system, built on five questions.

1. Who are we (corporate picture)?
2. What do we want to be good at (corporate words)?
3. How do we assess the external world that affects us (corporate analysis)?
4. How do we make choices and implement them (choosing and implementing corporate actions)?
5. How do we assess how we are doing (evaluating corporate outcomes)?

Each of the five strategic foci entails interlevel dynamics of change as an organization seeks to frame its corporate picture, name its corporate words, do its analysis, choose and implement corporate actions and evaluate outcomes. However, experience tells us that these levels are not only discrete, but also that they are interdependent and interrelated.

Levels of analysis in action research

Action research at the individual level

In Chapter 2 we explored how you can engage in first-person practice by attending to your own learning-in-action. First-person research in your own organization – how the research is for you – is linked to your own sense of *matching* to your organization. As we have seen, how the research contributes to your own development, role and future in the organization is a significant aspect of undertaking research in your own organization. Accordingly, your own self-awareness, closeness to the issues, how you frame the issues, and so on are critical first-person processes of which you need to be aware and to work on consciously as part of the action research project. Individual learning-in-action typically involves being able to reflect on your experience, understand it and enact chosen alternative behaviours, as well as learning to critique your assumptions in a manner which exposes your private inferences to public testing. The degree to which the project enhances your career, or to which it decreases your motivation to remain in the organization, is important.

Action research at the group or team level

Second-person research is characterized when researchers engage with others in conversation and action. This may be actualized in one-to-one situations where you engage in action and reflection with a single individual; more frequently, it is enacted in groups, whether in formal organizational hierarchical teams, temporary committees or taskforces that are built around the project. They may be collegial groups which you have set up to explore the task of your action research project, such as a cooperative inquiry or action learning group.

The experience of groups and teams in engaging in the action research steps is paramount. As they engage in the activities of constructing, planning and taking action they might experience some success in some of their activities, and not in others. They might experience internal conflict and destructive political behaviour by some members. They might struggle to reach agreement on strategies, action, and so on. What is important is that groups and teams learn to reflect on their experience in terms of *how* they function as groups and teams. This involves attending to task issues of how they do the task, and relational issues of how they manage communication among themselves, solve problems, make decisions, manage conflict, and so on (Schein, 1999). Exploring these issues means being able to go beyond personal blame and draw on useful constructs on effective group and team development to take remedial action where necessary, and develop effective team processes (Wheelan, 2012). For example, if you set up a group especially to work your insider action research project, you need to attend to how, in their early stages, groups struggle to deal with issues of inclusion, control and intimacy (Schutz, 1994). As Wicks and Reason (2009) explore, creating the psychological and social space for individual members to resolve these issues opens up a group's potential to become a unit rather than a collection of individuals, and to engage

INITIATING
ACTION
RESEARCH

in collaborative inquiry and joint action. These activities involve content, process and premise issues, as the issues on which they are working are studied, and the ways in which the teams work are reviewed and underlying assumptions uncovered and examined. Bartunek (2003) provides an illustration of the development of a change agent team over time in terms of identity, actions and stakeholder relationships. She narrates cognitive and affective links between:

- how identity has evolved over time in the face of member turnover, explicit reminders of identity and face-to-face contact;
- how the actions intended were taken, and how emotionally engaging the actions were; and
- how efforts to make these stakeholder relationships positive were taken.

Action research at the intergroup level

The research and change process cannot be restricted to learning and change by individuals and teams alone. A further application of second-person research is how the learning and change which takes place in individuals and teams needs to be generalized across the interdepartmental group, whereby other teams and units engage in dialogue and negotiation. A critical focus for attention in this regard is the impacts that cultural perspectives from different functions have on the change process (Schein, 2010). Intergroup dialogue needs to take account of how functional areas in organizations hold different assumptions from, and about, one another.

Groups and teams do not work in isolation. They are typically members of wider systems and such membership involves intergroup dynamics, such as being interdependent in a workflow or information process. The consequences of intergroup interdependence are intergroup dynamics such as sharing information, negotiation over resources, intergroup prejudice and intergroup conflict. You can expect to have intergroup dynamics in any project involving a complex system; indeed, working at the intergroup level is an extension of second-person research. The interdepartmental group experiences the differences between groups, as different groups are separated from one another by what they do, their location and interests. Accordingly, any action research work which involves members of separate departments working together must take account of how each department has its own concerns, view of the world, political interests in the work of the project and even terminology and language. We would argue that interdepartmental group-work is essentially intercultural (Schein, 2010).

A further instance of action research at the intergroup level is found in the burgeoning use of large group interventions in organizational change. Large group interventions are described as 'search conferences', 'future search', 'dialogue conferences', 'open space', 'real-time strategic change' and 'world café', among others

(Brown, 2005; Bunker and Alban, 2006; Holman et al., 2007; Martin, 2008), and are gatherings of the members of a system in a large group in order to create common ground for the future development of that system.

Action research at the organizational level

Finally, the action research project does not stop within the organization. Action research at the organizational level means that the project encompasses the organization as an entity in a competitive economic and social environment. Organizations as open systems have a dynamic two-way relationship with their external environments (Katz and Kahn, 1978). The second-person research process includes how the organization is affecting, and being affected by, its customers or clients, stakeholders, local community, competitors, wider society and other organizations. Therefore, the project is inclusive of the organization's relationship with its external stakeholders such as customers, clients and competitors, as well as internal stakeholders at the individual, group and intergroup levels.

To add further complexity, the project may involve inter-organizational work, typically called inter-organizational networking. Inter-organizational networking is where member organizations deliberately develop voluntary networks to help deal with complex issues, and devise collaborative ways of planning and taking action (Burns, 2007; Coughlan and Coghlan, 2011). The learning steps of the action research cycle need to be inclusive of reflection on how different mindsets and political interests in different organizations and groups are experiencing working together, how they process and interpret that experience and take action accordingly.

Conclusions

Levels of analysis are commonly used as frameworks for researching, understanding and intervening in organizational systems: typically, they refer to the identification of issues as units of complexity, such as the individual, group, intergroup and organization. They are an important dimension of action research, as traditionally they are seen as targets for action research. This chapter has reviewed the traditional focus of levels of analysis as targets for action research, and extends the notion to levels of aggregation or interlevel dynamics.

While many of the case examples cited through the book appear to focus on one unit of analysis, they actually contain interlevel dynamics. For example, while focusing on his own learning, Krim (1998) was embroiled in complex interlevel dynamics in his engagement with key political players and groups at a city hall. In OilCo, the CEO formed his managers into an executive council (Kleiner and

Roth, 2000). The managers had not worked together as a team before, so it was a new experience for them to do so. They formed sub-teams to work on particular projects. The executive council disseminated its work to the wider organization through a learning convention, at which people spoke frankly for the first time about their views of the company, and dialogue began to take place. The process continued through the company whereby the transformation of fundamental ways of thinking and feeling moved from the CEO to the executive council, and through the organization, impacted teams and individuals.

Interlevel dynamics are operative for you also as an action researcher in the action research process itself (Figure 6.1). You engage in interlevel dynamics as you encounter the process of the complex systems in which you enact action research projects. Your engagement in first- and second-person research typically requires enactment of your own learning-in-action along with work with groups, between groups and with organizations in their environments. The application of interlevel dynamics to first and second person is an important dimension of both understanding and enacting the experiential cycles of action research.

You can use the construct of the four levels to help you understand the interactive nature of your organization, being aware of the issues occurring at each level and how one level affects another, and to be able to work with individuals, teams and inter-team groups to evaluate the effect of one level on another. For example, the process of moving a change through an organization requires a systemic view

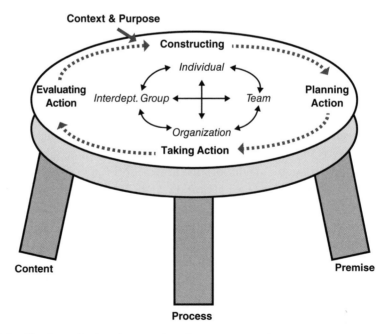

Figure 6.1 The Organizational Dynamics of Action Research

of the complex interrelationship and interdependence of the individual, face-to-face team, interdepartmental group and organization.

Interlevel dynamics are systemic processes. They provide frames for us to understand how participation in human systems is developed through increasing complexity as individuals, individuals in groups and teams, individuals in groups and teams which are part of an interdepartmental group with other groups and teams, the interdepartmental group within an organization which itself is a participant in a sector, market and global economy. These frames are not only for the purpose of understanding, but also the basis for action (Coghlan and Rashford, 2006). Hence your research-in-action can benefit from an awareness of, and skills in, working with interlevel dynamics.

Recommended reading

Arieli, D., Friedman, V.J. and Agbaria, K. (2009) 'The paradox of participation in action research', *Action Research*, 7 (3): 263–290.

Coghlan, D. with Brydon-Miller, M. (2014) *The SAGE Encyclopedia of Action Research*. London: Sage. (See especially: 'Cooperative inquiry', 'Dialogue', 'Dialogue conference', 'Inter-organizational action research', 'Large group action research', 'Learning window', 'Search conference', 'Strategic planning', 'World café'.)

McArdle, K. (2008) 'Getting in, getting on, getting out: On working with second-person inquiry groups', in P. Reason and H. Bradbury (eds), *The SAGE Handbook of Action Research* (2nd edn). London: Sage, pp. 602–614.

Wicks, P.G. and Reason, P. (2009) 'Initiating action research: Challenges and paradoxes of opening communicative space', *Action Research*, 7 (3): 243–262.

Access a selection of author videos, encyclopaedia entries and recommended reading on this topic at www.uk.sagepub.com/coghlanandbrannick

EXERCISE 6.1

Applying interlevel dynamics

1. (a) Who are the individuals involved in this project? How do I work with them?
   (b) Who are the teams involved in this project? How do I work with them?
   (c) What are the issues between these teams? How do I work at the inter-team level?
2. In the teams in the project, what impact are individuals having on the team in which they are members, and vice versa?
3. What are the significant patterns of relationships between individuals, teams, interdepartmental group and organization to which I need to be sensitive, and with which I need to work?

EXERCISE 6.2

Change issues

	Individual	Team	Interdepartmental group	Organization
Individual				
Team				
Interdepartmental group				
Organization				

1. Name a change issue with regard to an individual.
2. Now work diagonally along the shaded boxes. How does one level have an impact on the others?
3. Where would you put your energies to advance the progress of the change and heal dysfunctions?
4. Name a change issue which applies to the whole organization.
5. Now work diagonally along the shaded boxes. How does one level have an impact on the others?
6. Develop strategies to implement change at each level.

EXERCISE 6.3

The learning window

(The learning window is an adaptation of the famous JOHARI window, and is created by Lyle Yorks, Teachers College, Columbia University, New York. We are grateful to Lyle for permission to use it.)

The learning window can be used in an action research group, and aims to enable the group to distinguish between what it knows and what it is inferring, and thereby acting on the basis that it thinks it knows. Making these distinctions helps to keep the group focused on data.

- Quadrant 1: what the group knows has to contain solid data that have been tested and meets with consensual agreement among group members.
- Quadrant 2: what the group thinks it knows catches the inferences and attributions that group members are making, and challenges the group

LEARNING WINDOW

WHAT I KNOW & WHY I KNOW IT • What data do I have to support my view? • Do others accept my interpretation?	WHAT I THINK I KNOW & WHAT I NEED TO DISCOVER IN ORDER TO KNOW IT
WHAT I KNOW I DO NOT KNOW	I MUST BE OPEN TO WHAT I DO NOT EXPECT

KNOWING (vertical axis label)

DISCOVERING (horizontal axis label)

to make those inferences explicit, to locate them in directly observable behaviour through the ladder of inference, and to see them as hypotheses to be tested, rather than accepting them as facts.

• Quadrant 3: this identifies the gaps in knowledge that the group knows it needs to address, and opens up an agenda for further data collection and hypothesis testing in action.

• Quadrant 4: this is the blind area where the group does not know what it does not know.

Fill in the panes of the blank learning window in Exercise 6.3 below with your group. Discuss what goes into each pane and the evidence that you have that locates this information in each particular pane.

1 What we know	2 What we think we know
3 What we know that we don't know	4 What we don't know that we don't know

SEVEN
Using Frameworks to Study Organizations in Action

 See www.uk.sagepub.com/coghlanandbrannick for a short
introduction to the chapter from David Coghlan

We now turn our attention to the process of making sense of organizational dynamics by presenting some features of the use of frameworks in understanding organizational dynamics. The underpinning question is: 'How do I use frameworks to make sense of what I am seeking to understand?' This is a very difficult question to answer in the context of being in the 'swampy lowlands', as organizational frameworks typically suppose an outsider, objective stance. Organizational dynamics and the use of frameworks are subjects in themselves (Harrison, 2005; Bolman and Deal, 2008). There are innumerable frameworks which can be found in standard textbooks and the writings of those authors who have created them. For example, within the field of business strategy, you may be familiar with frameworks that enable you to analyse the competitive nature of an industry or relative position of a firm within it. Within marketing, you may draw on frameworks which help to position a product or service. In every field and subject area there are frameworks which enable you to make sense of the current situation and help you predict outcomes. In relation to doing action research in your own organization, we highlight the systems approach and give particular attention to constructs of organizational learning and change. We are not attempting to provide a list of such frameworks; rather, we aim to provide an introduction to their use.

Organizational diagnosis

Some textbooks use the term 'diagnosis' to express the activity of seeking to capture understanding of interrelated elements or processes.

We use the term *diagnosis* to refer to investigations that draw on concepts, models and methods from the behavioural sciences in order to examine an organization's current

state and help clients find ways to solve problems or enhance organizational effectiveness. (Harrison and Shirom, 1999: 7)

Underlying the principle of organizational diagnosis is a notion of organizational health that organizational clinicians use to compare with the present situation (Schein, 1997). Accordingly, frameworks which postulate key organizational variables and relationships are important diagnostic tools. At the same time, we remind you of our important point in Chapter 1, that we do not see an activity such as 'diagnosis' as an activity aimed at creating an objectivist truth. Rather, we understand the use of frameworks as providing a construction for conversation, and mechanisms for collaborative sense-making and joint action planning and action.

Organizational frameworks are presentations of organizations which help categorize data, enhance understanding, interpret data and provide a common shorthand language (Burke, 2011). They typically describe relationships between organizational dynamics such as purpose, strategy, structure, control systems, information systems, rewards systems and culture, help to organize data into useful categories, and point to the areas that need attention.

Some guidelines are useful for selecting and using frameworks. Weisbord (1988) advises that frameworks should have four features. They should be simple, fit members' values, highlighting the things they consider important, validate members' experience by putting recognizable things in a new light, and suggest practical steps. Burke (2011) provides three guidelines for selecting a framework. The first is that you should adopt a framework that you understand and with which you feel comfortable. The second is that the framework selected should fit the organization as close as possible: it should be comprehensive enough to cover as many aspects of the organization as appropriate, and clear enough for members of the organization to grasp. The third is that the framework should be sufficiently comprehensive to enable data-gathering and interpretation without omitting key pieces of information. In a word of caution, Burke points out that you may become trapped by your frameworks, so that your way of seeing becomes a way of not seeing – so as an action researcher you need to critique the frameworks that you use.

Systems thinking and practice

A significant contribution to situation analysis is systems thinking and practice. Systems thinking refers to seeing organizations as a whole, made up of interrelated and interdependent parts. The human body is a good example of a system whereby bones, muscles, tissues and organs perform interdependent and interrelated functions. While we might dissect the body and make an analysis of any particular part, the body's functioning depends on a holistic view of how all the parts work together.

Similarly, organizations may be viewed as systems in which planning, control, structural, technological and behavioural systems are interdependent and interrelated.

Understanding organizations as open systems – that is, being dependent on their external environment for survival – has been well established in organizational theory for many years (Katz and Kahn, 1978). What has received less emphasis is the 'recursive' systems model, which represents organizations as patterns of feedback loops and sequences of interaction that link and integrate the elements of a system (Senge, 1990; McCaughan and Palmer, 1994; Williams and Hummelbrunner, 2011). In systems thinking, linear cause-and-effect analysis is replaced by viewing patterns of interaction which mutually influence each other.

'Dynamic complexity' refers to situations where a system is complex, not due to a lot of detail, but due to multiple causes and effects over time (Senge, 1990). In situations of dynamic complexity, systems thinking provides a perspective of viewing and understanding how a system is held together by patterns of action and reaction, relationships, meanings, hidden rules and the role of time. In order to inquire into how a system functions, you can engage in systemic questioning (McCaughan and Palmer, 1994).

- *Establishing circuitry* – when A does [X], what does B do? What does A do next?
- *Establishing patterns* – what patterns are evident over time?
- *Exploring meaning* – what are the meanings held in the system? What are the common meanings attributed to events and actions?
- *Exploring covert rules* – what unarticulated and hidden rules govern behaviour?
- *Exploring the time dimensions* – how do time delays have an impact on the system?

It is not easy to find answers to questions posed by systemic questioning. Formulation of tentative working explanations as to what is happening in the system – the circuitry, patterns, covert rules, meanings and time – may uncover the dynamic complexity of the system and involve many iterations of collaborative inquiry before finding explanations that fit.

In his book on the socially constructed organization, Campbell (2000) makes the point that in the early 1980s a paradigm shift took place from what was traditional general systems theory, which is referred to as first-order cybernetics, to second-order cybernetics, which places the observer within the system that they are observing: the emphasis shifted towards the constructs that the observer was bringing. Rather than viewing the system as something connected by feedback and difference, there was a shift to understanding the system as meaning-generating. Social construction seeks to grasp how people work together to produce their realities. It distinguishes itself from systems thinking by moving to questions about what is happening to questions about how it happens, and from observations of action to explanations of action. It also poses questions about who is included or excluded in conversations, how the conversations are run and what they are about (Bushe and Marshak, 2009).

Systems thinking and action research

As an insider action researcher, you are seeking insight not only into the systemic patterns of thinking and acting in your system, but also the constructs and meanings that you bring to your inquiry. Hence, we offer systems thinking as a way of seeing the system and where you are in it, and engaging in collaborative dialogue about how multiple constructions affect what happens, and how what happens affects the constructions and meanings that people ascribe to their intentions and actions. Viewing the organization as a social construction is itself a social construction.

Systems thinking and the action research cycle play complementary roles. In a systems approach to action research, tentative insights are being formed as the story unfolds. These insights are provisional frames to articulate the elements of the system in order that they can be understood, and to consider interventions to change them where required. A very useful way of formulating systemic understanding is through the use of diagrammatic representation. A diagrammatic representation is a powerful way of expressing insight into how a system operates. When cycles of action and their consequences are drawn in a diagram, insight into the patterns of the system can be illuminated. Both the act of attempting to represent the system diagrammatically and the diagram itself are essential elements of the learning process: the very act of drawing the system's diagram is a learning process of explanation formulation and testing (Anderson and Johnson, 1997). In traditional research approaches, intuition is placed frequently against reasoning and considered alien from a research process. In Senge's (1990) view, the systems approach holds the key to integrating intuition and reason because intuition goes beyond linear thinking to recognize patterns, draw analogies and solve problems creatively.

Change and learning

As change and learning are central to action research, it is important for the action researcher to draw on knowledge of how change and learning take place (Schein, 1979). How change and learning take place applies not only to individuals, but also to groups, between groups and to organizations, as we saw in the previous chapter. Change theory has evolved from Lewin's (1999[1948]) model that the change process has three stages or sets of issues: being motivated to change, changing and making the change survive and work. Lewin argues that a system must unlearn before it can relearn, and that attention to all three stages is equally critical.

Any action researcher in an organization needs to understand how people in organizations can resist change. An important starting place is that resistance is a healthy, self-regulating manifestation which must be respected and taken seriously by the action researcher. Coghlan and Rashford (2006) present two psychological reactions to the initiation of a change. When a change agenda is first presented, people may *deny* its relevance. When denial is no longer sustainable it may be replaced by *dodging*, which is an effort to divert the change. Denial and dodging are natural reactions to a change agenda, especially when it is unexpected. In Coghlan and Rashford's view, they are a prelude to *doing* and *sustaining*, when the change agenda is accepted and implemented.

There are different levels of change and learning which have a particular relevance to action research. From the work of Bateson (1972) and others who have developed his work, a distinction between change or learning that deals with routine issues, and that involving a change of thinking or adoption of a different mental model, is defined typically as a distinction between single-loop and double-loop learning (Argyris and Schon, 1996) and first-, second- or third-order change (Coghlan and Rashford, 2006).

First-order change

This occurs when a specific change is identified and implemented within an existing way of thinking. For example, Bartunek et al. (2000) describe management-led action research on an issue of communication problems with clients in a bank. Through the action research process of participative data-gathering, data analysis, feedback and action planning, intervention and evaluation, the named problem was addressed and improvements made.

Second-order change

This occurs when a first-order change is inadequate, and the change requires both lateral thinking and questioning and altering the core assumptions that underlie the situation. In another example, Bartunek et al. (2000) describe a manager-led action research project which initially aimed to address improvement of a manufacturing system by increasing volume while maintaining flexibility, as well as enabling automated material control and improved planning. As the data were being analysed, it became evident that these changes would involve creating a radically new way that the company did business. Accordingly, through the action research cycle, materials personnel, assemblers, testers and supervisors and managers participated in diagnosis, analysis and feedback resulting in the implementation of a new integrated manufacturing system. Due to the success of this project, a similar methodology was applied to other change projects in the company.

Third-order change

It is realized that sometimes, concrete problems are symptoms of complex attitudinal and cultural problems which must be addressed, and that problem resolution involves organizational transformation. Third-order change occurs when the members of an organization learn to question their own assumptions and viewpoints, and develop and implement new ones.

The issues may not be obvious, as discussed in Chapter 4. First-order problems may persist unless there is second-order change. A recurrent demand for second-order change may point to the need for the development of third-order skills. Observation of a group at work may yield questions as to what particular behaviours or patterns of behaviour mean. What is critical is that you as the action researcher inquire into those patterns and facilitate the group in surfacing and examining them, rather than making a private interpretation that is untested and becomes the basis for action. Taking what is directly observable into the realm of meaning requires skills in inquiry and intervention (as discussed in Chapter 3).

Conclusions

In this chapter we have outlined how you would approach making sense of complex organizational data. We have presented some major themes with respect to how you might go about choosing a framework on which you would base your understanding of organizational data, and on the basis of which you would take action. At the same time, from the experience of messy iterative groping in the 'swampy lowlands', the frameworks may appear too simplistic and so you may search for other ones – or better still, construct your own. Here, the general empirical method enables you to name the experience, articulate your insights or understanding and test them in action.

It might be expected that in this chapter we would discuss topics such as data analysis, discourse analysis and other important techniques from the field of qualitative approaches to research. While some action researchers do engage in this form of analysis, out of having conducted interviews and engaged in participant observation activities as part of their action research project, we have refrained from such a discussion. We do not wish to distract you, as an insider action researcher, from the primary focus on describing, explaining and engaging in action. In our experience, a lack of familiarity or discomfort with the action research approach as presented in Part I of this book (a lack of familiarity or discomfort may apply to academic supervisors as well as to students) may tempt you to take refuge in these techniques.

Making sense has different applications in different contexts where the action research in your own organization is linked to academic accreditation. In a master's programme such as an MBA or its equivalent, frameworks such as those discussed in this chapter are used to help you see more clearly what is going on, and to design appropriate interventions to deal with the issues identified. In a master's by research and doctorate you go further. In this context, you not only use the frameworks to help you see what is going on and to plan further action, but also critique and extend theoretical frameworks in order to contribute to theory development.

Recommended reading

Coghlan, D. with Brydon-Miller, M. (2014) *The SAGE Encyclopedia of Action Research*. London: Sage. (See especially: 'Experiential learning', 'Social learning', 'Socio-technical systems', 'Soft systems methodology', 'Systemic action research', 'Systems psychodynamics', 'Systems thinking'.)

Access a selection of author videos, encyclopaedia entries and recommended reading on this topic at www.uk.sagepub.com/coghlanandbrannick

EXERCISE 7.1

Understanding your organization

Take any relevant organizational diagnostic framework from any textbook, and apply the categories and causal links lines to your own organization.

1. What picture is emerging?
2. What do you need to do, and with whom, to check the picture you have of the organization?
3. Where are the limitations of what the framework presents?
4. Where do you think you need to intervene?
5. How do you justify that understanding and intervention selection?

EXERCISE 7.2

Using systems thinking

Some useful books which can help you do some systems thinking and mapping are Senge et al. (1994), Anderson and Johnson (1997) and Williams and Hummelbrunner (2011).

On a sheet of paper, write the following.

1. Describe the issue or problem as you see it.
2. Tell the story.
3. Draw a map of the story. When A said/did [X], what did B do? What did A do next? What were the outcomes for C, and for D and E?
4. Connect the process of the story with arrows.
5. Include where you are in the story, and what your interests are.
6. Consider any number of explanations of the patterns.
7. Consider any number of interventions which might change the structure of the system, and see how each intervention has different outcomes across the system.

3

Issues and challenges in researching your own organization

EIGHT
Researching your Own Organization

 See www.uk.sagepub.com/coghlanandbrannick for a short introduction to the chapter from David Coghlan

Parts I and II have enabled you to enter into your insider action research project, and to advance on your action and inquiry into that action. We now turn to reflect on the specific topic of this book: namely, doing action research in your own organization. The questions underpinning this chapter are: 'What are the implications of engaging in action research in the backstage of the "swampy lowlands" of your own organization?' and 'What are the particular dynamics that accompany insider action research that you need to understand and take into account?' The following three chapters explore the issues and challenges that you face as you take an exciting venture into the 'swampy lowlands' of your own organization, engaging in the 'messy iterative groping' that Evered and Louis (1981) describe. Smyth and Holian suggest that insider research can be a little like abseiling: if you have abseiled you 'know the feeling when you defy gravity, lean back into the empty space parallel to the ground and step off a cliff space' (2008: 42).

Researching your own organization involves undertaking research in and on your own organization while being a 'complete member' (Adler and Adler, 1987). As 'permanent' is a term increasingly less applicable to today's workplace, we are using 'complete member' to refer to being a full member of your organization, and wanting to remain a member within their desired career path when the research is completed.

The 'complete member role' as outlined by Adler and Adler (1987) is closest to researchers studying their own organization. Such researchers have an opportunity to acquire 'understanding in use' rather than 'reconstructed understanding'. Riemer (1977) argues that rather than neglecting 'at hand' knowledge or expertise, researchers should turn familiar situations, timely events and/or special expertise into objects of study. This orientation was abandoned partly by ethnographers during the classical era, when participant observation replaced life history, and the emphasis shifted toward greater objectivity and detachment. Participation, and for some, the research process, involved becoming a temporary member of the organization in order to observe at first hand how life was lived, accepted and accorded legitimacy, but subjectivity, involvement and commitment were thrust aside. What is central to this book is how complete members may undertake action research in and on their own organizations.

In Chapter 3 we provided a brief introduction to the notion of collaborative management research, which involves shared exploration between practitioners and researchers to improve the performance of a system and to add to the broader body of knowledge in the field of management (Shani et al., 2008). The collaboration of practitioners and researchers is paralleled by collaboration between insiders and outsiders. While it might be generally assumed that the insider is the practitioner and the outsider is the researcher, this is not necessarily the case (Bartunek, 2008). The insider perspective is integral to the process of collaborative management research and, as Coghlan and Shani (2008) explore, the challenge is to create a community of inquiry from the collaboration of practitioners and researchers, and insiders and outsiders. We invite you to note here that the issues that we explore in this and the following chapters (8, 9 and 10) pertain not only to the context of this book – i.e. you as an individual undertaking insider action research – but also to the insider perspective of collaborative management research.

Focus of the researcher and the system

Doing action research in your own organization is opportunistic: you may be selecting an issue for research that is occurring anyway, irrespective of whether or not your inquiry takes place. We have described these as the *core* action research project and the *thesis* action research project (Zuber-Skerritt and Perry, 2002). Hence, we need to distinguish between the two projects as respective responsibilities may differ. For example, we know of a case of insider action research in which, in effect, the researcher is doing action research on a major project for which she is responsible. In this case, her academic supervisor has challenged her to differentiate between the actions of the project and the quality of her inquiry into how that project progresses, and what knowledge can be extrapolated. Her research is evaluated on the quality and rigour of her inquiry, rather than on the extent and success of the organizational project that she manages, and for which she is accountable to her organizational superiors. In contrast, we know of another case in which the insider-researcher is working as an internal facilitator in a change project, but is not responsible for its overall management – a role assigned to a senior project manager.

Accordingly, we need to differentiate between the researcher and the system in and on which the action research is taking place, whether that system is a large organization, community, department or unit. We can reflect on the intended goals of both the researcher and the system. As we reflect on cases that we know of insider research projects, we notice that the focus of the researcher and system can vary. For example, we know of an individual manager whose master's action research project was about the organizational change he was leading. His second-person intervention work to manage the politics, power dynamics and conflicts between key protagonists was central to both his managerial role in leading change in his organization and his action research dissertation. His reflection in action was central to his dissertation. At the same time, the members of his organization had little consciousness of the fact that he was doing a dissertation for a postgraduate degree; in their eyes he was simply doing his job. We know of another case of an individual in the same master's programme, who studied how his organization managed information. In this case, the individual's research focused on what was happening around him and was of great interest to his superiors and other members of the organization, but it did not involve him in any form of deliberate self-reflection in action.

Given there can be a range of foci on the part of both the researcher and system, can these foci be captured in a useful way? We understand that research can be viewed along a continuum which reflects the intended focus of the research for both researcher and system (Figure 8.1). Here, we are distinguishing a commitment to intended self-study in action by either or both researcher and system, from no such commitment.

Quadrant 1

Quadrant 1 is defined by the absence of intended self-study in action by both researcher and system. There is study but it is not deliberately in-action. This is

Figure 8.1 Focus of Researcher and System

a situation where the researcher is focusing on a perspective, issue or problem within the system as if external to themselves, and is not engaging in any deliberate self-reflection-in-action as part of the research process (Anderson et al., 1994; Flyvbjerg, 2001; Flyvbjerg et al., 2012). At the same time, the system itself is not committed to engaging in any intended self-study-in-action. The researcher may be researching patterns of statistical information, customer preferences or writing a case study around a particular strategic initiative or a period of time. For the researcher, this is data which are gathered and analysed using established methodologies.

Alvesson (2003) addresses the situation of doing ethnographical research in one's own organization: he calls it 'self-ethnography' rather than insider-ethnography or home-culture ethnography. 'Self-ethnography' involves studying a setting in which the researcher is a participant on more or less equal terms with other participants. Participation comes first and is complemented only occasionally by research-focused observation, hence 'observing participant' is a more appropriate term than participant-observer. The self-ethnographer relies on familiarity with the setting as the empirical starting point. If you are an insider-researcher working within the ethnography tradition, you have to work hard at liberating yourself from subjectivity in order to meet the intellectual requirements of this research tradition. Young (1991) provides a good case of doing ethnography in his own organization. He reports how there was a culture of secrecy within the police force of which he was a member. Social science research was equated with 'claptrap', and anyone engaged in it ran the risk of being labelled a 'traitor', with their promotion put in jeopardy. Therefore, he had to undertake his study surreptitiously and refers to his work as 'writing espionage'.

The ethnographic role and the action researcher role are closely interconnected and sharply distinguished (Schein, 1987). The ethnographic observer attempts to be an unobtrusive observer of the inner life of an organization, while the action researcher works at enabling obtrusive change. Since the self-ethnography approach is not the subject of this book, we are not including any further exploration of this quadrant; rather, we are addressing the research projects contained in quadrants 2, 3 and 4.

Quadrant 2

Quadrant 2 applies where there is no intended self-study-in-action on the part of the researcher, while what is being studied is the system-in-action. We see this as organization development action research, which comprises management action, internal consulting projects and some action learning. Coghlan (2003) refers to this as 'mechanistic-oriented' action research, where the research is framed in terms of managing change or solving a problem: it is directed at confronting and resolving a pre-identified issue.

There are many examples of quadrant 2 insider action research. Coghlan et al. (2004) provide a broad range of cases in which managers engaged in action research on particular issues confront their companies: improving influence and performance in a multinational subsidiary, building interorganizational relationships in a global virtual community, implementing a 360-degree feedback programme and managing human resources, among others. Bartunek et al. (2000) also present three case examples of such research. Three of the authors, acting in their organizational managerial capacity, carried out action research projects in their own organizations: in a bank, manufacturing company and public utility, respectively. The research projects were oriented towards improving operational action, and there is no reported self-study-in-action on the part of the authors.

There is a broad range of accounts of quadrant 2 action research in healthcare and nursing (Coghlan and Casey, 2001). Examples of action research in the clinical area illustrate interventions to improve palliative care (Hynes et al., 2012; Hockley et al., 2013), midwifery (Deery, 2011), knee replacement (Lucas et al., 2013) and intensive care (Soh et al., 2011).

Action research in quadrant 2 is typically the type of research undertaken in MBA and other master's programmes, where the focus is manager-led operational projects within a limited, specified timeframe. These may well be projects already under way in an organization, and accordingly are adopted opportunistically by manager-MBA students as their action research project. Clearly, such opportunistic adoption is not confined to MBA situations, but may be undertaken by teachers, nurses, social workers, clinicians and similar situations, where course participants choose pre-existing projects for their own research topic. In these situations, action researchers attempt to bring the action research cycles of inquiry to a project which has not been set up as an action research project. This may make severe demands on action researchers' ability to manage organizational politics. Depending on the origin and scope of the project within this quadrant, the internal researcher may be working with an external consultant who has been hired to facilitate the change.

From their three case experiences of manager-led action research projects, Bartunek et al. (2000) generalize a number of relevant issues and themes.

1. The initial assignment to carry out work that leads to the action research project is likely to come from the manager's superiors, and to be part of the manager's job description.
2. The other participants in the intervention are likely to be subordinates who need to buy into the change project.
3. The intervention is likely to be aimed at increased productivity.
4. Managers may find it helpful to constitute a consulting team to assist in the intervention.
5. Data-gathering can take place through a variety of formal and informal means.
6. Feedback sessions can be integrated into the workday, or conducted separately.
7. The manager is likely to have a personal stake in the outcome of the intervention.
8. The managers were all receiving training in action research while carrying out their interventions.

Quadrant 3

Quadrant 3 applies where the researcher is engaged in an intended self-study of themselves in action, but the system is not. The researcher may be engaging in a study to improve professional practice: they are engaging simultaneously in a process of self-reflection and examining their own assumptions in action and learning about themselves as events unfold. The researcher becomes a 'reflective practitioner' (Schon, 1983) or, as described in Chapter 1, a scholar-practitioner. Coghlan (2003) refers to this as 'organistic-oriented' action research, where the inquiry process is a value in itself. In organistic-oriented action research researchers engage in an action inquiry process in which inquiry into their own assumptions and ways of thinking and acting is central to the research process. As mentioned previously, Marshall (1999, 2001) describes this first-person research or practice in terms of:

1. inquiring into the inner and outer arcs of attention;
2. engaging in cycles of action and reflection; and
3. being active and receptive.

If you are locating yourself in this quadrant, then the processes described in Chapter 2 are paramount for you.

> Krim (1988) provides a case example of quadrant 3 action research. In a somewhat dramatic account of an action inquiry project in action, he outlines the context of change in a city hall power culture and describes both the political and conflictual dynamics within that culture and the processes of his own personal learning. He reports how, as the initiator and coordinator of a new labour management cooperation programme based on employee participation in a city hall, he sought to use himself as the key learning strategy, whereby his management style would be central to the inquiry process. He outlines the context of change in a city hall power culture, and describes both the political and conflictual dynamics within that culture and the processes of his own personal learning. He describes his reflection process in terms of a pyramid of five steps:
>
> 1. recording and observing on a daily and hourly basis;
> 2. weekly selection and analysis of critical incidents;
> 3. exploration of these issues with his academic supervisor;
> 4. rehearsal and role-playing with his supervisor in anticipation of further critical incidents; and
> 5. public testing in the real-life situation (Krim, 1988).
>
> He reports how this cycle of continuous rehearsal and performance allowed him to improve his performance in highly political and conflictual situations. From this process he received feedback on his management style, particularly how he tended to 'de-authorize' himself, and so he adopted some practical rules of thumb to help him develop new behaviours. He reports how he was accused of spying when his research notes were pilfered from his computer and circulated among his antagonists. You can read Krim's own account to have a fuller picture of his insider action research.

Questions for reflection and discussion

- What did it mean for Krim to 'use himself' as the key learning strategy? How does this example give you insights into quadrant 3 insider action research?
- If quadrant 3 work fits for you, how might you structure your own learning-in-action process?

A quadrant 3 research may be pre-selected, or it may emerge. Where the research agenda is self-selected by the researcher it may focus on the researcher's job or role within the organization; it may be that the quadrant 3 research emerges out of a quadrant 2 project. Meehan and Coghlan (2004) provide such an example. They describe a case in which Meehan, in his organizational role, was asked by his superior to evaluate the addiction counselling service in his regional health area. The service was primarily treatment-focused, providing a service to help those with addiction problems end their dependence on mood-altering substances and rebuild their relationships with their families, friends and colleagues.

Meehan met the group of counsellors. As the group explored the issue of evaluation, resistance emerged. There was concern that no matter how good the evaluation was, the organization would not accept it. A feeling of alienation that the group felt was surfacing, with an air of futility about the process being articulated. At this time Meehan found himself actively listening to the group, and he speculated that if an effective evaluation was to take place, the participants' feelings needed to be heard and dealt with in some way. He was becoming aware that he was utilizing listening and counselling skills in the process. The counselling skills were those he had learned as a clinical psychiatric nurse, and it enabled the group to explore the feelings they had about these issues. As time went on he became more convinced that he was working on a project that would really benefit from an action research approach, and he entered into discussions with the group on the issue. His thinking in this regard was that the action research approach would be likely to produce insights that could not be gleaned in other ways. He hoped that the process would enable the group to get new and innovative insights into the service, and to take action based on them.

Meehan introduced the group to the notion of cooperative inquiry, and the group agreed to pursue the issues pertaining to themselves and the service in that mode of reflection on experience through a cooperative inquiry group process. Over a six-month period the group met 11 times and explored three themes: feelings of alienation and powerlessness, the lack of strategic direction in the service and professional identity and autonomy. They carried out a SWOT (Strengths, Weaknesses, Opportunities and Threats) analysis of the service and identified areas for change, both within themselves and in the management of the service.

As he led the group through the formulation of an action plan to initiate a service evaluation, Meehan found himself confronted by a feeling of futility within the group. On one level he was getting feedback that his intervention was helpful, but how it was helpful was not articulated. On another level the group was sceptical about the usefulness of the evaluation. The manager assumed that there was a feeling it had all been done before, and 'what's the point?' He then began to see his role as a go-between or an arbitrator between the management team and the addiction counsellors, and in some way perceived that if he could get a good evaluation of the process utilizing management input, addiction counselling input and from a service users' perspective, that would solve the issue. However, intuitively he was picking up resistance and vibes saying that this was not going to work.

The group of addiction counsellors worked in the group to reflect on their experience and to develop new and creative ways of looking at things. They also learned how to act to change the things that they wanted to change, and explored how to do things better. Each member acted as a co-subject in the reflection phases and a co-researcher in the action phases. They enacted the action research cycles of reflection and action in a psychologically safe environment, which enabled them to make sense of their experience and take steps to initiate change. Overall, the outcomes of the cooperative inquiry process were that there was a reduction in feelings of alienation and powerlessness in the group, which was evidenced in the enthusiasm with which the group subsequently engaged in the evaluation. A commitment grew to work in partnership with all stakeholders and service users in evaluation and developing the service. The group was beginning to look at issues from other perspectives, and this appeared to reduce hostility and fear. There were also real issues about their power in the organization: at one level they felt like victims in the process, yet it was obvious that unless they agreed with changes, these were unlikely to be implemented.

Meehan found the whole process difficult yet rewarding. It was an ongoing dynamic, and he found that he learned a lot in the process. It was the first time that he had consciously bridged the gap between his role as a clinician and as a manager. It showed him how to utilize his skills as a clinician in management. He found the action research cycles to be very useful and that it produced insights that he believed could not be gleaned other ways. The process was also a healing one, and he believed that it empowered the group to deal with underlying difficulties in the service.

Through this process Meehan believed that he received insights into how he could develop further as a manager and a person. One particular change in his behaviour and role as a manager that occurred in this process was how he now perceived his role differently. Traditionally he had viewed his role as an agent of control; now he viewed himself in a different way. The process enabled him to explore new and interesting ways of viewing his role as a manager: it gave him an insight into potential ways of working with alienation and powerlessness in the workplace. Hitherto he had functioned as what Frost and Robinson (1999) described as a 'toxic handler', which he now viewed as an unhealthy way of managing organizational pain. He now saw one of his managerial roles as that of a healer (Quick et al., 1996).

In hindsight he was able to manage many of the political elements, because as an insider he understood the process politics of the organization. He found himself as a middle manager who has to understand internal and external pressures on the organization, and satisfy personal or competing interests. The personal and emotional issues remained confidential to the group, but the broader learning from the group was discussed. Changes to management structures, issues regarding supervision, renegotiations regarding timeframes for completion were all dealt with well, and there was no conflict on these issues.

You can read Meehan and Coghlan to obtain a fuller picture of Meehan's insider action research project.

Questions for reflection and discussion

- How did Meehan's work in quadrant 2 lead to work in quadrant 3? Did he leave quadrant 2 behind in his pursuit of quadrant 3 learning?
- If you are beginning in a quadrant 2 setting, what possibilities and options are there for you to move into quadrant 3? Do you want to move to quadrant 3, or do you prefer to remain in quadrant 2? Is being in both possible, as it was for Meehan?

Quadrant 4

Quadrant 4 is where both the researcher and the system are engaged in intended study-in-action. The system has made, or is making, a commitment to change. For example, the system may undertake a system-wide, transformational change programme in which everything in the system is open to review: as instanced in a movement to quality of working life, business process re-engineering and organization development project, or any of those through a learning history approach. In this instance, there is a broad commitment to reflecting on experience and learning. The researcher's role involves being part of this collective reflection and learning and articulating what is happening. There is active participation by both the system and the individual. In a large-scale system change project, it is likely that there will be external consultants, hence the need for insider–outsider collaboration (de Guerre, 2002; Adler et al., 2004; Bartunek, 2008; Shani et al., 2008). Quadrant 4 is clearly the most difficult and demanding in terms of scale, complexity, conceptual, analytic and practical knowledge and skill.

The research process itself may provoke a move from one quadrant to another. For example, an action researcher operating in quadrant 2 may find that the technical problem being researched is a symptom of underlying cultural assumptions, and so its resolution carries more far-reaching implications than was envisaged at the outset. The dimensions of research in quadrant 3 may evolve into quadrant 4. It may be that the researcher's personal development through the research process involves a gradual movement from quadrant 2 to quadrant 3. For example, participants in the Master's Programme in Management Practice at the Irish Management Institute, University of Dublin, which was a part-time, action research-oriented programme, reported that they perceived the two-year programme as a journey from quadrant 2 to 3, with quadrant 4 the desired outcome in the long term.

Eddie reflects on his experience

I would have to say that it began in quadrant 3. I, as a classroom teacher, was engaged in an intentional self-study-in-action to gain insight with respect to the inquiry questions of how the learning of beginning algebra can be made more meaningful to students, especially those who have faced prior difficulties with mathematics. However, the larger system that I found myself in was not engaging in this type of inquiry. As a result the project took the form of me, as an individual, engaging in a reflective study of my own professional practice.

As the project ran its course, however, I feel as though it moved into quadrant 4. I followed my supervisor's suggestions and engaged my fellow teachers in the analysis of the Foundations of Algebra I curriculum. After writing it, I gave it to them and asked them, in the spirit of co-inquiry, whether or not what I had prepared connected to their reality. I was especially interested in what they would add and how they would describe the same things. As a consequence I witnessed my project gain momentum and buy-in. Not only were my colleagues interested in gaining an understanding about the question that was at the heart of my project, but the school's administration also reacted by expressing interest in the work and a willingness to provide any necessary support. For these reasons I am excited to say that the system eventually participated with me in an intended study-in-action, the result of which will hopefully be a large-scale transformational change in the way in which introductory algebra is taught at my school.

George reflects on his experience

Much of the project would be placed in quadrant 3, since I was engaging in an intended self-study of myself in action, but my department was not. Since my department was pursuing a year-long goal, many of their actions could be characterized as quadrant 2, internal consulting and action learning. In the middle of launching the initiative I became our department's team leader, so in the process of developing the agenda for our weekly meetings and reporting on the progress made toward our goals, the administration and the teachers began to participate in the cycle of observing, planning, implementing and reflection. This occurrence had some characteristics of quadrant 4, whereby the researcher and the system are engaging in an intended self-study. While we never explicitly articulated the engagement in self-study, this is what we were doing. This understanding leads me to realize that you may be able to motivate people more readily to develop professionally by appealing to their own curiosities in reflecting on goals that they feel are beneficial to their practice. Dropping the term 'project' removed a psychological burden. To many people the word 'project' means a 'lot of hard work'. It wasn't necessary to define this initiative as a project in order for the teachers to engage.

The grid acts as a mechanism for subject selection. You can select a subject based on:

1. a desired outcome for yourself and/or your system;
2. the opportunity or access to areas of the organization; and
3. your sense of your possession of the level of skill required to work in any particular quadrant.

Action research at home

Not all action research in your own organization is done at places of work. The following example illustrates action research at home.

Goode and Bartunek (1990) described a self-initiated action research project in an apartment complex, where Goode initiated a process to address a problem of direct personal concern. In the apartment complex where Goode was a resident, there were problems relating to mail delivery and security. Single efforts to address resident concerns had been unsuccessful. Goode approached several concerned residents, discussed the problem with them and explained action research in order to foster an environment that would enable collaboration and search for multiple causes of the problem, rather than unitary blaming of the complex's caretakers, which was common. Goode then formulated a plan for gathering information, which involved producing an informational letter which she distributed to all residents; conducting preliminary meetings with some of the residents and caretakers; conducting an informational session with anyone interested in participating; and interviewing all interested individuals. All these actions took place and the data generated was analysed under such headings as: 'organization strengths', 'existing mail security problems' and 'existing group-level structures and problems'. A feedback session was held at which taskforces were formed to address particular issues, and actions implemented.

Goode and Bartunek reflect on this case in terms of two issues. First, this case is an example of action research in an underbounded system (as this subject is not central to the theme of this book we will not reflect further on this point). Second, and the one which concerns us in the context of action research in your own organization, is how the action researcher initiated research in an organization where she had a personal stake. Goode and Bartunek point to two roles that the action researcher played. One role was that of a long-term participant in the system, which meant that she shared the concerns of the fellow residents and had credibility. The other role was a short-term consultant role, where her knowledge of action research provided guidance for the process. She was willing to take an educative, directive and participative approach to enable the resolution of problems and emergence of new structures.

Questions for reflection and discussion

- What insights are you receiving from this informal action research initiative?
- Are there opportunities for you to practice your insider action research skills in situations outside of the dissertation setting?

Conclusions

In this chapter we have reflected on the subject of doing research in and on your own organization. Researching your own organization involves undertaking research in and on your own organization while being a complete member. In undertaking action research in and on your own organization, the commitment to learning-in-action by both the system and yourself is a useful defining construct. If the research project is accompanied by the system's commitment to learning in action, then secondary access is easier. On the one hand, if your organizational role is that of an internal consultant, then your research role is integral to that role. On the other hand, if you are a manager, then you are taking on the researcher role in addition, and this may create confusion.

As an insider action researcher you are engaged in first-person research, using your preunderstanding of organizational knowledge and organizational studies for your own personal and professional development. You are engaging in second-person research by working on practical issues of concern to your organization in collaboration with colleagues and relevant others. You are engaging in third-person research by generating understanding and theory which is extrapolated from the experience.

Doing action research in your own organization involves clarifying the action research project in terms of both your and the system's commitment to learning-in-action, and managing issues of role and secondary access.

Recommended reading

Bartunek, J.M. (2008) 'Insider/outsider team research: The development of the approach and its meanings', in A.B. Shani, S.A. Mohrman, W. Pasmore, B. Stymne and N. Adler (eds), *Handbook of Collaborative Management Research*. Thousand Oaks, CA: Sage, pp. 73–92.

Coghlan, D. (2003) 'Practitioner research for organizational knowledge: Mechanistic- and organistic-oriented approaches to insider action research', *Management Learning*, 34 (4): 451–463.

Coghlan, D. with Brydon-Miller, M. (2014) *The SAGE Encyclopedia of Action Research*. London: Sage. (See especially: 'Insider action research'.)

Access a selection of author videos, encyclopaedia entries and recommended reading on this topic at www.uk.sagepub.com/coghlanandbrannick

EXERCISE 8.1

Assessing your research focus

Drawing on Figure 8.1, reflect on your current position.

- What quadrant are you in?
- What quadrant do you think that you are in?
- Which quadrant are you best at?
- Which quadrant would best serve your dissertation requirements?

NINE
Preunderstanding, Role Duality and Access

 See www.uk.sagepub.com/coghlanandbrannick for a short introduction to the chapter from David Coghlan

The dynamics of doing action research in your own organization in quadrants 2, 3 and 4 involve building on the insider knowledge that you have already (preunderstanding), managing the two roles that you have (your standard organizational roles and now, in addition, the action researcher role) and negotiating access. The questions underpinning this chapter are: 'How do you build on the closeness that you have to the organization and maintain distance?' and 'How do you balance the potential dilemmas ands tugs between your established organizational roles and your researcher role?' We now explore these.

Preunderstanding

'Preunderstanding refers to such things as people's knowledge, insights and experience before they engage in a research programme' (Gummesson, 2000: 57). Knowledge refers to what is generated during the research. The knowledge, insights and experience of the insider-researcher apply not only to theoretical understanding of organizational dynamics, but also to the lived experience of your own organization. Some misunderstand the notion of preunderstanding and equate it with tacit knowledge. Preunderstanding includes both explicit and tacit knowledge. Personal experience and knowledge of your own system and job are a distinctive preunderstanding for the insider-researcher.

One advantage that you have as an insider-researcher over an outsider-researcher is that you have valuable knowledge about the cultures and informal structures of your organization. Organizations lead two lives. Their formal or public life is presented in terms of formal documentation: mission statement, goals, assets, resources, annual reports, organizational chart and so on. Their informal or private life is experiential, the life as experienced by its members: its cultures, norms, traditions, power blocs, and so on. In their informal lives, organizations are centres of love, hate, envy, jealousy, goodwill and ill-will, politics, in-fighting, cliques, political factions, and so on – a stark contrast to the formal, rational image organizations tend to portray. You have valuable experience of this, although you do not know it all. While this knowledge is an advantage, it is also a disadvantage, as you are likely to be part of the organization's culture and find it difficult to stand back from it in order to assess and critique it. You may need to be in tune with your own feelings as an organizational member: where your feelings of goodwill are directed, where your frustrations are, and so on.

Nielsen and Repstad (1993) outline some examples of such experience and pre-understanding. You have knowledge of your organization's everyday life. You know the everyday jargon. You know the legitimate and taboo phenomena of what can be talked about and what cannot. You know what occupies colleagues' minds. You know how the informal organization works, and who to turn to for information and gossip. You know the critical events and what they mean within the organization. You are able to see beyond objectives which are merely window dressing. When you are inquiring you can use internal jargon and draw on your own experience in asking questions and interviewing, and be able to follow up on replies and so obtain richer data. You are able to participate in discussions, or merely observe what is going on without others being necessarily aware of your presence. You can participate freely without drawing attention to yourself and creating suspicion. You are decidedly backstage.

However, there are some disadvantages to be being close to the data. When you are interviewing you may assume too much, and so not probe as much as if you were an outsider or ignorant of the situation. You may think that you know the answer and not expose your current thinking to alternative reframing. In insider research, epistemic reflexivity is the constant analysis of your lived experience, as well as your own theoretical and methodological presuppositions. This helps you to retain an awareness of the importance of other people's definitions and understandings of theirs. You may find it difficult to obtain relevant data, because as a member you have to cross departmental, functional or hierarchical lines, or because as an insider you may be denied deeper access which might not be denied an outsider. Ferguson and Ferguson (2001) caution against insider action researchers believing that they fully understand their own contexts, when in fact their perspectives are only partial. In their view, the moral is to be honest about the perspectives from which you operate, and to be open to disconfirming evidence, perhaps seeking it out through interviews.

Table 9.1 Preunderstanding in first-, second- and third-person practice

	Task	Process
First person	Developing a spirit of inquiry in familiar situations where things are taken for granted	Attending, questioning own assumptions; self-awareness reflection skills
Second person	Developing collaborative inquiry/ action in familiar situations where the spirit of inquiry may be diminished	Collaborative inquiry/action: • Combine advocacy with inquiry • Has a range of intervention options • Testing assumptions and inferences • Learning window
Third person	Developing practical knowledge of how to inquire as a 'native'	Link practice with theory

Table 9.1 outlines the essential tasks and skills required to work with the strengths and limitations of preunderstanding. The task at first person is to develop a spirit of inquiry so as to receive insights into familiar situations where things are taken for granted because they are so familiar. This requires self-awareness reflection skills, as we explored in Chapter 2, so that you learn to attend to and question your own assumptions. At second person, the challenge is to develop collaborative inquiry or action with relevant colleagues in familiar situations where the spirit of inquiry may be diminished. Here, you need to be able to combine advocacy with inquiry, test assumptions and inferences through having a range of intervention options, and be skilled at using each of them appropriately. The learning window is a useful framework for both first- and second-person work on preunderstanding. Your third-person contribution may include an understanding of developing practical knowledge of how to inquire as a 'native', and so to be able to link theory with practice.

Schein (2010) describes organizational culture as patterns of basic assumptions which have been passed on through generations of organizational members, and which are unnoticed and taken for granted. Accordingly, the approach to uncovering cultural assumptions is a dialogue between organizational members and an external process consultant who facilitates exploration of what assumptions underlie artefacts and values. As an insider-researcher you may need an external facilitator to help you make sense of your experience; an academic supervisor may play this role. Krim (1988) reported how, in his meetings with his academic supervisor, he would role-play critical incidents. These role-plays were important in his reflective learning process.

Gorinski and Ferguson (1997) share a conversation about their respective experiences of being an insider action researcher. They identify positive aspects of accessibility, credibility, trustworthiness, commitment and familiarity with the research context and personnel. They found the barriers to be communication difficulties, time limitations, power positions and how cultural openness changed as they found themselves being left out of things. Their conclusion is that they had to 'make the road by walking'.

The quest for authenticity with respect to preunderstanding requires attention to your own inner and outer dynamics. Outer dynamics pertain to the familiarity of the settings, and inquiring as to how they may be different and what further insights are required where the ritual appears to be the same. You may be different this week due to what you have thought, felt and done, or due to what has been done to you; likewise the other participants. The context may have shifted slightly or subtly. Inner dynamics point to your thoughts and feelings in such familiar settings, which may be familiar feelings of powerlessness or other feelings or thoughts that accompany being in these regular situations with the same people. Being intelligent refers to asking what evidence you are being presented with as you work in a familiar setting, and what it is that you take for granted. Being reasonable means weighing the evidence and distinguishing inferences and attributions in deciding what conditions are fulfilled, in order to make a confident judgement. Being responsible means that you take responsibility for what you decide to do and what you do.

Journalling is an important mechanism for learning to reflect on and gain insights into your preunderstanding. Through recording your experiences, thoughts and feelings over time as you move through your project, you can begin to identify gaps between what you think you know and then find that you don't, or between explicit and tacit knowledge. You can begin to learn to stand back and critique what you have taken for granted previously. The journalling process helps your meta-learning of content, process and premise in the arena of your preunderstanding as it can expose what you know and do not know due to your closeness to the issues and the organization.

Role duality: organizational and researcher roles

In action research the traditional distinction between the researcher and the researched diminishes. Working in quadrants 2, 3 and 4 of Figure 8.1, the insider action researcher role is added to the complete member role, as discussed earlier.

In a detailed and insightful reflection on role duality, Wirth reflects that negotiating between her various roles and identities was the greatest challenge, as it was difficult to develop a balance between being a colleague, schoolteacher, friend and researcher (Ravitch and Wirth, 2007). In one role she acted as a leader supporting colleagues in a literacy programme, ensuring that she did not act as an evaluator.

In her researcher role she needed to be more direct in presenting the expectations of the research initiative. She notes that what was important was that she was an insider: as colleagues knew her and she knew them, they seemed to assume fairly that she had no hidden agenda and that the more sensitive issues involving culture, 'race', social class and equity could be approached. Because she knew and respected them, she understood the suggestions that they made about the design and implementation of the initiative, so she felt able to recognize their concerns and work to address them. At the same time, there were some significant challenges and disadvantages. She wondered that because they knew her, some seemed to think that they could ignore her requests.

Wirth reports that one of her most significant struggles was to maintain a collaborative mode of working with the teachers in a school climate that did not foster collaboration. Being familiar with the various personalities, perspectives and dynamics between the teachers was helpful in setting up the collaborative effort and facilitating change, but she noted that in other ways her preconceived notions about the teachers compromised her ability to see them more objectively, and constrained possibilities for building new kinds of relationships and processes.

Questions for reflection and discussion

- Do you recognize the challenges that Wirth presents? We suggest that you read the complete article, reflect on it for yourself, and discuss with your group the issues that she identifies and how she dealt with them.
- What roles do you play in your organization? When you add the researcher role, what challenges do you expect to face or are facing?

Williander and Styhre (2006) reflect on the role of the insider action researcher as a dual channel between academia and practice: information flows in both directions. In their experience, the first role of the insider action researcher was to act as a bridge between academia and the company, and in translating information between the two worlds of research and practice. The second role was that of traditional researcher, but using the benefits of being an insider, constructing case studies about the company and its parent company. Studies on one and the same case from a network perspective, marketing perspective, consumer behaviour perspective, and so on provided a multidisciplinary understanding of the issue and became an important foundation for emerging ideas and how to address them. The third role of the insider action researcher was to use the company as an object of experimentation. Academia would have the opportunity of testing, observing, intervening and validating, while the company would gain competitive advantage from the firsthand knowledge created. We suggest you read Williander and Styhre (2006) for a fuller exploration of their reflection on the role of the insider action researcher.

Ashforth et al. (2000) explore the nature of roles, presenting a number of useful constructs. Role boundary is defined as the scope of a role. Role boundaries can be flexible (that is, their boundaries can be pliable spatially and temporally) and permeable (you may be physically in one role, and psychologically and/or behaviourally in another). For Ashforth et al. these constructs of role flexibility and permeability enable transition from one role to another. In terms of doing action research in your own organization, you may be in your office or at a meeting in your organization exercising your organizational role (physical and spatial), while at the same time probing for answers to questions in your research role. Ashforth et al. also explore the notion of role identity: how a role cues specific goals, values, behaviour, and so on. Role identities are socially constructed definitions of self-in-role, consisting of contrasts between core and peripheral features. In their view, combining the construct of role boundary in terms of flexibility and permeability, with that of role identity in terms of contrast between core and peripheral features, can be arranged along a continuum from high role segmentation to high role integration.

> Roth et al. (2004) apply Ashforth et al.'s framework as they enacted insider action research roles in both the organizational and the academic setting of the action research. For example, they applied frames of reference from the academic setting to the organizational setting. They note that each of them acted as a bridge between industry and the academy which could facilitate the joint knowledge creation necessary for both settings, albeit in a different way in each project. In their reflection, they viewed that the nature of the insider action researcher's dual role facilitated the creation of a stable bridge between the academy and industry, through extensive knowledge of the company being studied and the research process.

Augmenting your normal organizational membership roles with the research enterprise can be difficult and awkward, and can become confusing and overwhelming. You may find as, Keegan and Lahey (2001) put it, that you have 'competing commitments'. As a result, in trying to sustain a full organizational membership role and the research perspective simultaneously, you are likely to encounter role conflict. Your organizational role may demand total involvement and active commitment, while the research role may demand a more detached, theoretic, objective and neutral observer position. This conflict may lead you to experience role detachment, where you begin to feel like an outsider in both roles (Adler and Adler, 1987).

> Humphrey (2007) reflects that her insider–outsider status was a valuable resource for her, as she could mobilize both insider wisdom and outsider research to explain the rationale of self-organization. Some expressed relief that issues had been exposed by an 'insider' rather than an 'outsider', that they were now 'on the table' for debate and there were 'theories' to make use of them. She reflects:

The perils of the insider-outsider are that she can be pushed and pulled along an invisible insider-outsider continuum by others who have a vested interest in who she is and what she is doing and she is cast now as an 'insider' and now as an 'outsider' by different actors and audiences and can lose her sense of herself. To actively take charge of the hyphen is to appreciate one's uniqueness as an insider-outsider and to cultivate the art of crossing between life-worlds. (2007: 23)

Questions for reflection and discussion

- Do you recognize the perils that Humphrey presents? We suggest that you read the complete article, reflect on it for yourself, and discuss with your group the issues that she identifies and how she dealt with them.
- What pulls and tugs are you experiencing in your insider action research project? Are they pushing you to choose one role identity over another? How do you deal with them?

Your organizational relationships typically are lodged and enmeshed in a network of membership affiliations, as you have been and continue to be a participant in the organization. These friendships and research ties can vary in character, from openness to restrictiveness. You are likely to find that your associations with various individuals or groups in the setting will influence your relations with others that you encounter, affecting the character of the data you can gather from them.

Table 9.2 outlines the essential tasks and skills required to work with the challenges of role duality. The task at first person is to hold and value both sets of roles simultaneously, and to learn to catch your internal responses to conflicting demands and learn to deal with them. This challenge may be played out in second person, where you try to hold and manage the demands of both roles, particularly in situations of conflicting role demands. In such situations your ability to negotiate your

Table 9.2 Role duality in first-, second- and third-person practice

	Task	Process
First person	Holding and valuing both sets of roles simultaneously	Catching internal responses to conflicting demands and dealing with them
Second person	Holding and managing demands of both roles, particularly in situations of conflicting role demands	Role negotiation with significant others
Third person	Developing practical knowledge of how dual roles impact on action research and contribute to insider action research role identity theory	Linking experience of role duality with theory

role with significant others will be important. At third person you will have developed practical knowledge of how dual roles impact on action research, and so you may contribute to insider action research role identity theory.

Your organizational role or roles will influence the degree of role confusion or ambiguity that you will experience as an insider action researcher, as well as your ability to cope with your situation. On the one hand, if your sole job in your organization is that of internal change consultant, then you are already a researcher in your own organization. We see this as a single role with low potential for role confusion. Quadrants 2 and 4 of Figure 8.1 incorporate such internal researchers. On the other hand, if your job is that of manager, then you are taking on a researcher's role in addition to your managerial job. Hence you have to manage dual roles – manager and researcher – and there is high potential for role confusion. Quadrant 3 of Figure 8.1 is a good example of this situation. Where their job involves research-type activities, single-role researchers are quite distinct from dual-role researchers, where their research activity is a separate role from their standard functional role. In terms of the cases that we discuss throughout this book, we can see that Krim (1988) and Moore (2007) are examples of dual-role researchers, while Humphrey (2007) is a single-role researcher.

Feelings of detachment can be oriented toward one or other of these roles, and increase or decrease as the research progresses. When you are caught between loyalty tugs, behavioural claims and identification dilemmas, you initially align yourself with your organizational role. Elizur (1999) uses the term 'self-differentiation' to review how he, as an insider consultant, managed to contain emotions and relate to emotionally charged issues in a balanced way, maintaining his own autonomy and self-identity in these situations. Your involvement in the two roles affects your relations with organizational members (Adler and Adler, 1987). The new dimension of your relationship to members and/or your new outside interests set you apart from ordinary members.

Reflecting on their insider action research work, Roth et al. (2007) identify challenges with regard to multiple roles. They noted that the insider action researcher has three roles:

[The insider action researcher] is first an employee of his/her organization and the second is a researcher. In addition to these two roles a third role evolved when the insider action researcher was seen as an internal consultant to the organization. (2007: 51)

They identified four challenges.

1. Knowing how to operate successfully within each role.
2. Translating ideas into the appropriate language for each world.
3. Knowing the language of the organization and the academic community – this is important for reporting back data from relevant interventions in the proper context.
4. Learning to 'put on different hats', so that multiple roles are an asset rather than a burden (Roth et al., 2007).

Questions for reflection and discussion

- In what roles are you finding yourself?
- How are you crossing the boundaries between the organization and the scholarly community, and translating language from one community to the other?
- How are your multiple roles an asset rather than a burden?

Nielsen and Repstad (1993) cite a number of specific role duality-related advantages and disadvantages of insider research. You may have a strong desire to influence and want to change the organization. You may feel empathy for your colleagues, and so be motivated to keep up the endeavour. These are beneficial in that they may sustain your energy, and a drawback in that they may lead to erroneous conclusions. You have to deal with the dilemma of writing a report of what you have found, and dealing with the aftermath from superiors and colleagues, on the one hand; or doctoring your report to keep your job, on the other. When you are observing colleagues at work and recording your observations, you may be perceived as 'spying' or breaking peer norms. Probably the most crucial dilemma for you as an action researcher in your own organization, particularly when you want to remain and progress in the organization, is managing organizational politics (we will return to this subject in Chapter 10).

Roth et al. (2004) recount how a conflict between the two roles arose in terms of timing. In the organizational setting there was pressure to present conclusions from the research setting, even though in research terms the insider action researcher thought that the data had not been fully reflected on, and that it was too early. In their view: 'In doing so the insider action researcher tried to legitimize the researcher role before it was mature in that setting, giving the opposite result' (2004: 212).

A practical issue you have to deal with is that you may be too close to the issues and people in the organization, and so you have to work more consciously and explicitly at the process of inquiry. If you have been trained in a particular discipline or are familiar with a particular function, you may not be open to seeing problems from other perspectives. You may be too close to the people and situations that you are researching. What if the research involves critiquing your friends or close colleagues? It may be difficult for you to stand back from the situation and question your own assumptions, which have been previously unquestioned. Epistemic reflexivity correctly enacted incorporates challenging presuppositions derived from closeness to people and issues.

Homa (1998) reflected on what it was like to combine the roles of CEO and researcher. He provided a number of useful pieces of potential advice.

1. You need to be reasonably on to p of your job as it is hard to switch psychologically from management responsibility to research without it. Therefore, selecting the right time in your career to do research is an important choice. You need to

achieve effective personal organization – time management and the ability to create a distance between work and study so that you can leave the organization for
period of uninterrupted study.

2. You need excellent secretarial support, particularly if you don't do your own typing.
3. Over time you need to balance the achievement of being a manager and working
   through others with the solitary work of a researcher.
4. You need a strong management team and a strong and supportive chairman.

The quest for authenticity with respect to role duality requires attention to the
inner and outer dynamics of holding both sets of roles. Outer dynamics pertain
to the roles expected of you and those you seek to adopt, and the ambiguity or
conflict between them. Inner dynamics refer to how you think and feel about any
such role ambiguity or conflict, and the implications that you internalize. Being
intelligent refers to understanding the structural nature of roles and how they are
played out in this organizational setting. Being reasonable means weighing the evidence and judging the demands of conflicting role expectations. Being responsible
means you take responsibility for what you decide to do and what you do.

Access

Primary access refers to the ability to get into the organization and to be allowed
to undertake research. As you are already a member of the organization, you have
primary access: you are already in there. While you have primary access, you may or
may not have secondary access: that is, you may or may not have access to specific
parts of the organization which are relevant to your research. This is especially true
of research in quadrant 3, where the system is not committed to self-study-in-action.
By parts of the organization we mean not only functional areas such as departments,
but also hierarchical areas whereby there is restricted access to specific privileged
information which may not be available otherwise. However, insider-researchers do
find that membership of the organization means that some avenues are closed to
them due to their position in the organization. Clearly, any researcher's status in
the organization has an impact on access. Access at one level may lead automatically to limits or access at other levels. The higher the status of the researcher, the
more access they have or the more networks they can access, particularly downward
through the hierarchy. Of course, being in a high hierarchical position may exclude
access to many informal and grapevine networks. Fundamentally, secondary access
means access to documentation, data, people and meetings. In relation to research
in quadrants 2 and 4, the system takes responsibility for secondary access because it
is committed to self-study-in-action.

An important aspect of negotiating the research project is to assess the degree
of secondary access to which one is allowed. Dual-role researchers may experience
more problems than single-role researchers. Of course, what is espoused at the

outset and then actually allowed may be different once the project is under way and at a critical stage. There may be a significant gap between an aspiration towards 'purity' of research and the reality. How access is realized may depend on the type of research being undertaken and the way that information is disseminated.

Negotiating access with your superiors is a tricky business, particularly if the research project aims at good work and not something bland. It raises questions about the different needs which must be satisfied through the project. As an insider action researcher you have needs around doing a solid piece of research that will contribute to your own career and development (first-person research, for me). You also have needs around doing a piece of research in the organization that will be of benefit to the organization (second-person research, for us), and contribute to general theory for the broader academic community (third-person research, for them). Balancing these three audiences is difficult. In general, researchers' superiors have needs around confidentiality, sensitivity to others and organizational politics.

For you, the researcher, who is undertaking research as part of a degree programme or who seeks to publish, a particular issue relating to access is the fact that what is researched will be going outside the organization. Theses and dissertations are read by people external to the organization and are filed in libraries, with their abstracts disseminated to a wider audience. Bartunek (2008) sees this as an 'outsider' role that the insider also plays. In its extreme, organizations can be paranoid about information going outside them, or at least be nervous about it.

Once again, we emphasize the value of journalling in exploring role duality. Role ambiguity and role conflict can challenge how your role identity is flexible and permeable. Locating yourself on the continuum between role integration and role segmentation, and exploring the forces whereby you are enabled or inhibited in exercising both your organizational roles and your insider action researcher role, are key to first- and second-person inquiry and practice.

Conclusions

Role duality and secondary access tend to be research project-specific and organizationally dependent, whereas preunderstanding tends to be researcher-specific. Therefore, preunderstanding is not directly linked to the quadrant schema presented in Figure 8.1. As the word suggests, preunderstanding is what the insider brings to the research process. In summary, secondary access pertains to the specific nature of the research project. In quadrants 2 and 4 the system takes responsibility for secondary access, and it may be more readily available if all the relevant parts of the system are committed to the project. It is more problematic in quadrant 3, where the system does not necessarily have a commitment to your action research.

Recommended reading

Coghlan, D. with Brydon-Miller, M. (2014) *The SAGE Encyclopedia of Action Research*. London: Sage. (See especially: 'Insider action research'.)

Access a selection of author videos, encyclopaedia entries and recommended reading on this topic at www.uk.sagepub.com/coghlanandbrannick

EXERCISE 9.1

Assessing your preunderstanding

Apply the learning window to the area of your own preunderstanding and understanding.

1. Take a particular issue within your insider action research project.
2. Fill in the boxes, distinguishing between what you know that you know; what you think you know and need to test your assumptions, inferences and attributions; what you know that you don't know, and so need to inquire more in order to find out and be open to new areas of discovery.
3. Apply this process to other specific issues.

1 What I know	2 What I think I know
3 What I know that I don't know	4 What I don't know that I don't know

TEN
Managing Ethics and Organizational Politics

 See www.uk.sagepub.com/coghlanandbrannick for a short introduction to the chapter from David Coghlan

In Chapter 2 we introduced the first-person process of valuing and making value judgements about how we judge something to be good. Such judgements are the grounds for ethical decision-making and action. In this chapter we move to second- and third-person processes, where we seek to explore building collaboration with others on creating consensus about what is good to do and implementing it, while at the same time being attentive to concomitant political dynamics that inevitably are operative. The questions underpinning this chapter are: 'How do I expose my first-person process of coming to value with others, so that we can come to a shared judgement of value and develop shared action?' and 'How do I act politically in a mode within my own values and the ethics of action research?' In this chapter we examine the ethics and politics involved in doing action research in your own organization.

As Table 10.1 illustrates, there are tasks and processes for first-, second- and third-person practice. In first-person terms, the task is to learn to act authentically

Table 10.1 Politics and ethics in first-, second- and third-person practice

	Task	Process
First person	Learning to act politically in a mode within the ethics of action research	Acting politically and authentically
Second person	Surviving and thriving political dynamics	Performing and backstaging
Third person	Articulating knowledge out of action that is actionable politically; contributing knowledge of what organizations are really like	Linking political experience with theory

and politically in a mode within your own values and those of action research. In second-person terms, the task is to collaborate with others in framing the value of your project, and to survive and thrive in the political dynamics of your own organization. In third-person terms, the contribution is to articulate actionable knowledge out of ethical and political action.

Ethics

Ethics procedures are part of life, and so are a part of research. There are increasing strictures being placed on research by universities and organizations through institutional review boards or ethics committees. In many settings researchers are required to fill out an ethical approval form prior to commencing work. Over the past few years a literature on ethics in action research has emerged that may help you to think through the issues you face and to design your research (Coghlan and Shani, 2005; Brydon-Miller, 2008a; Holian and Coghlan, 2013). The special issue of *Action Research* devoted to the subject of ethics and action research is a particularly valuable source (Brydon-Miller et al., 2006), as are the other works referenced in this chapter. As action research has an unfolding nature, as it attempts to integrate inquiry with everyday organizational action, one may argue that the ethical issues of action research are not different from those of a good life. Eikeland (2006b) distinguishes between philosophical and applied levels of ethical aspects of action research. Action research is grounded in principles of democracy, justice, freedom and participation, although as Boser comments, 'democratic intentions do not obviate the need for thoughtful examination of the ethical implications of the research on individuals and other stakeholders groups' (2006: 14). Hilsen (2006) argues that ethics in action research may be based on three pivots: human interdependency, co-generation of knowledge and fairer power relations.

Quality of relationships

Rowan (2000) presents a series of five concentric circles that describe ethical issues in different forms of research in psychology. The first circle is the 'natural inquiry' arena, in which researchers engage in what we typically term positivist research: here, the researcher and participant engage at a single point of contact, namely the researcher's agenda to obtain information from the participant. The ethical issues that arise in this one-sided relationship typically focus on doing good, not doing harm and respecting the person (what Eikeland, 2006b refers to as 'condescending ethics'), and these issues are met through communication. Participation observation, which often involves disguising the purpose of the researcher's involvement, does mean that deceit is part of the research process. The second circle is the 'human inquiry', which is captured by the hermeneutics and phenomenology. In this approach the participants are treated as fully human and not simply a set of variables to be measured. There is an emphasis on empathy, identification, trust and non-exploitative relationships.

For Rowan there is a major shift when one moves to the third circle. Rather than the researcher meeting participants at one carefully stage-managed point of the research process, the researcher involves participants in planning the research and processing the results. This is the arena of action research. Ethical issues not only concern individuals, but also the whole community or organization, and unintended consequences are a deliberate focus. The researcher's self-understanding and social vision come into play, with issues of power central to the process. The fourth circle is transcendent research, which focuses on transpersonal research, spirituality and mindfulness (Bentz and Shapiro, 1998). Ethical issues attend to the spiritual level in people. Rowan's fifth circle is comprehensive, systematic inquiry, which encompasses all the others and demands being able to think and act appropriately in each research setting, with a concern for the researcher, participants and wider system, taking into account the spiritual implications of what is being undertaken. Rowan provides a framework for thinking about the forms and quality of relationship that action researchers have with participants in different research settings. It directs the ethical behaviour in which action researchers must engage in the democratic, participative values on which action research is grounded.

Williamson and Prosser (2002) pose three ethical questions which, in their view, action researchers and participants need to be clear about, discuss and agree the answers.

1. If researchers and participants collaborate closely, how can confidentiality and anonymity be preserved? As action research is a political enterprise and has consequences for the participants and researchers, it is difficult to guarantee anonymity and confidentiality, as others can easily know who participated and may be able to identify who said or contributed what.
2. If action research is a 'journey' and 'evolves', how can informed consent be meaningful? Neither action researcher nor participants can know in advance where the journey will take them, and cannot know to what they are consenting. As a change process can create its own resistance, action researchers cannot be expected to withdraw in the face of opposition (albeit by small groups within the project).
3. As action research can have political consequences, how can action researchers avoid doing harm to participants? Williamson and Prosser point to two ways of answering this question: the establishment of an ethical code for action researchers; and the extent to which the collaboration and negotiation occurs, so that participants own the findings as much as the researcher.

Walker and Haslett (2002) ground the issues of ethics in action research in the action research cycle itself. They suggest that ethical questions may be posed in

terms of possible and actual ethical questions around the cyclical activities of planning, action and reflection. Processes of obtaining consent, ensuring anonymity
and confidentiality, balancing conflicting and different needs, are actualized in
planning, taking action, collecting data and interpreting. They cite Stringer's two
important questions as central questions running through the whole project: who
will be affected, and how will they be affected? Gellerman et al. (1990) articulate
four ethical principles.

1. Serve the good of the whole.
2. Treat others as we would like them to treat us.
3. Always treat people as ends, never only as means; respect their being and never use
   them for their ability to do; treat people as persons and never as subjects.
4. Act so we do not increase power by more powerful stakeholders over the less powerful.

Second-person co-inquiry into valuing

Barden (1991) argues that it is more fruitful to engage with others on what is
common – our own operations of knowing, valuing and doing – than to debate positions or answers. Debates about positions and answers, of themselves, are likely to be
incomplete and frequently lead to polarization. Co-inquiry into what we have experienced, how we have understood, what we have experienced and how we have made
value judgements provide a fruitful second-person application of the first person focus
described in Chapter 2. It provides a foundation for engaging in covenantal ethics
which, as Brydon-Miller (2008b) describes, is a commitment to act for the good of
others and requires deep commitment to working together to address issues of importance. Articulating how we come to value and identify the good, how we have weighed
options in making concrete choices, and how we decided what action to take, perform
a valuable third-person contribution to the field of action research. The articulation of
these operations facilitates the transparency that Reason (2006) discusses, and in these
terms contributes to the quality of action research.

Protocols and ethics committees

In general, the role of ethics committees and institutional review boards is to avoid
or prevent abusive behaviour and to prevent violations and lawsuits against universities, and so they act as guardians of ethical practice. Interestingly, from an
action research perspective, they do not ask questions such as: 'Who developed
the research question?', 'Who will own the knowledge generated?' or 'Who is pay-
ing for the research?' By and large, the members of these committees come out
of the conventional positivist research tradition and expect hypotheses, methods and expected outcomes to be well articulated in advance, and so the review

of research proposals is fairly straightforward. When they are confronted with action research proposals they are frequently at a loss as to how to understand this form of research and evaluate a proposal (DeTardo-Bora, 2004). Given that action research is an unfolding, emergent process which evolves through cycles of action and reflection, it is not feasible to map out a detailed anticipation of ethical issues in advance that will cover all eventualities (Morton, 1999; Walker and Haslett, 2002). Lincoln (2001) suggests that protocols are inadequate and insufficient to meet the face-to-face, participative close work of action research. However, at the same time it is possible to articulate some ethical principles to guide your work as an action researcher. Boser (2006) proposes that attention to ethics needs to be:

- guided by a set of externally developed guidelines that direct attention to the set of relations among those participating in, or affected by, the research;
- integrated into each stage of the action research cycle to inform decision-making by stakeholders; and
- transparent to the larger community.

Brydon-Miller and Greenwood (2006) are optimistic about the difficulties in going before such committees, and suggest that action research actually holds out more guarantees for the ethical treatment of human subjects than conventional research does. This is because action research is built on a voluntary partnership with stake-holders who form a collaborative team, who learn, apply and implement the methods together, and analyse the outcomes together. Brydon-Miller and Greenwood suggest a dialogue between the faculty that is supporting the action research and ethics committees and/or institutional review boards. This dialogue fruitfully may explore the dialectic tensions between predictability and process, protection and participation, confidentiality and credit and coercion and caring.

ETHICS AND
ACTION
RESEARCH

Insider action research and ethics

There are ethical and credibility issues associated with reporting findings from insider action research (Smyth and Holian, 2008; Holian and Coghlan, 2013). These findings may include commercially confidential, personally confidential or potentially embarrassing information related to the organization, members and stakeholders, or yourself as the researcher. When publishing or reporting the findings it may be necessary to go beyond anonymity by removing details that could permit identification of the organization or the people involved. This may be necessary in any write-up that is submitted for assessment as a case study or assignment as part of academic studies, or what is included in a master's or doctoral thesis sent to external examiners, as well as any papers or reports submitted for publication or dissemination.

As you are an existing member of your organization and probably have multiple roles to which you are adding the researcher role, as we explored in the previous chapter, role clarification around your researcher tasks, such as gathering information and analysing data, is complex (Holian and Brooks, 2004). In addition, not only may the notion of action research be strange for ethics committees and institutional review boards, but the idea of doing action research in your own organization may be even stranger. For example, when her research proposal was turned down by the ethics committee for the second time, Joan, an insider action research student, retorted to the committee: 'You are telling me now that I cannot do my job – the job that I have been doing for eight years. What I am seeking approval for is what I do every day.' Joan's dilemma with regard to doing action research within her own organizational role clarified a central point with regard to ethics approval for insider action research, a point reinforced by Brydon-Miller and Greenwood (2006).

- A distinction needs to be made between engaging in action research and reporting on that action research. The action research activity may be integral to your day-to-day work, and as such does not require ethical approval. What does require approval is the process of taking this action and transforming it into research for publication or academic credit. This distinction is crucial, and it is for the latter that ethical approval may be directed.
- Faculties needs to work with ethics approvals committees to incorporate the development of proposal forms and consent forms into the action research process, and for the forms to incorporate the action research paradigm. This is a process of collaboration-in-action, and action research faculties are on familiar ground in engaging on this issue.
- Ethical approval is only one step in the process and, as Boser (2006) argues, ethics need to be integrated into each stage of the action research cycle. So the questions and issues identified above are critical to keep in mind as the research progresses.

Humphrey reflects:

I tottered on the tightrope of the insider-outsider hyphen, torn between the views and values of academic and activists camped on either side of me and overlooking the murky waters below. There is no Code of Ethics which could have offered a safety net in this situation and as I found myself sacrificing some principles to others, I consoled myself by repeating the mantra [that] it was only my clothing that had become mud-splattered rather than my core self. (2007: 16–17)

Politics

While doing any research in an organization is very political (Punch, 1994), doing research in and on your own organization is particularly so. Power is a subject that is well explored from multiple perspectives and in various literatures. It is not our intention in this book to retrace the research and discussion of power and politics in society and organizations. However, we do recommend strongly that you undertake some reading in this area so as to ground your own first-, second- and third-person inquiry and practice. Buchanan and Badham (2008) provide an excellent exploration of the subject of power and politics that we think that you as an insider action researcher will find very useful, and which we hope will facilitate insights.

The politics of researching your own organization

Clearly, any form of research in any organization has its political dynamics. Political forces can undermine research endeavours and block planned change. Gaining access, using data, disseminating and publishing reports are intensely political acts. Take, for example, the act of constructing, which we discussed in Chapters 3 and 7. Constructing is never a neutral act, it rarely affects stakeholders in the same way. Some may benefit and some may feel threatened, and they may be harmed because it exposes weaknesses in performance. So, while in action research constructing is a collaborative activity, raising certain questions and applying judgements to particular issues may have severe political implications.

Insider action researchers have ethical responsibilities associated with their normal work roles and ethical responsibilities in their additional role as a researcher, even when the research role is for a limited period. As Hilsen (2006) points out, power and responsibility are unavoidable issues for those who hold positions that make a difference in other people's lives, and they have ethical responsibilities for the consequences of both what they do and do not do. Ethical dilemmas arise as part of normal work, particularly for those with decision-making roles. However, role duality in insider action research can provide additional ambiguity and role conflict (Holian and Coghlan, 2013).

'AND THEY SHALL BE KNOWN BY THEIR DEEDS'

Therefore, doing action research in your own organization is political. Indeed, it might be considered subversive – action research has a subversive quality about it. It examines everything. It stresses listening. It emphasizes questioning. It fosters courage. It incites action. It abets reflection and endorses democratic participation. Any or all of these characteristics may be threatening to existing organizational norms, particularly in those organizations that lean towards a hierarchical control culture. Goffman (1959) refers to insider roles as 'informer', 'confidant' and 'renegade': clearly, you do not want to be viewed as a 'renegade'. Meyerson (2001) calls those who quietly enact change in their own organizations as 'tempered radicals'. Cooklin (1999) refers to the insider change agent as the 'irreverent inmate', one who is a supporter of the people in the organization, a saboteur of the organization's rituals and a questioner of some of its beliefs. While as the action researcher you may see yourself as attempting to generate valid and useful information in order to facilitate free and informed choice, so that there will be commitment to those choices in accordance with the theory and practice of action research (Argyris and Schon, 1996), you may find that, as Kakabadse (1991) argues, what constitutes valid information is intensely political.

Accordingly, you need to be politically astute in engaging in action research, becoming what Buchanan and Badham (2008) call a 'political entrepreneur'. In their view, this role implies a behaviour repertoire of political strategies and tactics and a reflective self-critical perspective on how those political behaviours may be deployed, and emphasizes the risk-taking and creative role of the change agent. Buchanan and Boddy (1992) describe the management of the political role in terms of two activities, *performing* and *backstaging*. *Performing* involves you in the public performance role of being active in the change process, building participation for change and pursuing the change agenda rationally and logically; while backstage activity involves the recruitment and maintenance of support and reduction of resistance. *Backstaging* comprises skills in intervening in the organization's political and cultural systems through justifying, influencing and negotiating, defeating opposition, and so on. Because you are an insider you have a preunderstanding of the organization's power structures and politics, and are able to work in ways that are in keeping with its political conditions without compromising the project or your own career.

As you engage in your action research project, you need to be prepared to work the political system, which involves balancing the organization's formal justification of what it wants in the project, with your tacit personal justification for political activity. Throughout the project you will have to maintain your credibility as an effective driver of change and an astute political player. The key to this is assessing the power and interests of relevant stakeholders in relation to aspects of the project. One particular manager may have a great deal of influence with regard to strategic decision-making, but little influence with regard to budget allocation. The person who supports you on A may not support you on B.

Pettigrew (2003) reflects on his own role as a political entrepreneur. He notes that it can be exhilarating when it appears that your advocacy, enthusiasm and energy have created desired effects towards some defined outcomes, and equal and opposite despair when things go wrong. He reflects that there is a fine line between acting in a politically astute manner, and acting unethically. In his view, action researchers have to build relationships and trust with people who operate from different mental models and at different levels. Yet, working as a change agent cannot always be done with openness, honesty and transparency. He judges that the real skill for the political entrepreneur is knowing that the game is everything, and that 'theories-in-action' rather than espoused theories are what count.

Roth et al. (2007) describe their experience of acting in the political landscape and come up with four strategies.

1. Anchor the project in the organization, and find the right stakeholders and sponsors.
2. Be 'street smart' and know how to get things done.
3. Ensure that the first interventions and change in the project have a wide impact on a wide range of organizational members.
4. Describe action research projects as organizational change programmes.

Managing political relationships

In order to be able to manage the content and control agendas of the action research project, and the power political processes of influencing and ensuring the legitimacy of your project, you need to be able to manage your superiors, peers and colleagues. We have identified ten key power relationships. All of the ten key power relationships need to be considered and managed when carrying out a quadrant 3-type action research project, where the system is not committed to self-study-in-action. The first two relationships may not be of great importance for quadrant 2 and 4 research projects, where the system is committed to self-study-in-action.

Relationship with your sponsor

It is most likely that if you have a middle or low organizational rank, you will probably have a sponsor: one who provides permission and primary access to undertake the research, both in the initial and latter stages of the project. Where the research is part of a degree programme, the sponsor grants you permission to have time off to attend the course, take study leave and use organizational materials for research. The sponsor may be your immediate superior within the same department: in this case, the relationship may be close and supportive. Alternatively, the sponsor may be elsewhere in the organization, in a position of higher management: you need to work at maintaining this relationship, as continuation of the research project may depend on it. This may become particularly difficult if it emerges that the sponsor is a source of problems within the organization. You need to keep your sponsor abreast of developments and seek their counsel: in this way you keep them informed and on your side.

Sponsor's relationship to other executives

Your credibility and access may depend on the sponsor's status and standing within the organization. If your sponsor is not considered favourably by other executives, it may have a negative effect on how your research project is perceived. Your sponsor's power relationship with other powers in the organization is critical in gaining acceptance for that research from higher levels of management or administration. Secondary access may be granted or denied at this level. You may have to leave your sponsor to do your access negotiation for you, or you may be allowed to approach these other executives yourself – this will depend on the nature of the project. It may be that you are helpless in this regard. Whatever the project, you will have to work independently at establishing the credentials and value of the research project.

Executives' relationship with each other

The power dynamics between departments or individual heads of departments may be a relevant feature in promoting or blocking the research. If you are from one department, it may inhibit cooperation from other departments. This may be the most significant political force for you as an insider-researcher, and the one over which it may be most difficult to exercise control. The key is to build personal relationships with significant people in other departments so that they will cooperate. Perhaps some of them will be members of your project team.

Relationship between you and significant others

Whatever the relationship between the sponsor and other executives, you must be able to establish your own relationship with significant others, many of whom may be key executives. This is particularly relevant if you wish to interview senior executives and ask what might be experienced as awkward questions. If your sponsor falls from favour, you will need to have established relationships with significant others in order to maintain your profile and project.

Relationship between executives and higher management

Senior management at a corporate level may undermine the research or withdraw consent. The relationship tends to be remote, in that the executives are unlikely to know you personally. Usually it is unnecessary for them to have any detailed knowledge of your project. You may not have access to these people, so you may find it difficult to exercise influence over them.

Relationship between executives and organizational members

This relationship includes relationships between management and workers and management and trade unions, so that the research is accepted by the relevant parts of the organization. The research project may fall victim to ongoing organizational relationships, where employees might use lack of cooperation with you as a power tool to express dissatisfaction with some unrelated aspect of organizational life with which there is a dispute, in order to gain political leverage. In these situations you are powerless and dependent on others for resolution of the dispute.

Interdepartmental relations

In this case, some departments have more power than others, and there may be different sub-cultures – all of which may work for or against a research project. If, for example, you work in head office or corporate centre, you may have to deal with the attitudes of those in regional offices who view anyone from corporate headquarters with a prejudiced eye. The key is to establish a personal relationship with significant people who will cooperate with you.

Relationship of the researcher with subordinates

This is a relationship on which you may be relying for significant information. Subordinates may feel the need to be less than honest with their boss, who is undertaking the research. It may be that your own behaviour and management style is a critical factor in the issues under investigation, and so subordinates may be reticent in providing accurate information or feedback. In such a case, where you are a superior, having a third party gather data may be essential.

Relationship with customers or clients

These may be the ultimate beneficiaries of the research, or may be involved in the actual research process. Approaching clients and customers has political complexities, as it may raise expectations about the service provided to them.

Relationship between you and your peers

Engaging in research which involves your peers, some of whom may be friends, is particularly sensitive and may make the research process stressful. If peers and colleagues are the subject of observation and comment, they need to be informed and actively involved. They also need to be protected from possible retaliation by superiors. At the same time, you need to be wary of how you may be biased in favour of peers and colleagues or seduced by the closeness of the relationship, and hence unable to reflect and critique. Peers, colleagues and superiors may be asking the following sorts of questions: 'What are you observing?', 'What are you writing about me?', 'Am I being criticized?' For those unfamiliar with an action research approach the idea of doing research in the everyday job may be hard to grasp. How can you work and include research at the same time? This question comes not only from a limited notion of what constitutes research, but also from a fear of being criticized in writing behind one's back. The management of insider action research project involves attention to significant relationships by building support and involving key others. For example, if the CEO wants to be a member of your inquiry group, would it work? Would you be able to tell them that you think it is a bad idea?

Bjorkman and Sundgren (2005) reflect on being political entrepreneurs and relate their respective insider action research projects to the ten key relationships. They note that finding 'red and hot' issues is closely linked to relations with sponsors and executives, with the sponsors' relationship to other executives, and the relationship of executives with each other. They refer to building a *relational platform* to address the needs of managing these relationships directly. They suggest extending the list of ten power relationships further to include the utilization of external networks.

Friedman (2001) reflects that in cases of individual research where issues are non-technical, there are likely to be insurmountable obstacles and high degrees of defensive routines. How, then, do you work as a political entrepreneur engaging in public performance and backstaging activities? Kakabadse (1991) presents six useful guidelines.

1. Identify the stakeholders. This means identifying those who have a stake or interest in the project and its outcomes, and approaching them so as to identify their intentions.
2. Work on the comfort zones. This means working on those behaviours, values and ideas which a person can accept, tolerate or manage. As long as these are not threatened, people will be able to focus on wider concerns.
3. Network. This means going beyond formal hierarchies or structures where necessary to coalitions of interests which may exert greater influence on key stakeholders than the hierarchical structure.
4. Make deals. This is common in organizations, as individuals and groups agree to support one another on a particular issue in return for support on others. This is a common way of reaching agreement on policies.
5. Withhold and withdraw. It may be useful on occasion to withhold information in order not to fuel opposition, although you would not want to withhold information constantly. It is also useful on occasion to withdraw from conflictual situations and allow others to sort out the issue.
6. Have some fallback strategies if all else fails. Obviously, these depend on the demands of the situation and what you can personally handle and manage.

Friedman (2001) provides more specific guidelines.

1. Describe your own reality and situation as concretely as possible.
2. Ask senior and middle management if this explanation fits as they see it.
3. If there are significant differences, inquire into the sources of these differences.
4. Continuously inquire into the reasoning behind actions.
5. Design strategies dealing with the current situation and similar future ones.

Ramirez and Bartunek (1989) reflect on role conflict explicitly in their case of an insider action research project in a healthcare organization. They cite two specific instances. In one instance, they note that the insider action researcher had to deal with the twin role of facilitating meetings while at the same time acting as a department head whose status was junior, relative to other participants. The second role conflict was more explicitly political. Other organizational members spread rumours about the action researcher to the effect that she was engaging in the research to set up a position for herself. The researcher's experiences of being the recipient of such political behaviours caught her off guard and were hurtful to her.

Researchers often think that they have little power in the research process because they are dependent on powerful others for access. Others may see the researcher as powerful because they are knowledgeable, have initiated the research and are selecting whom to involve. In effect they may see the researcher's view of reality as being given public visibility. Therefore, we need to examine some ethical issues of doing action research in your own organization accordingly.

Williander and Styhre (2006) implicitly explore the nature of the social construction of Williander's project through reflecting and how it was perceived by senior managers. The lack of a budget could be said to be a reason why the project could not start, but this also could be due to managers' unwillingness to budget. As long as the insider action researcher had difficulties in expressing the specific need and resulting transformational state of the suggested research project sufficiently explicitly, and preferably in financial terms, it remained too vague for senior management to act on it. They report that one manager referred to the project as 'your scientific hocus-pocus', while another suggested that 'this sounds too theoretical and time-consuming – why don't we just come up with some innovations'.

Questions for reflection and discussion

- Does this reaction to Williander's action research initiative sound familiar? What is your experience?
- How might you seek to address and change the constructions that others put on your project?

Integrating roles, politics and ethics

There are ethical dilemmas attached to how action researchers hold their researcher and organizational action roles. In terms of organizational action, they are bound to provide a quality service to the organization's management; as researchers they have a responsibility to go beyond the boundaries of the particular project to contribute to knowledge generation. In addition to the ethical dilemmas pertaining to these separate roles, there are dilemmas which pertain to integration of the roles held together by action researchers (Benne, 1959; Lippitt, 1961; Kelman, 1965). Applying Katz and Kahn, White and Wooten (1986) refer to this as 'role episode', by which they mean studying an ethical dilemma through an ambiguity or conflict between the 'sending role' and 'role receiver'. The 'sending role' comprises expectations of what the action research role will fulfil. The 'receiving role' has perceptions of both the role and the sending role, and then either complies or resists. As White and Wooten (1986) illustrate, this role episode model is a useful one to investigate and explain the behaviour of change agents and client systems, and as such is relevant to our consideration of action researchers. They apply the role episode model to five categories of ethical dilemmas:

1. misrepresentation and collusion;
2. misuse of data;
3. manipulation and coercion;
4. values and goals conflict; and
5. technical ineptness.

With regard to the dual role of action research, Morton (1999) describes four ethical dilemmas in terms of 'role contamination'.

1. What might action researchers promise clients? Action researchers should not promise beyond what they can reasonably deliver, yet the process of action research is innovative and involves a degree of risk. So, action researchers have a dilemma in holding both promise and risk.
2. How theoretical can action researchers be on organizations' time and money? Action researchers, more than consultants, value reflection and theorizing which satisfy their own intellectual interests but may be of little value to organizational management. Action researchers need to balance their research-oriented activities with their action-oriented activities.
3. How do action researchers present themselves? Presenting themselves primarily as academic researchers who also do consulting or primarily as consultants who have academic interests, has its own pitfalls, depending on the audience and the audience's view and expectation of either role.
4. How can action researchers resolve the conflict between the quality of organizational action and the quality of research? While one expects them to be in harmony, this may not be necessarily so. A failure in the organizational action may generate rich research data. If an organizational action is heading for possible failure, action researchers may be confronted with having to prioritize one over the other.

Humphrey concludes her reflection on the political dilemmas of her insider action research:

> It is the activation of the hyphen which enhances one's chances of surviving and thriving in complex territories. The perils of the insider-outsider are that she can be pushed and pulled along an invisible insider–outsider continuum by others who have a vested interest in who she is and what she is doing, as she is now cast as an 'insider' and now as an 'outsider' by different actors and audiences. She can lose her sense of herself. To actively take charge of the hyphen is to appreciate one's uniqueness as an insider-outsider and to cultivate the art of crossing between life-worlds. It is only when the researcher cherishes herself as an insider-outsider and commits herself to journeying between lifeworlds that she can protect herself and her project from others. (2007: 23)

Journalling is a most valuable tool for coping with and exploring political and ethical issues. As described in Chapter 3, it can be a vehicle for dumping painful experiences as well as for articulating and reflecting on them in a more reflective space.

Humphrey describes what journalling meant for her.

It is not surprising that my journal came to function as a 'friend' in the sense of 'confidante', since the more I censored and silenced myself with my comrades, the more I disclosed to my journal. A journal absorbs our disturbing thoughts and feelings without pronouncing judgement upon them; it allows us to draw pictures in accordance with the language of our body and to write poetry in accordance with the language of our soul; it also stores these archives for our own subsequent processing. My journal contains references to being 'shipwrecked on a desert island' and 'seeking refuge in the desert'. (2007: 18–19)

Integrative case

Holian (1999) provides a case which integrates some of the themes of Chapters 9 and 10. She reports how her additional researcher role added a complex dimension to her senior executive role. She found that when organizational members provided information to her 'in confidence', there was some doubt as to whether it was in confidence to her as a researcher, or as a senior executive. Merely asking informants which hat they saw her wearing at the time did not resolve the uncertainty. If information was provided to her as a senior executive, she may have been authorized or even obliged to act on it to prevent harm to others. If it was provided to her as a researcher, she might not have the right to do so. Whatever the role, organizational members knew that she was the same person, knew what they had told her and that she could not forget it.

When organizational members gave her information that she did not know if she could use in her researcher role, but which she thought she should use in her executive role, she faced an ethical dilemma. In terms of role duality this dilemma can be understood as a role conflict between her senior executive position and the action researcher role. As Holian's research subject was ethical decision-making she faced a double dilemma: a content one for her organization, and a process one for the research. She established and participated in a cooperative inquiry group comprising people of decision-making roles from a diverse range of organizations. The members of this group discussed ethical issues that they were experiencing, and encouraged one another to reflect on their own experience and find new ways of working with ethical issues in their own organizations.

Holian reported how she felt unprepared for the backlash which resulted from surfacing 'undiscussables' within the organization related to cover-ups, perceived abuse of power, nepotism, harassment, allocation of rewards and unfair discrimination. While these issues were deeper, more shocking and troubling than anticipated, she reflected that she was not adequately prepared to look after herself or others when the backlash came. Consequently, she was not able to balance the multiple roles of researcher, senior executive and programme facilitator, and after one last stand-up fight with some of her fellow senior executives, she resigned.

Authenticity involves attention to and reflection on the personal questions and dilemmas that arise in the political dynamics of action research projects. The outer dynamics pertain to attention to the political behaviour of others, while the inner dynamics refer to how you think and feel about engaging in political activity. Being intelligent refers to understanding the structural patterns of political action and how they are played out in this organizational setting. Being reasonable means weighing the evidence and judging the demands of political action. Being responsible means you take responsibility for what you decide to do and what you do in second-person action.

Conclusions

When you are engaging in action research in your own organization, politics are powerful forces. You need to consider the impact of the process of inquiry, who the major players are, and how you can engage them in the process. Ethics involve not deceiving or doing harm, and being true to the process. This does not mean telling everyone everything or being politically naïve, but recognizing who the key political players are and how they can value the research by participating in it. It may seem that political dynamics are the major obstacle to doing action research in your own organization, and it may put you off. At the same time there are those who revel in political behaviour and enjoy the cut and thrust of attempting to make a difference through their action research project.

Recommended reading

Brydon-Miller, M. (2008a) 'Covenantal ethics and action research: Exploring a common foundation for social research', in D. Mertens and P. Ginsberg (eds), *Handbook of Social Research Ethics*. Thousand Oaks, CA: SAGE, 243–258.

Brydon-Miller, M. (2008b) 'Ethics and action research: Deepening our commitment to social justice and redefining systems of democratic practice', in P. Reason and H. Bradbury (eds), *The SAGE Handbook of Action Research* (2nd edn). London: Sage, pp. 199–210.

Brydon-Miller, M., Greenwood, D. and Eikeland, O. (2006) 'Ethics and action research' (special issue), *Action Research*, 4 (1): 5–121.

Coghlan, D. with Brydon-Miller, M. (2014) *The SAGE Encyclopedia of Action Research*. London: Sage. (See especially: 'Ethics and moral decision-making', 'Feminist ethics', 'Institutional review boards'.)

Hilsen, A.I. (2006) 'And they shall be known by their deeds: Ethics and politics in action research', *Action Research*, 4 (1): 23–36.

Reason, P. and Bradbury, H. (eds) (2008) *The SAGE Handbook of Action Research* (2nd edn). London: Sage, pp. 199–210.

Access a selection of author videos, encyclopaedia entries and recommended reading on this topic at www.uk.sagepub.com/coghlanandbrannick

EXERCISE 10.1

Assessing ethics and politics

Exercise A. Ethical issues

1. When you collaborate with others, how can confidentiality be maintained?
2. If your action research project is a 'journey' and 'evolves', how can informed consent be meaningful?
3. As action research can have political consequences, how can you avoid doing harm to others?

Political issues

1. Challenging the status quo: how can you do things differently?
2. Changing existing power relations: do you have the power to change this for yourselves?
3. The system reasserting existing power relations: what do you do if you don't have the authority to change this for yourself?

Exercise B: Assessing ethics and politics

As a concrete application of Table 10.1 to your project, answer the following questions and fill out the table for yourself.

	Task	Process
First person	What are your specific political and ethical tasks in your project?	How are you to achieve your goals ethically and politically?
Second person	Who are the political stakeholders of your action research project? What interests do they have that need to be served?	How do you work with the different stakeholders to achieve the purpose of the project?
Third person	What knowledge are you generating from this project that informs your understanding of the political dynamics of organizations?	How do you build this actionable knowledge about the political dynamics of organizations from your first- and second-person inquiry and practice?

EXERCISE 10.2

Force field analysis

Kurt Lewin's force field analysis is a most useful tool to use for assessing and constructing interventions with respect to organizational political forces. As it is presented in many organization development texts, force field analysis is a technique created by Lewin for problem-solving or managing change. It is based on the assumptions that in every situation there are forces driving change and forces restraining change, and that an emphasis on reducing restraining forces is more effective than increasing driving forces. While a force field might look like what we might do in listing reasons for and against taking an action, it is actually quite different. Reasons for and against are static and rational: they have to be justified. In force field analysis, forces impinging on a situation are listed. Hence, with regard to organizational politics a force field of political driving and restraining forces may provide you with a useful insight into what is going on, and help you construct interventions to reduce restraining forces.

Force field analysis comprises five steps.

Step 1. Describe the change issue and the desired direction of the change.
Step 2. List the political forces driving change and those restraining in a diagram which has the forces in opposition to one another.
Step 3. Give a weighting to the forces – those that are stronger and more powerful than others.
Step 4. Focus on the restraining forces, and assess which of the significant ones that *need* to be worked on, and those which *can* be worked on.
Step 5. Develop plans for reducing these forces.

ELEVEN
Writing up your Insider Action Research Work

 See www.uk.sagepub.com/coghlanandbrannick for a short introduction to the chapter from David Coghlan

In this chapter we explore writing up and disseminating your insider action research work. We do this in terms of two contexts; writing a dissertation for academic accreditation, such as a master's or doctorate, and writing a report or article. Regarding the former, there are valuable publications on action research dissertation writing (notably Dick, 1999; Zuber-Skerritt and Perry, 2002; Herr and Anderson 2005; Coghlan and Pedler, 2006; Zuber-Skerritt and Fletcher, 2007; van der Meulen, 2011). We draw on their work and bring our own reflection on insider action research to bear on their respective work. Regarding the latter, we discuss this issue later in the chapter.

An action research dissertation

At the end of the academic-oriented action research project you have to write a dissertation. In non-academic contexts you may write a report or want to write an article or paper. We assume that you have been writing all through your project, as you have written up accounts of events and kept your own personal journal and reflections up to date. It is important that you keep records and notes in real time, close to events, so that you have an accurate record of what took place, what you were thinking about them at the time, and the insights and the judgements you made.

Remember that action research is a different form of research to traditional research.

- Traditional research begins with what we know and seeks to find what we don't know.
- Action research begins with what we don't know, and seeks to find what we don't know.
- What we don't know that we don't know is the particular fruit of action research.

As we discussed in Chapter 2, there are two action research projects running concurrently, what Zuber-Skerritt and Perry (2002) call the *core* action research project and the *thesis* action research project. Now we are focusing on writing up the *thesis* action research, which is the inquiry-in-action into how the *core* action research project was designed, implemented and evaluated, how you enacted your role in it and how you now reflect on it.

A dissertation is an academic document and therefore needs to conform to academic requirements around justification of topic and approach, description and defence of rigour in methodology and methods of inquiry, familiarity with existing content and process literature and contribution to knowledge. An action research dissertation is no different, although its presentation and argument differ from traditional presentations.

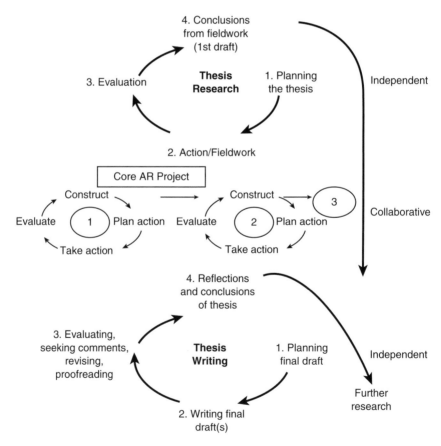

Figure 11.1 Conceptual Model of an Action Research Thesis

(adapted with permission from Zuber-Skerritt and Fletcher, 2007: 421)

Zuber-Skerritt and Fletcher (2007) elaborate the interrelationship between *core* action research and *thesis* action research. From Figure 11.1, you can see that the core action research project is a collaborative venture whereby the cycles of action and reflection are enacted in multiple successive and concurrent cycles in first- and second-person practice, as discussed in Chapters 2 and 3. The *thesis* research project involves you in independent work at both ends of the entire process. In this chapter we focus on the thesis writing cycle.

Constructing and writing your dissertation

Practices describing action research dissertations typically suggest that it is structured to deal with:

- the purpose and rationale of the research;
- context;
- methodology and method of inquiry;
- story and outcomes;
- self-reflection and learning of the action researcher;
- reflection on the story in light of experience and theory;
- extrapolation to a broader context and articulation of usable knowledge.

This is not to say that such a structure necessarily would mean that each of these headings has to be a chapter in itself; rather, that these issues need to be clearly dealt with formally. For example, the story may be spread over several chapters, depending on its length and complexity and the extent of the research project.

Purpose and rationale of the research

When you present the purpose and rationale of your research, in effect you are presenting its academic context. This involves stating why the action you have chosen is worth doing, why it is worth studying and what it contributes to the world of theory and practice. The most critical issue for you at the outset of writing an action research dissertation is to make an academic case for what you are doing. This is not just an argument for credibility, but a formal effort to locate your work in an academic context.

Context

We have outlined the main strands of a discussion of context in Chapter 4. While there you were outlining it in a proposal, here you are writing about it in depth. Academic context is also important: not only are you reviewing the social and organizational context of your project, you also need to review and critique the research that has been done in that context. We refer to this literature as *outset literature*: the literature that you read, discuss and critique at the outset of your research, which helps ground your research in existing work and opens the door to your contribution.

Williander and Styhre (2006) outline the main contextual issues that underpin Williander's insider action research work in creating the eco-benign car in Volvo. They explicitly discuss external factors pertaining to the car manufacturing industry and to the challenges facing Volvo. They conclude that Volvo needed two types of change: what they refer to as 'locking-up minds from the lock-in effects of the technological paradigm in order to be more objectively able to assess the possibilities of going green', and 'the creation of the capabilities required to exploit these possibilities' (2006: 243).

Methodology and methods of inquiry

This is your major section on methodology, in which you outline and justify your approach. Here you describe your action research approach, methodology and methods of inquiry. Methodology is your philosophical approach; methods describe what you actually did. Accordingly, you need to articulate both your methodology and your methods of inquiry.

As with any research dissertation, first, you need to review the theory and practice of your methodology – in this instance, action research. This is a matter of providing definitions, some history and its main philosophical tenets. Second, you then review the practice of action research in your own field, such as nursing, education, information systems research, and so on. Third, you need to describe and review the particular approach within action research that you might be using, particularly if you are using one approach predominantly. Accordingly, for example, you will review and critique the theory and practice of appreciative inquiry, cooperative inquiry, action learning, and so on as appropriate.

Regarding methodology, you need to convey that you are using a normal and natural research paradigm with a long tradition and adequate rigour that is suitable for the project on which you have worked. As Dick (1999) very usefully points out, it is important to argue positively for your approach, rather than to criticize negatively the limitations of other approaches. As we presented in the earlier chapters, the action research literature provides extensive justification of how action research is scientific and rigorous. While all research demands rigour, action research has to demonstrate its rigour more particularly. This is because in action research you typically start out with a fuzzy question, are fuzzy about your methodology in the initial stages, and have fuzzy answers in the early stages. As the project develops, your methods and answers – and so your questions – become less fuzzy. This progression from fuzziness to clarity is the essence of the spirals of action research cycles (Gummesson, 2000). Accordingly, you need to demonstrate clearly the procedures you have used to achieve rigour and defend them. As Dick (1999) emphasizes, this means that you show:

- your use of action research learning cycles;
- how you accessed multiple data sources to provide contradictory and confirming interpretations;
- evidence of how you have challenged and tested your own assumptions and interpretations continuously throughout the project; and
- how your interpretations and outcomes are challenged, supported or disconfirmed from existing literature.

Discussing quality

As we discussed in Chapter 1, it is important to be explicit about how you have tried to ensure quality in your action research project. There are several frameworks that are useful in establishing quality criteria and for exploring quality in action research, and which can be applied to your dissertation work (Levin, 2003; Herr and Anderson, 2005; Reason, 2006; Zuber-Skerritt and Fletcher, 2007; Pasmore et al., 2008).

In terms of Shani and Pasmore's (2010[1985]) complete theory of action research, the quality of your project rests on how you have presented:

- context;
- quality of relationships;
- the quality of the action research process itself; and
- outcomes.

This is a simple four-point framework that is easy to use, particularly in a master's thesis. An equally simple framework is Levin's (2003) four criteria: participation, real-life problems, joint-meaning construction and workable outcomes.

- Participation – how well does the action research reflect cooperation between you and the members of the system?
- Real-life problems – is the action research project guided by a concern for real-life, practical outcomes, and is it governed by constant and iterative reflection as part of the process?
- Joint meaning construction – is the process of interpreting events, articulating meaning and generating understanding a collaborative process between you and the members of the system?
- Workable solutions – does the action research project result in significant work and sustainable outcomes?

Herr and Anderson (2005) use the term 'validity' and explore five types: outcomes, process, democratic, catalytic and dialogic. In terms of Reason's (2006) choice points, you may ask how your study may be judged in terms of:

- being explicitly both aimed at and grounded in the world of practice;
- being explicitly and actively participative: research *with*, *for* and *by* people rather than *on* people;
- drawing on a wide range of ways of knowing – including intuitive, experiential, presentational as well as conceptual – and linking these appropriately to form theory;
- being worthy of the term 'significant';
- emerging towards a new and enduring infrastructure.

As Reason (2006) points out, your research cannot rate all of these equally highly, so he argues that as an action researcher you need to be aware that these are choice points. As you construct your dissertation you need to relate how you made the choices that you did when you were researching in the present tense. Here, as we outlined in Chapter 2, you can draw on the general empirical method and show what understanding of events you had, how you tested these insights and weighed up the evidence, and how you made the value judgements and decisions that you did. Accordingly, you can select which choice points you want to be judged against, and make them clear and transparent.

In your section on methods you describe how you are doing action research. Methods of inquiry refer to the content and process issues of how you:

- constructed and selected the issue;
- built participation and support;
- accessed and generated data;
- recorded data – notes and minutes of meetings, journal, where and how you used observation, interviews or survey instruments;
- engaged others in the action research cycles of implementing the project;
- dealt with the political and ethical dimensions presented in Chapter 6, particularly with regard to reflective learning, and so on.

Story and outcomes

The heart of the dissertation is the story or course of events. In the early drafts, you are likely to construct the story around a chronological narrative and structure it in terms of significant time periods or particular projects. At these draft stages you might have narratives which cover periods of time or particular projects. This is an important structure to follow at the early stages of your write-up, as it enables you to get the story down on paper in a logical sequence. The next stage of writing the story is to reflect on it and test your insights as to what themes emerge. Then you may find that you are surfacing images or themes for the time periods or projects which capture your sense of the meaning of the project, and lead you to a synthesis.

Often, action researchers are surprised at what happens during the writing of a dissertation. They think that it is simply a mechanical task of writing up what is in their notes and files. Experience shows that the writing-up period is a whole new learning experience. It is where synthesis and integration takes place. From what previously have been isolated masses of details of meetings, events and organizational data, notes on your laptop, scraps of paper and disks, notes from books and articles, a new reality emerges. Things begin to make sense, meanings begin to form. For many researchers this is the time that they realize what they have been doing all along.

Writing the story is the key to synthesis. You are likely to have far more detail than you need or can use. Therefore, as you begin to select what to include and exclude, you are beginning to form a view of what is important in the story. You are at the next stage of reflective practice and, indeed, of action research itself. The writing project becomes an action research project, as you engage in cycles of drafting and revising, seeking comments from your supervisor, reflecting, understanding how what you have written fits into the whole, and then formulating conclusions (Zuber-Skerritt and Perry, 2002; Zuber-Skerritt and Fletcher, 2007). It is far from being the mechanical task of writing up your notes that you might have thought.

A critical issue in presenting the story is to distinguish the events that took place, about which there is no dispute, and the meanings that you attribute to these events. It is important to present the basic story separately, as if it were a news bulletin or a video camera had recorded what had taken place. As McTaggart (1998) points out, the narrative needs to be sufficiently comprehensive and transparent so that the reader can arrive at the end of it able to judge for themselves the validity of the research, its claims to creation of knowledge and any claims for its extrapolation. This form of presentation presents the evidence in a factual and neutral manner. Your view of these events and theorizing as to what they mean should not be mixed in with telling the story. This should come later, perhaps at the end of the chapter or a particular phase of the story. By separating the story from its sense-making, and by clearly stating which is story and which is sense-making, you are demonstrating how you are applying methodological rigour to your approach. Combining narrative and sense-making leaves you open to the charge of biased storytelling, and makes it difficult for readers to evaluate your work.

Winter (1989) argues that your presentation should reflect your own process of learning and not be a judgement of others. He makes the relevant point that you should avoid making commentaries which place you as the researcher in the superior role of one whose analysis of other people's words show that you understand what took place, while they do not. He suggests that your commentary should place you at risk, as the single voice of the author in a context where many people participated in the work.

> A useful technique for using your own reflections as you are telling the story is to insert a *reflective pause* in a box at periodic intervals, giving your own reflections on what you have just recounted. Here you can reflect in public, show your train of thought and insights, and share what you plan to do next and why. This technique provides a mechanism for having accounts of your own reactions, interpretations and action planning alongside factual narrative in a way that does not confuse the two. The reader can see what is happening in the story, and then in the boxes read what you are thinking and how you are interpreting the situation as it unfolds, following the logic of your thoughts and actions. This is a tool for inserting first-person narrative alongside the second-person narrative. It provides a concrete demonstration of your use of general empirical method and your quest for first-person authenticity.

In an action research dissertation, your account of your sense-making often takes three forms. The first form is where you make sense of particular events within the narrative as it progresses, for example, the reflective pause technique described in the box above. Bourner (2003) suggests that to demonstrate reflective learning and critical thinking it is useful to note how events 'surprised' you, 'disappointed' you, and so on. These notes, which may be shared in the reflective pauses, illustrate the application of your first-person inner arc of attention to second-person external events, and to the insights that accompany them to create third-person insights. The second form is at the end of a chapter or section, where you can present how you make sense of that event. You do that clearly so that the reader may know what you are doing and go back to the story to see how your interpretations make sense. It is important that your sense-making sections are not too far from the story narrative. It makes it difficult for the reader to remember what you are referring to, if you leave all your sense-making to chapters at the end, particularly in a doctoral dissertation. The third form is to have a general chapter towards the end of the dissertation which integrates the more specific interpretations that you have made, and provides an overview of your sense-making of the whole story, linking it back to the purpose of the research, its context and contribution to actionable knowledge.

It is at this stage that you may have to draw on further content literature. This is what we call *emergent* literature. As you are progressing through the story and making sense of it you will find that you are being drawn into more specific or even new areas of content and process whose literature you now need to read and review. In action research projects, specific relevant content areas emerge as the project progresses, so you often do not quite know what the focus of your synthesis is until the project is well in progress. Content literature becomes more focused through the story and directly relates to what is being framed in the story. Angela, whom we encountered in Chapter 4, found that as her action research progressed, team dynamics became central. So she read some books and articles on teamwork and stages of team development to help her make sense of what was going on in her team, and to assist her in her team role in leading the project. This was an area of literature that emerged in her project, and could not have been anticipated at the outset.

Self-reflection and learning of the action researcher

An important part of the action research dissertation is reflection on your own learning. As you have been intervening in the organizational system over the period of the action research project, you need to articulate what you have learned, not only about the system you have been working to change, but about yourself as an action researcher. The project may have challenged many of your assumptions, attitudes, skills and existing organizational relationships, as we have seen in the cases of Humphrey (2007) and Moore (2007). Many of these points of learning have been expressed in the reflective pause boxes discussed above, which try to capture your reflection-in-action. This first-person material is important, as it contributes to the integration of the three voices – first, second and third person.

Reflection on the story in light of experience and theory

One of the most common criticisms of published action research is that it lacks theory. In other words, action research accounts tell a story, but do not address issues of emergent theory and so contribute to knowledge. Accordingly, your action research project needs to apply some established theory, or extend or develop theory. The scope of the academic project, whether master's or doctorate, is an important determinant of what is to be expected in this regard.

If you are a participant in a master's programme engaging in classical action research, such as an action-oriented MBA programme, you use frameworks to make sense of what is happening. You may be drawing on frameworks which help you make sense of an industry analysis, firm performance, and the like. Your use of these frameworks aligns the story to the theory, and through this alignment you demonstrate your understanding of the theory and its application.

If you are engaged in a more research-oriented programme, such as a master's by research or doctorate, you are not only aligning the story with theory, but also extending that theory or developing it. This extension is an inductive process, coming out of your meta-learning of reflecting on implementation of the action research cycles with the members of the systems as they enact the action research project. This extension or development of existing theory may be in content or process.

Extrapolation to a broader context and articulation of usable knowledge

As a consequence of your reflection on the story and articulation of usable knowledge, you need to articulate how your research project can be extrapolated (or transported) to a wider context. Such an extrapolation answers the 'So what?' question in relation to your research, and completes the agenda that good research is for me, for us and for them: that it integrates first-, second- and third-person research. This section is answering the question: 'Why should anyone who has not been involved directly in my research be interested in it?'

Action research projects are situation-specific and do not aim to create universal knowledge. At the same time, extrapolation from a local situation to more general situations is important. As an action researcher you are not claiming that every organization will behave as the one you have studied. However, you can focus on some significant factors, consideration of which is useful for other organizations, perhaps similar organizations or organizations undergoing similar types of change processes.

For readers whose action research is directed at both a practical organizational outcome and an academic assessment, it may be useful for you to produce two documents. Organizational readers tend to be interested primarily in the story and its analysis, and less interested in academic citations, critiques of methodology, literature reviews and discussions of theoretical differences between schools of thought, which are central to an academic dissertation. For organizational readers, the researcher may produce a report which contains the core story and its analysis, omitting the academic requirements.

Dissemination

Dissemination of action research occurs in ways similar to all forms of research dissemination. A dissertation is held in a library, with its abstract circulated on abstract indexes. Articles and papers may be submitted to journals and books. Throughout this book we have referenced many such published accounts.

As we mentioned previously, political sensitivities are typically critical issues in writing a research report and disseminating it. The content of the report may contain classified material or data of interest to competitors. Individual actors may be identifiable, and their reported role in the events of the story may not be complimentary. Conventions relating to disguising the identity of the case and the actors may be applied. Krim (1988) and Moore (2007) do not identify the organizations in which their research took place and probably, for most readers, their identity is irrelevant and subordinate to the theme and methodology of the research. Williander and Styhre (2006) and Roth et al. (2007) identify their organizations as Volvo and AstraZeneca respectively.

A particular application of action research dissemination involves those who have participated as co-researchers in the project. You may have a moral obligation to involve them in your formulation of conclusions. For example, when he had drafted his thesis, Meehan circulated a copy of his story and reflection chapters to the group and incorporated their comments. Subsequently, when he was writing his article with Coghlan, he circulated a draft to the group (Meehan and Coghlan, 2004).

Nielsen and Repstad (1993) advise the following.

- Do not promise greater anonymity than you can keep.
- Take actors' analyses seriously.
- Point to potential solutions.
- Take the opportunity to discuss with as many as possible.

Publishing

Returning to Shani and Pasmore's (2010[1985]) definition of action research in Chapter 1, you might draw on the four factors from that chapter as the structure and basis for your report or article:

- how the context was assessed;
- the quality of collaborative relationships between researchers and members of the system;
- the quality of the action research process itself as cycles of action and reflection were enacted; and
- the dual outcomes reflect some level of sustainability, the development of self-help and competencies out of the action, and the creation of new knowledge from the inquiry.

This involves discussing how these four factors are engaged rigorously, reflectively and relevantly. For example, from some perspectives rigour is understood as upholding the standards of scientific proof in assessing the impact of a specific organizational issue on performance. If you are in this environment, then you need to show how the discussions that took place in your project were rigorous in analysing and interpreting scientifically generated data. Also, if reflection is viewed as the process of jointly and collectively creating new insights and theories by referring to the related work of others, the discussion needs to include how contextual factors might impact on the quality of reflection, as well as the design choices of the dialogical process that can facilitate the most appropriate context for that reflection. Finally, if relevance is understood as addressing the concerns of both the practitioner and academic communities, then the processes of inquiry and action and the outcomes need to address both communities.

From the field of action learning, Mann and Clarke (2007) have articulated a provocative slogan for practitioners who wish to publish accounts of their practice. 'Writing it down–writing it out–writing it up' captures an insightful approach that is a useful construct for reflecting on what you might want to say in an article out of your action research work, and how you might say it. While Mann and Clarke's article uses action learning terminology, its core message of working through what your work is about, what it is really about and what it is really, really about, is stimulating and enabling.

One particular dilemma that action researchers face in publishing their work is whether to use the personal first-person or the impersonal third-person narrative style when referring to themselves as the researcher or author. There is no consensus. For example, Krim (1988), Holian (1999), Humphrey (2007) and Moore (2007) use the personal 'I' throughout. Williander and Roth, as they are writing in collaboration, use the impersonal third-person form (Williander and Styhre, 2006; Roth et al., 2007). A useful guideline in our experience is that if the report contains extensive reflection on the personal learning of the author-researcher as agent of the action in the story (as instanced by Krim, Humphrey and Moore, respectively), then the first-person narrative adds a considerable strength to the published report. Third-person narrative gives a sense of objectivity and remove, while using the first-person demands that the distinction between the story's narrative and the researcher's interpretation and sense-making is very clearly distinct.

FINDING FORM
IN WRITING
FOR ACTION
RESEARCH

Marshall (2008) reflects on the role of form in her action research writing and suggests the following practices.

- Accept and seek to express what is, rather than what should be.
- Employ disciplines and respect emergence.
- Invoke the writer in you and your own direct voice, whatever shape it takes.
- Create resonant spaces and conditions for writing.
- Defend emergent form and claim authority.
- Value the imaginal and the metaphorical as guides to form.

Conclusions

With respect to practitioner doctoral programmes that are built on insider action research, Coghlan (2007) argues that it is precisely the integration of first-, second- and third-person inquiry and practice by scholar-practitioners that gives their work its integrity. The first-person process of executives learning-in-action, combined with the second-person collaborative processes of building and implementing change in a spirit of co-inquiry, address the twin imperatives for third-person practice. The action imperative for the organization, and the knowledge generation imperative for the academic community, are met as third-person contribution emerges from first- and second-person inquiry and practice.

Writing up and publishing your action research work is an act of learning and itself an action research project. Whether you are writing an article or a dissertation, you draw together the complexities of all your experiences, insights and judgements, data which integrate your own personal learning, as well as what took place in the system in which you work. Telling the story, making sense of it and applying a rigorous methodology to that sense-making, are directed toward the generation of useful knowledge which must produce outcomes of value to others.

Recommended reading

Bradbury, H. (2008) 'Quality and "actionability": What action researchers offer from the tradition of pragmatism', in A.B. Shani, S.A. Mohrman, W.A. Pasmore, B. Stymne and N. Adler (eds), *Handbook of Collaborative Management Research*. Thousand Oaks, CA: Sage, pp. 583–600.

Coghlan, D. with Brydon-Miller, M. (2014) *The SAGE Encyclopedia of Action Research*. London: Sage. (See especially: 'Disseminating action research', 'Dissertation writing'.)

Levin, M. (2012) 'Academic integrity in action research', *Action Research*, 10 (2): 133–149.

Marshall, J. (2008) 'Finding form in writing for action research', in P. Reason and H. Bradbury (eds), *The SAGE Handbook of Action Research* (2nd edn). London: Sage, pp. 682–695.

Pasmore, W.A., Woodman, R. and Simmons, A.L. (2008) 'Toward a more rigorous, reflective, and relevant science of collaborative management research', in A.B. Shani, S.A. Mohrman, W.A. Pasmore, B. Stymne and N. Adler (eds), *Handbook of Collaborative Management Research*. Thousand Oaks, CA: Sage, pp. 567–582.

Shani, A.B. and Pasmore W.A. (2010[1985]) 'Organization inquiry: Towards a new model of the action research process', in D. Coghlan and A.B. Shani (eds), *Fundamentals of Organization Development*, Vol. 1. London: Sage, pp. 249–260.

Access a selection of author videos, encyclopaedia entries and recommended reading on this topic at www.uk.sagepub.com/coghlanandbrannick

TWELVE
In Conclusion

In this book we have explored a subject which continues to represent very common practice in post-experience master's and doctoral programmes within business education, healthcare, social work and third-sector organizations.

Action research is about undertaking action and studying that action as it takes place. It is about improving practice through intervention and demands rigorous preparation, planning, action, attention to process, reflection, re-planning and validating claims to learning and theory generation. It is collaborative, involving working with others as co-researchers. We have focused on the dynamics of how this might be done when action research is undertaken in the organization of the action researcher, who is aiming both to achieve personal goals from the project and to contribute to the organization. We have drawn on several key images. The first is of researching in your own organization as being in the 'swampy lowlands' (Schon, 2004[1995]), where inquiry involves 'messy, iterative groping' in the dark (Evered and Louis, 1981). The second, adapted from Weisbord (1988), is of the actor-director in the act of making a film. We have portrayed the insider action researcher as an actor-director in the 'swampy lowlands' of their own organization.

Action research operates within the realm of practical knowing, where the concern is practical outcomes, and what is familiar in one setting may be unfamiliar in another. Accordingly, our knowing in everyday situations is always incomplete and can be completed only by attending to the particular tasks and situations in which we are at a given time. A remembered set of insights is only approximately appropriate to the new situation. They are insights into situations which are similar, but not identical. No two situations are identical as time has passed: other events have taken place and we remember differently. This is why we reason, reflect and judge in a practical pattern of knowing in the present tense, in order to make sense of the situations in which we find ourselves and deciding what to say and do.

We began our exploration by locating action in the three core foundational elements:

1. how action research works through the spirals of cycles of constructing, planning, taking and evaluating action, and the meta-cycle of content, process and premise reflection;
2. how the individual researcher knows in action; and
3. how the whole process is genuinely collaborative.

In all this the critical skills are introspective reflection and, when engaging with others, combining advocacy with inquiry. While many of the issues of any research project pertain to researching your own organization, the particular challenges posed by researching your own organization are around managing the closeness–distance tension in preunderstanding, managing role duality and competing commitments, and managing politics in order that you have a future in the organization when the research is completed.

Engaging in insider action research poses serious challenges to first-person inquiry for you as an insider action researcher. You are confronted primarily with the familiar: the people and organizational rituals that you encounter on a daily basis. As familiarity inhibits inquiry, the challenge is to develop ways of knowing what is familiar, and to develop practical knowledge that enables you to understand what is taking place and to act in the shifting situations of organizational life. Inquiring and acting within the familiar evokes issues of role – the existing organizational roles and the adopted researcher role – and the accompanying challenges to hold both sets of roles concurrently and manage the tension between them. All such activity is political, so managing the political dynamics which pertain to being a change agent in an organization is critical for survival and success.

We have invited you to bring the general empirical method to your work. In essence, this method shows us that there are four basic, unfolding and interrelated operations that fit into a pattern that characterizes the human experience of data, the effort to understand them, the judgement after relating the insight back to the evidence of data, and a decision about what to do about it. In first-person terms, you are starting with yourself and the dynamic structure of knowing that is integral to being human. Once you understand how you know, you can transpose that dynamic operational structure into the basic, normative patterns of insider action research. Attention to the experience, understanding and judgement that leads to action provides a methodology through which you can affirm what and how you know. Quality and rigour can be formulated by the quest for authenticity, that is: to struggle to engage in being attentive, intelligent, reasonable and responsible in confronting the challenges of preunderstanding, role duality and organizational politics (Table 12.1). We introduced the notion of interiority, whereby you can distinguish different forms of knowing and through which you can remain grounded in your actual knowing processes, rather than being trapped by the often-conflicting ideologies of different philosophical positions.

Table 12.1 Authenticity in insider action research

Process imperatives	Preunderstanding	Role duality	
Be attentive	What is familiar/how is it different when the ritual is the same	Role expecta... ambiguity/conflict	P... Politica... others
Be intelligent	Evidence you are being presented with as you work with the familiar	Understand the structural nature of roles	Understand the structural pattern of political action
Be reasonable	Weigh the evidence/ distinguish inferences	Weigh the evidence and judge conflicting role and demands	Weigh the evidence and judge the demands of political action
Be responsible	Take responsibility for what you do	Take responsibility for what you do	Take responsibility for what you do

What you can do in an action research project in your own organization depends on the formal and psychological contract that you have with the system on its commitment to learning-in-action juxtaposed with yours. This is critical to the nature of the project that you can undertake. You draw on your preunderstanding of the organization and how you can manage the twin roles of your regular organizational role with the researcher role. With that foundation we explored some important and useful issues: managing organizational politics, framing and selecting a project, implementing it and finally, writing an action research dissertation.

In the past we have been asked questions such as: 'Given that doing insider research seems to be so complex and can be fraught with danger, wouldn't it be better to advise people not to select this approach as a means to do any academic research, particularly a major thesis for a postgraduate qualification?' In our view, while it can be difficult at times, the challenges that have to be overcome are usually well worth the effort. Intending insider-researchers do need to be aware of the issues that they may face, both to help prepare them to address these when they arise, and to know that this is a 'normal' part of the process. As Wirth reflects:

> This research has been the most exciting and challenging learning process I have experienced professionally. It changed the way I view teaching and instruction and it certainly changed my views on collaboration. The research has made me realize how much more we need to foster collaboration within the school system. (Ravitch and Wirth, 2007: 81)

n and Repstad (1993) describe the notion of researching your own organization erms of a journey from nearness to distance and back, and provide some practical dvice. In terms of maintaining distance, they advise researchers to be aware of pre-conceived ideas and prejudices about the organization, and to find rational theories to explain the organization as a way of distancing yourself. They suggest that you perform the role of devil's advocate by finding alternative theories which contradict the rational theories you have selected to explain the organization. This you can do through conversations with other members of the organization, especially those who do not share your perspective. In their view, you need to consider seriously the prevailing explanation of organizational problems, which might reflect analyses of symptoms. Typically these would be the scapegoat syndrome, 'Who is to blame?'; too little information, and too few resources, 'If only we had more'.

For some readers, doing action research in their own organizations is an exciting, demanding and invigorating prospect that will contribute considerably to their own learning and help their career development. For others it may seem daunt-ing, with a high potential for self-destruction. In the words of Brookfield (1994), it smacks of impostorship, cultural suicide, lost innocence, road-running and, in a more positive vein, community. Can you survive doing action research in your own organization? Shepard (1997) provides a few rules of thumb for change agents which are useful for insider action researchers:

Stay alive.

Care for yourself. Keep a life outside of the project so be able to turn yourself on and off. Stay in touch with the purpose of the project and go with the flow.

Start where the system is.

Have empathy with the system and the people in it, particularly as it won't like being 'diagnosed'.

Never work uphill.

Keep working at collaboration and work in the most promising arena.

Innovation requires a good idea, initiative and a few friends.

Find the people who are ready to work on the project and get them working together.

Load experiments with success.

Work at building success steps along the way.

Light many fires.

Remember the notion of systems. Any part of a system is the way it is because of how the rest of the system is. As you work towards change in one part, other parts will push the system back to the way it was. Understand the interdependencies among sub-systems and keep movement going in as many of them as you can.

Keep an optimistic bias.

Stay focused on vision and desired outcomes.

Capture the moment.

Stay in tune with yourself and the situation.

Friedman (2001) suggests four attributes: be proactive and reflective, be critical and committed, be independent, work well with others and have aspirations, and be realistic about limits. With these in mind we are confident that not only can you survive doing action research in your own organization, but you can flourish and be successful.

We close with David's words.

I understand the subversive nature of action research and I like it. I like the counter-culturalness to it all. It seems all at once to be natural and unnatural, something so right and primal, so comforting and familiar, yet something that seems to have been taken away from us in some way. We have learned to be inactive, even in the face of injustice, and we are aware of it. We know it, yet we continue to be inactive. Action research, even in my little context in my little school in the suburbs, was in some way revolutionary, for it allowed people to feel more in control of their work lives, to be more in control of their day-to-day being, to be more connected with their reality that they experience every day. Something else I like about action research: I did not have the assistant's journal, take notes, read books or participate in any activity other than those that helped them become better at what they do. We all knew in our hearts and souls that we were making our present situations better by working together, and that is one very good reason to use action research.

References

Adler, N., Shani, A.B. and Styhre, A. (2004) *Collaborative Research in Organizations*. Thousand Oaks, CA: Sage.

Adler, P.A. and Adler, P. (1987) *Membership Roles in Field Research*. Thousand Oaks, CA: Sage.

Aguinis, H. (1993) 'Action research and scientific method: Presumed discrepancies and actual similarities', *Journal of Applied Behavioral Science*, 29 (4): 416–431.

Alvesson, M. (2003) 'Methodology for close up studies: Struggling with closeness and closure', *Higher Education*, 46 (2): 167–193.

Anderson, G., Herr, K. and Nihlen, A. (1994) *Studying Your Own School*. Thousand Oaks, CA: Corwin.

Anderson, V. and Johnson, L. (1997) *Systems Thinking Basics: From Concepts to Causal Loops*. Cambridge, MA: Pegasus.

Argyris, C. (1993) *Knowledge for Action*. San Francisco, CA: Jossey-Bass.

Argyris, C. (2003) 'Actionable knowledge', in T. Tsoukas and C. Knudsen (eds), *The Oxford Handbook of Organization Theory*. Oxford: Oxford University Press, pp. 423–452.

Argyris, C. (2004) *Reasons and Rationalizations: The Limits to Organizational Knowledge*. New York: Oxford University Press.

Argyris, C. and Schon, D.A. (1974). *Theory in Practice: Increasing Professional Effectiveness*. San Francisco, CA: Jossey-Bass.

Argyris, C. and Schon, D. (1996) *Organizational Learning II*. Reading, MA: Addison-Wesley.

Argyris, C., Putnam, R. and Smith, D. (1985) *Action Science*. San Francisco, CA: Jossey-Bass.

Arieli, D., Friedman, V.J. and Agbaria, K. (2009) 'The paradox of participation in action research', *Action Research*, 7 (3): 263–290.

Ashforth, B., Kreiner, G. and Fugate, M. (2000) 'All in a day's work: Boundaries and micro role transitions', *Academy of Management Review*, 25 (3): 472–491.

Barden, G. (1991) *After Principles*. South Bend, IN: Notre Dame University Press.

Bargal, D. (2006) 'Personal and intellectual influences leading to Lewin's paradigm of action research', *Action Research*, 4 (4): 367–388.

Bargal, D. (2012) 'Kurt Lewin's vision of organizational and social change: The interdependence of theory, research and action/practice', in D. Boje, B. Burnes and J. Hassard (eds), *The Routledge Companion to Change*. Abingdon: Routledge, pp. 31–45.

Bartunek, J.M. (2003) *Organizational and Educational Change. The Life and Role of a Change Agent Group*. Mahwah, NJ: Erlbaum.

Bartunek, J.M. (2008) 'Insider/outsider team research: The development of the approach and its meanings', in A.B. Shani, S.A. Mohrman, W. Pasmore, B. Stymne and N. Adler (eds), *Handbook of Collaborative Management Research*. Thousand Oaks, CA: Sage, pp. 73–92.

Bartunek, J.M., Crosta, T.E., Dame, R.F. and LeLacheur, D.F. (2000) 'Managers and project leaders conducting their own action research interventions', in R.T. Golembiewski (ed.), *Handbook of Organizational Consultation* (2nd edn). New York: Marcel Dekker, pp. 59–70.

Baskerville, R. and Pries-Heje, J. (1999) 'Grounded action research: A method for understanding IT in practice', *Accounting, Management and Information Technology*, 9 (1): 1–23.

Bateson, G. (1972) *Steps to an Ecology of Mind*. San Francisco, CA: Ballantine.

Beckhard, R. (1997) *Agent of Change: My Life, My Work*. San Francisco, CA: Jossey-Bass.

Beckhard, R. and Harris, R. (1987) *Organizational Transitions: Managing Complex Change* (2nd edn). Reading, MA: Addison-Wesley.

Beckhard, R. and Pritchard, W. (1992) *Changing the Essence: The Art of Creating and Leading Fundamental Change in Organizations*. San Francisco, CA: Jossey-Bass.

Bell, S. (1998) 'Self-reflection and vulnerability in action research: Bringing forth new worlds in our learning', *Systemic Practice and Action Research*, 11 (2): 179–191.

Benne, K.D. (1959) 'Some ethical problems in group and organizational consultation', *Journal of Social Issues*, 15 (2): 60–67.

Bentz, V.M. and Shapiro, J.J. (1998) *Mindful Inquiry in Social Research*. Thousand Oaks, CA: Sage.

Bjorkman, H. and Sundgren, M. (2005) 'Political entrepreneurship in action research: Learning from two cases', *Journal of Organizational Change Management*, 18 (5): 399–415.

Bolman, D. and Deal, T. (2008) *Reframing Organizations* (3rd edn). San Francisco, CA: Jossey-Bass.

Boser, S. (2006) 'Ethics and power in community–campus partnerships for research', *Action Research*, 4 (1): 9–22.

Boud, D. (2001) 'Using journal writing to enhance reflective practice', in L.M. English and M.A. Gillen (eds), *Promoting Journal Writing in Adult Education*. San Francisco, CA: Jossey-Bass, pp. 9–18.

Boud, D., Keogh, R. and Walker, D. (1985) *Reflection: Turning Experience into Learning*. Abingdon: Routledge.

Bourner, T. (2003) 'Assessing reflective learning', *Education and Training*, 45 (5): 267–272.

Bradbury, H. (2008) 'Quality and "actionability": What action researchers offer from the tradition of pragmatism', in A.B. Shani, S.A. Mohrman, W.A. Pasmore, B. Stymne and N. Adler (eds) *Handbook of Collaborative Management Research*. Thousand Oaks, CA: Sage, pp. 583–600.

Bradbury, H. and Mainmelis, C. (2001) 'Learning history and organizational praxis', *Journal of Management Inquiry*, 10 (4): 340–357.

Bradbury, H., Mirvis, P., Neilsen, E. and Pasmore, W. (2008) 'Action research at work: Creating the future following the path from Lewin', in P. Reason and H. Bradbury (eds), *The SAGE Handbook of Action Research* (2nd edn). London: Sage, pp. 77–92.

Brannick, T. and Coghlan, D. (2007) 'In defense of being "native": The case for insider academic research', *Organizational Research Methods*, 10 (1): 59–74.

Brookfield, S. (1994) 'Tales from the dark side: A phenomenography of adult critical reflection', *International Journal of Lifelong Education*, 13 (3): 203–216.

Brown, J. (2005) *The World Cafe*. San Francisco, CA: Jossey-Bass.

Brydon-Miller, M. (2008a) 'Covenantal ethics and action research: Exploring a common foundation for social research', in D. Mertens and P. Ginsberg (eds), *Handbook of Social Research Ethics*. Thousand Oaks, CA: Sage, pp. 243–258.

Brydon-Miller, M. (2008b) 'Ethics and action research: Deepening our commitment to social justice and redefining systems of democratic practice', in P. Reason and H. Bradbury (eds), *The SAGE Handbook of Action Research* (2nd edn). London: Sage, pp. 199–210.

Brydon-Miller, M. and Greenwood, D. (2006) 'A re-examination of the relationship between action research and human subjects review process', *Action Research*, 4 (1): 117–128.

Brydon-Miller, M., Greenwood, D. and Eikeland, O. (2006) 'Special issue: Ethics and action research', *Action Research*, 4 (1): 5–131. Special Issue.

Brydon-Miller, M., Greenwood, D. and Maguire, P. (2003) 'Why action research?', *Action Research*, 1 (1): 9–28.

Buchanan, D. and Badham, R. (2008) *Power, Politics and Organizational Change: Winning the Turf Game* (2nd edn). London: Sage.

Buchanan, D. and Boddy, D. (1992) *The Expertise of the Change Agent*. London: Prentice-Hall.

Bunker, B. and Alban, B. (2006) *The Handbook of Large Group Methods*. San Francisco, CA: Jossey-Bass.

Buono, A.F. and Kerber, K.W. (2008) 'The challenges of organizational change: Enhancing organizational change capacity', *Revue Sciences de Gestion*, 65: 99–118.

Burgoyne, J. (2011) 'Evaluating action learning: A perspective informed by critical realism, networks and complex adaptive system theory', in M. Pedler (ed.), *Action Learning in Practice* (4th edn). Farnham: Gower, pp. 427–468.

Burke, W.W. (2011) *Organization Change: Theory and Practice* (3rd edn). Thousand Oaks, CA: Sage.

Burnes, B. (2007) 'Kurt Lewin and the Harwood Studies: The Foundations of OD', *Journal of Applied Behavioral Science*, 43 (2): 213–231.

Burnes, B. and Cooke, B. (2012) 'The past, present and future of organization development: Taking the long view', *Human Relations*, 65 (11): 1395–1429.

Burns, D. (2007) *Systemic Action Research*. Cambridge: Polity Press.

Bushe, G.R. (2012) Appreciative inquiry: Theory and critique', in D. Boje, B. Burnes and J. Hassard (eds), *The Routledge Companion to Organizational Change*. Abingdon: Routledge, pp. 87–103.

Bushe, G.R. and Marshak, R. (2009) 'Revisioning organization development: Diagnostic and dialogic premises and patterns of practice', *Journal of Applied Behavioral Science*, 45 (3): 248–268.

Bushe, G.R. and Shani, A.B. (1991) *Parallel Learning Structures*. Reading, MA: Addison-Wesley.

Campbell, D. (2000) *The Socially Constructed Organization*. London: Karnac.

Cassell, C. and Johnson, P. (2006) 'Action research: Explaining the diversity', *Human Relations*, 59 (6): 783–814.

Chandler, D. and Torbert, W.R. (2003) 'Transforming inquiry and action: Interweaving 27 flavors of action research', *Action Research*, 1 (2): 133–152.

Chevalier, J.M. and Buckles, D.J. (2013) *Participatory Action Research: Theory and Methods for Engaged Inquiry*. New York: Routledge.

Coch, L. and French, J.R.P. (1948) 'Overcoming resistance to change', *Human Relations*, 1 (1): 512–532.

Coghlan, D. (1993) 'Learning from emotions through journaling', *Journal of Management Education*, 17 (1): 90–94.

Coghlan, D. (2002) 'Interlevel dynamics in systemic action research', *Systemic Practice and Action Research*, 15 (4): 273–283.

Coghlan, D. (2003) 'Practitioner research for organizational knowledge: Mechanistic- and organistic-oriented approaches to insider action research', *Management Learning*, 34 (4): 451–463.

Coghlan, D. (2004) 'Managers as learners and researchers', in D. Coghlan, T. Dromgoole, P. Joynt and P. Sorensen (eds), *Managers Learning in Action*. London: Routledge, pp. 183–189.

Coghlan, D. (2007) 'Insider action research doctorates: Generating actionable knowledge', *Higher Education*, 54 (2): 293–306.

Coghlan, D. (2008) 'Authenticity as first person practice: An exploration based on Bernard Lonergan', *Action Research*, 6 (3): 399–343.

Coghlan, D. (2009) 'Toward a philosophy of clinical inquiry/research', *Journal of Applied Behavioral Science*, 45 (1): 106–121.

Coghlan, D. (2010a) 'Seeking common ground in the diversity and diffusion of action research and collaborative management research action modalities: Toward a general empirical method', in W.A. Pasmore, A.B. Shani and R.W. Woodman (eds), *Research in Organization Change and Development*, Vol. 18, Brinkley: Emerald, pp. 149–181.

Coghlan, D. (2010b) 'Interiority as the cutting edge between theory and practice: A first person perspective', *International Journal of Action Research*, 6 (2+3): 288–307.

Coghlan, D. (2011) 'Action research: Exploring perspective on a philosophy of practical knowing', *Academy of Management Annals*, 5: 53–87.

Coghlan, D. (2012a) 'Organization development and action research: Then and now', in D. Boje, B. Burnes and J. Hassard (eds), *The Routledge Companion to Organizational Change*. Abingdon: Routledge, pp. 46–58.

Coghlan, D. (2012b) 'Understanding insight in the context of Q', *Action Learning: Research and Practice*, 9 (3): 247–258.

Coghlan, D. (2013) 'Messy, iterative groping in the swampy lowlands: The challenges of insider scholar-practitioner inquiry', in A.B. Shani, W.A. Pasmore and R.W. Woodman (eds), *Research in Organization Change and Development*, Vol. 21, Brinkley: Emerald, pp. 121–147.

Coghlan, D. and Casey, M. (2001) 'Action research from the inside: Issues and challenges in doing action research in your own hospital', *Journal of Advanced Nursing*, 35 (5): 674–682.

Coghlan, D. and Holian, R. (2007) 'Insider action research: Special issue', *Action Research*, 5 (1): 5–91. Special Issue.

Coghlan, D. and Jacobs, C. (2005) 'Kurt Lewin on reeducation: Foundations for action research', *Journal of Applied Behavioral Science*, 41 (4): 444–457.

Coghlan, D. and Pedler, M. (2006) 'Action learning dissertations: Structure, supervision and examination', *Action Learning: Research and Practice*, 3 (2): 127–140.

Coghlan, D. and Rashford, N.S. (1990) 'Uncovering and dealing with organizational distortions', *Journal of Managerial Psychology*, 5 (3): 17–21.

Coghlan, D. and Rashford, N.S. (2006) *Organization Change and Strategy: An Interlevels Dynamics Approach*. Abingdon: Routledge.

Coghlan, D. and Rigg, C. (2012) 'Action learning as praxis in learning and changing', in A.B. Shani, W.A. Pasmore and R. Woodman (eds), *Research in Organizational Change and Development*, Vol. 20. Brinkley: Emerald, pp. 59–90.

Coghlan, D. and Shani, A.B. (2005) 'Roles, politics and ethics in action research design', *Systemic Practice and Action Research*, 18 (6): 533–546.

Coghlan, D. and Shani, A.B. (2008) 'Collaborative management research through communities of inquiry', in A.B. Shani, S.A. Mohrman, W. Pasmore, B. Stymne and N. Adler (eds), *Handbook of Collaborative Management Research*. Thousand Oaks, CA: Sage, pp. 601–614.

Coghlan, D. and Shani, A.B. (2013) 'Organization development research interventions: Perspectives from action research and collaborative management research', in S. Leonard, R. Lewis, A. Freedman and J. Passmore (eds), *The Wiley-Blackwell Handbook of the Psychology of Organization Development and Leadership*. New York: Wiley, pp. 443–460.

Coghlan, D. with Brydon-Miller, M. (2014) *The SAGE Encyclopedia of Action Research*. London: Sage.

Coghlan, D., Dromgoole, T., Joynt, P. and Sorensen, P. (2004) *Managers Learning in Action: Research, Learning and Education*. London: Routledge.

Cooklin, A. (ed.) (1999) *Changing Organizations: Clinicians as Agents of Change*. London: Karnac.

Cooperrider, D.L. and Srivastva, S. (1987) 'Appreciative inquiry in organizational life', in R. Woodman and W. Pasmore (eds), *Research in Organizational Change and Development*, Vol. 1. Greenwich, CT: JAI Press, pp. 129–169.

Cornell, A.W. (1996) *The Power of Focusing*. Oakland, CA: New Harbinger Publications.

Costley, C., Elliott, G. and Gibbs, P. (2010) *Doing Work-based Research*. London: Sage.

Coughlan, P. and Coghlan, D. (2009) 'Action research', in C. Karlsson (ed.), *Researching Operations Management*. New York: Routledge, pp. 236–264.

Coughlan, P. and Coghlan, D. (2011) *Collaborative Strategic Improvement Through Network Action Learning*. Cheltenham: Edward Elgar.

Darling, M. and Parry, C. (2000) *From Post-mortem to Living Practice: An In-depth Study of the Evolution of the After Action Review*. Boston, MA: Signet.

Deane, C. (2004) 'Learning to change', in D. Coghlan, T. Dromgoole, P. Joynt and P. Sorensen (eds), *Managers Learning in Action: Research, Learning and Education*. London: Routledge, pp. 9–23.

Deery, R. (2011) 'Balancing research and action in turbulent times: Action research as a tool for change', *Evidence-based Midwifery*, 9: 89–94.

de Guerre, D. (2002) 'Doing action research in one's own organization: An ongoing conversation over time', *Systemic Practice and Action Research*, 15 (4): 331–349.

DeTardo-Bora, K. (2004) 'Action research in a world of positivist-oriented review boards', *Action Research*, 2 (3): 237–253.

De Vos, H. (1987) 'Common sense and scientific thinking', in F. van Hoolthoon and D.R. Olsen (eds), *Common Sense: The Foundation for Social Science*. Lanham, MD: University Press of America, pp. 345–359.

Dick, B. (1999) 'You want to do an action research thesis?' Available at: http://www.aral.com.au/resources/arthesis.html (accessed 3 October 2013).

Dickens, L. and Watkins, K. (1999) 'Action research: Rethinking Lewin', *Management Learning*, 30 (2): 127–140.

Docherty, P., Ljung, A. and Stjernberg, T. (2006) 'The changing practice of action research', in J. Lowstedt and T. Stjernberg (eds), *Producing Management Knowledge*. Abingdon: Routledge, pp. 221–236.

Dunne, T. (2010) *Doing Better: The Next Revolution in Ethics*. Milwaukee, WI: Marquette University Press.

Dutton, J.E., Fahey, L. and Narayanan, V.K. (1983) 'Toward understanding strategic issue diagnosis', *Strategic Management Journal*, 4: 307–323.

Dworkin, R. (2011) *Justice for Hedgehogs*. Cambridge, MA: Belknap Press.

Dymek, C. (2008) 'IT and action sensemaking: Making sense of new technology', in P. Reason and H. Bradbury (eds), *The SAGE Handbook of Action Research* (2nd edn). London: Sage, pp. 573–588.

Eden, C. and Huxham, C. (2006) 'Researching organizations using action research', in S. Clegg, C. Hardy, T. Lawrence and W. Nord (eds), *The SAGE Handbook of Organization Studies*. Thousand Oaks, CA: Sage, pp. 388–408.

Eikeland, O. (2006a) 'Phronesis, Aristotle and action research', *International Journal of Action Research*, 2 (1): 5–53.

Eikeland, O. (2006b) 'Condescending ethics and action research', *Action Research*, 4 (1): 37–48.

Eikeland, O. (2007) 'Why should mainstream social researchers be interested in action research?', *International Journal of Action Research*, 3 (1+2): 38–64.

Eikeland, O. (2008) *The Ways of Aristotle: Aristotelian Phronesis, Aristotelian Philosophy of Dialogue and Action Research*. Bern: Peter Lang.

Elizur, Y. (1999) '"Inside" consultation through self-differentation: Stimulating organization development in the IDF's care of intractable, war-related, traumatic disorders', in A. Cooklin (ed.), *Changing Organizations: Clinicians as Agents of Change*. London: Karnac, pp. 141–168.

Evans, M. (1997) 'An action research enquiry into reflection in action as part of my role as a deputy headteacher'. PhD dissertation, Kingston University.

Evered, M. and Louis, M.R. (1981) 'Alternative perspectives in the organizational sciences: "Inquiry from the inside" and "inquiry from the outside"', *Academy of Management Review*, 6 (3): 385–395.

Ferguson, P. and Ferguson, B. (2001) 'Shooting oneself in the foot: An investigation of some issues in conducting insider research', Paper presented at the 24th HERDSA conference, Newcastle, Australia, July 2001.

Fisher, D., Rooke, D. and Torbert, B. (2000) *Personal and Organizational Transformations Through Action Inquiry*. Boston, MA: Edge\work Press.

Fisher, R. and Sharp, A. (1999) *Getting It Done*. New York: Harper.

Fisher, R. and Ury, W. (2012) *Getting to Yes* (2nd edn). London: Business Books.

Flanagan, J. (1997) *Quest for Self-knowledge: An Essay in Lonergan's Philosophy*. Toronto: University of Toronto Press.

Flyvbjerg, B. (2001) *Making Social Science Matter*. Cambridge: Cambridge University Press.

Flyvbjerg, B., Landman, T. and Schram, S. (2012) *Real Social Science*. Cambridge: Cambridge University Press.

Foster, M. (1972) 'An introduction to the theory and practice of action research in work organizations', *Human Relations*, 25 (6): 529–556.

French, W. and Bell, C. (1999) *Organization Development: Behavioral Science Interventions for Organization Improvement* (6th edn). Englewood Cliffs, NJ: Prentice-Hall.

Fricke, W. and Totterdill, R. (2004) *Action Research in Workplace Innovation and Regional Development*. Amsterdam: John Benjamins.

Friedman, V. (2001) 'The individual as agent of organizational learning', in M. Dierkes, J. Child, I. Nonaka and A. Berthoin Antal (eds), *Handbook of Organizational Learning*. Oxford: Oxford University Press, pp. 398–414.

Friedman, V. and Rogers, T. (2008) 'Action science: Linking causal action and meaning making in action research', in P. Reason and H. Bradbury (eds), *The SAGE Handbook of Action Research* (2nd edn). London: Sage, pp. 252–265.

Frost, P. and Robinson, S. (1999) 'The toxic handler: Organizational hero – and casualty', *Harvard Business Review*, 77 (4): 97–106.

Gellerman, W., Frankel, M. and Ladenson, R. (1990) *Values and Ethics in Organization and Human System Development*. San Francisco, CA: Jossey-Bass.

Gendlin, E. (1981) *Focusing*. New York: Bantam.

Gergen, K. and Gergen, M. (2008) 'Social construction and research on action', in P. Reason and H. Bradbury (eds), *The SAGE Handbook of Action Research* (2nd edn). London: Sage, pp. 159–171.

Gibbons, M., Limoges, C., Nowotny, H., Schwartzman, S., Scott, P. and Trow, M. (1994) *The New Production of Knowledge*. London: Sage.

Goffman, E. (1959) *The Presentation of Self in Everyday Life*. New York: Doubleday.

Goode, L.M. and Bartunek, J.M. (1990) 'Action research in an underbounded setting', *Consultation*, 9 (3): 209–228.

Gorinski, R. and Ferguson, P. (1997) '(Ex)changing experiences of insider research'. Paper presented at the NZARE conference. Auckland, New Zealand, December 1997.

Greenwood, D. (2007) 'Pragmatic action research', *International Journal of Action Research*, 3 (1+2): 131–148.

Greenwood, D. and Levin, M. (2007) *Introduction to Action Research* (2nd edn). Thousand Oaks, CA: Sage.

Gummesson, E. (2000) *Qualitative Methods in Management Research* (2nd edn). Thousand Oaks, CA: Sage.

Gustavsen, B. (2003) 'New forms of knowledge production and the role of action research', *Action Research*, 1 (2): 153–164.

Harrison, M. (2005) *Diagnosing Organizations: Methods, Models and Processes* (3rd edn). Thousand Oaks, CA: Sage.

Harrison, M. and Shirom, A. (1999) *Organizational Diagnosis and Assessment: Bridging Theory and Practice*. Thousand Oaks, CA: Sage.

Hatchuel, A. and David, A. (2008) 'Collaborating for management research: From action research to intervention research in management', in A.B. Shani, S.A. Mohrman, W. Pasmore, B. Stymne and N. Adler (eds), *Handbook of Collaborative Management Research*. Thousand Oaks, CA: Sage, pp. 143–161.

Heron, J. (1996) *Cooperative Inquiry*. London: Sage.

Heron, J. and Reason, P. (2008) 'Extending epistemology with a co-operative inquiry', in P. Reason and H. Bradbury (eds), *The SAGE Handbook of Action Research* (2nd edn). London: Sage, pp. 367–380.

Herr, K. and Anderson, G. (2005) *The Action Research Dissertation*. Thousand Oaks, CA: Sage.

Hilsen, A.I. (2006) 'And they shall be known by their deeds: Ethics and politics in action research', *Action Research*, 4 (1): 23–36.

Hirschhorn, L. (1988) *The Workplace Within: Psychodynamics of Organizational Life*. Cambridge, MA: MIT Press.

Hockley, J., Froggatt, K. and Heimerl, K. (eds) (2013) *Participatory Research in Palliative Care: Actions and Reflections*. Oxford: Oxford University Press.

Holian, R. (1999) 'Doing action research in my own organization: Ethical dilemmas, hopes and triumphs', *Action Research International*, Paper 3. Available at: http://www.aral.com.au/ari/p-rholian99.html (accessed 3 October 2013).

Holian, R. and Brooks, R. (2004) 'The Australian National Statement on Ethical Conduct in Research: Application and implementation for 'insider' applied research in business', *Action Research International*, Paper 7. Available at: http://www.aral.com.au/ari/p-rholian04.html (accessed 3 October 2013).

Holian, R. and Coghlan, D. (2013) 'Ethical issues and role duality in insider action research: Challenges for action research degree programmes', *Systemic Practice and Action Research*, 26: 399–415.

Holman, P., Devane, T. and Cady, S. (2007) *The Change Handbook: Group Methods for Shaping the Future* (2nd edn). San Francisco, CA: Berrett-Koehler.

Homa, P. (1998) Re-engineering the Leicester Royal Infirmary healthcare process. Henley Management College and Brunel University. PhD dissertation,.

Humphrey, C. (2007) 'Insider-outsider: Activating the hyphen', *Action Research*, 5 (1): 11–26.

Hynes, G., Coghlan, D. and McCarron, M. (2012) 'Participation as a multi-voiced process: Action research in the acute hospital environment', *Action Research*, 10 (3): 293–312.

Jarvis, P. (1999) *The Practitioner-Researcher*. San Francisco, CA: Jossey-Bass.

Johansson, A. and Lindhult, E. (2008) 'Emancipation or workability? Critical versus pragmatic scientific orientation in action research', *Action Research*, 6 (1): 95–115.

Kahneman, D. (2011) *Thinking Fast and Slow*. New York: Penguin.

Kakabadse, A. (1991) 'Politics and ethics in action research', in N. Craig Smith and P. Dainty (eds), *The Management Research Handbook*. London: Routledge, pp. 289–299.

Kaplan, R.S. (1998) 'Innovation action research: Creating new management theory and practice', *Journal of Management Accounting Research*, 10: 89–118.

Katz, D. and Kahn, R.L. (1978) *The Social Psychology of Organizations* (2nd edn). New York: McGraw-Hill.

Keegan, R. and Lahey, L.L. (2001) *How the Way We Talk Can Change the Way We Work*. San Francisco, CA: Jossey-Bass.

Kelley, T. and Kelley, D. (2012) 'Reclaiming your creative confidence', *Harvard Business Review*, 90 (12): 115–118.

Kelman, H.C. (1965) 'Manipulation of human behavior: An ethical dilemma for the social scientist', *Journal of Social Issues*, 21 (2): 31–46.

Kemmis, S. (2001) 'Exploring the relevance of critical theory for action research: Emancipatory action research in the footsteps of Jurgen Habermas', in P. Reason and H. Bradbury (eds), *The SAGE Handbook of Action Research*. London: Sage, pp. 91–102.

Kleiner, A. and Roth, G. (1997) 'How to make experience your company's best teacher', *Harvard Business Review*, 75 (5): 172–177.

Kleiner, A. and Roth, G. (2000) *Oil Change*. New York: Oxford University Press.

Klev, R. and Levin, M. (2012) *Participative Transformation: Learning and Development in Practising Change*. Farnham: Gower.

Koch, N. (2007) *Information Systems and Action Research*. New York: Springer.

Kolb, D. (1984) *Experiential Learning*. Englewood Cliffs, NJ: Prentice-Hall.

Koshy, E., Koshy, V. and Waterman, H. (2011) *Action Research in Healthcare*. London: Sage.

Krim, R. (1988) 'Managing to learn: Action inquiry in city hall', in P. Reason (ed.), *Human Inquiry in Action*. London: Sage, pp. 144–162.

Ladkin, D. (2005) 'The enigma of subjectivity: How might phenomenology help action researchers negotiate the relationship between "self", "other" and "truth"?', *Action Research*, 3 (1): 108–126.

Levin, M. (2003) 'Action research and the research community', *Concepts and Transformation*, 8 (3): 275–280.

Levin, M. (2012) 'Academic integrity in action research', *Action Research*, 10 (2): 133–149.

Lewin, K. (1997[1943, 1944]) 'Problems of research in social psychology', in *Field Theory in Social Science*. Washington, DC: American Psychological Association, pp. 279–288.

Lewin, K. (1997[1946]) 'Action research and minority problems', in *Resolving Social Conflicts: Selected Papers on Group Dynamics* (ed. G. Lewin). Washington, DC: American Psychological Association, pp. 144–154.

Lewin, K. (1999[1948]) 'Group decision and social change', in M. Gold (ed.), *The Complete Social Scientist: A Kurt Lewin Reader.* Washington, DC: American Psychological Association, pp. 265–284.

Lincoln, Y. (2001) 'Engaging sympathies: Relationships between action research and social constructivism', in P. Reason and H. Bradbury (eds), *The SAGE Handbook of Action Research.* London: Sage, pp. 124–132.

Lippitt, R. (1961) 'Value-judgement problems of the social scientist in action research', in W. Bennis, K. Benne and R. Chin (eds), *The Planning of Change.* New York: Holt, Rinehart & Winston, pp. 689–694.

Lippitt, R. (1979) 'Kurt Lewin, action research and planned change', paper provided by the author.

Lipshitz, R., Friedman, V.J. and Popper, M. (2007) *Demystifying Organizational Learning.* Thousand Oaks, CA: Sage.

Lonergan, B.J. (1992[1957]) *Insight: An Essay in Human Understanding. The Collected Works of Bernard Lonergan*, Vol. 3 (eds F. Crowe and R. Doran). Toronto: University of Toronto Press.

Lucas, B., Cox, C., Perry, L. and Bridges, J. (2013) 'Pre-operative preparation of patients for total knee replacement: An action research study', *International Journal of Orthopaedic and Trauma Nursing*, 17 (2): 79–90.

Ludema, J. and Fry, R. (2008) 'The practice of appreciative inquiry', in P. Reason and H. Bradbury (eds), *The SAGE Handbook of Action Research* (2nd edn). London: Sage, pp. 280–296.

Lykes, M.B. and Mallona, A. (2008) 'Towards transformational liberation: Participatory and action research and praxis', in P. Reason and H. Bradbury (eds), *The SAGE Handbook of Action Research* (2nd edn). London: Sage, pp. 106–120.

MacLean, D., MacIntosh, R. and Grant, S. (2002) 'Model 2 management research', *British Journal of Management*, 13 (2): 189–207.

Macmurray, J. (1957) *The Self as Agent.* London: Faber and Faber.

Mann, P. and Clarke, D. (2007) 'Writing it down–writing it out–writing it up: Researching our practice through action learning', *Action Learning: Research and Practice*, 4 (2): 153–171.

Marquardt, M. (2004) *Optimizing the Power of Action Learning.* Palo Alto, CA: Davies-Black.

Marrow, A.J. (1969) *The Practical Theorist.* New York: Basic Books.

Marshall, J. (1999) 'Living life as inquiry', *Systemic Practice and Action Research*, 12 (2): 155–171.

Marshall, J. (2001) 'Self-reflective inquiry practices', in P. Reason and H. Bradbury (eds), *The SAGE Handbook of Action Research.* London: Sage, pp. 433–439.

Marshall, J. (2008) 'Finding form in writing for action research, in P. Reason and H. Bradbury (eds), *The SAGE Handbook of Action Research* (2nd edn). London: Sage, pp. 682–695.

Marshall, J. and Reason, P. (2007) 'Quality in research as taking an "attitude of inquiry"', *Management Research News*, 30 (5): 368–380.

Martin, A. (2008) 'Action research on a large scale: Issues and practices', in P. Reason and H. Bradbury (eds), *The SAGE Handbook of Action Research* (2nd edn). London: Sage, pp. 394–406.

McArdle, K. and Reason, P. (2008) 'Organization development and action research', in T. Cummings (ed.), *Handbook of Organization Development*. Thousand Oaks, CA: Sage, pp. 123–136.

McCaughan, N. and Palmer, B (1994) *Systems Thinking for Harassed Managers*. London: Karnac.

McGill, I. and Brockbank, A. (2004) *The Action Learning Handbook*. London: Routledge Falmer.

McMullan, W. and Cahoon, A. (1979) 'Integrating abstract conceptualizing with experiential learning', *Academy of Management Review*, 4 (3): 453–458.

McNiff, J., Lomax, P. and Whitehead, J. (2009) *You and Your Action Research Project* (3rd edn). Abingdon: Routledge.

McTaggart, R. (1998) 'Is validity really an issue in PAR?', *Studies in Culture, Organization and Societies*, 4 (2): 211–237.

Meehan, C. and Coghlan, D. (2004) 'Managers as healing agents: A cooperative inquiry approach', *Systemic Practice and Action Research*, 17 (2): 407–423.

Melchin, K.R. and Picard, C.A. (2008) *Transforming Conflict through Insight*. Toronto: Toronto University Press.

Meyerson, D. (2001) *Tempered Radicals: How People use Difference to Inspire Change at Work*. Boston, MA: Harvard Business School Press.

Meynell, H. (1999) *Postmodernism and the New Enlightenment*. Washington, DC: Catholic University of America Press.

Mezirow, J. (1991) *Transformative Dimensions of Adult Learning*, San Francisco, CA: Jossey-Bass.

Mitki, Y., Shani, A.B. and Stjernberg, T. (2000) 'A typology of change programs and their differences from a solid perspective', in R.T. Golembiewski (ed.), *Handbook of Organizational Consultation* (2nd edn). New York: Marcel Dekker Inc., pp. 777–785.

Mohrman, S.A., Lawler, E.E. and Associates (2011) *Useful Research: Advancing Theory and Practice*. San Francisco, CA: Berrett-Koehler.

Moon, J. (1999) *Learning Journals: A Handbook for Academics, Students and Professional Development*. London: Kogan Page.

Moore, B. (2007) 'Original sin and action research', *Action Research*, 5 (1): 27–39.

Morton, A. (1999) 'Ethics in action research', *Systemic Practice and Action Research*, 12 (2): 219–222.

Nadler, D.A. (1977) *Feedback and Organization Development: Using Data-based Methods*. Reading, MA: Addison-Wesley.

Nadler, D.A. (1998) *Champions of Change*. San Francisco, CA: Jossey-Bass.

Neilsen, E. (2006) 'But let us not forget John Collier: Commentary on David Bargal's personal and intellectual influences leading to Lewin's paradigm of action research', *Action Research*, 4 (4): 389–399.

Nielsen, J.C.R. and Repstad, P. (1993) 'From nearness to distance – and back: Analyzing your own organization'. Papers in Organizations No. 14, Copenhagen Business School, Institute of Organizational and Industrial Sociology.

Nielsen, K.A. and Svensson, L. (2006) *Action Research and Interactive Research: Beyond Theory and Practice*. Maastricht: Shaker.

Parkin, P. (2009) *Managing Change in Healthcare: Using Action Research*. London: Sage.

Pasmore, W.A. (2001) 'Action research in the workplace: The socio-technical perspective', in P. Reason and H. Bradbury (eds), *The SAGE Handbook of Action Research*. London: Sage, pp. 38–47.

Pasmore, W.A. (2011) 'Tipping the balance: Overcoming persistent problems in organizational change', in A.B. Shani, R.W. Woodman and W.A. Pasmore (eds), *Research in Organizational Change and Development*, Vol. 19. Bingley: Emerald, pp. 259–292.

Pasmore, W.A., Woodman, R. and Simmons, A.L. (2008) 'Toward a more rigorous, reflective and relevant science of collaborative management research', in A.B. Shani, S.A. Mohrman, W.A. Pasmore, B. Stymne and N. Adler (eds), *Handbook of Collaborative Management Research*. Thousand Oaks, CA: Sage, pp. 567–582.

Pedler, M. (2008) *Action Learning for Managers*. Aldershot: Gower.

Pedler, M. (2011) *Action Learning in Practice* (4th edn). Farnham: Gower.

Pedler, M. and Burgoyne, J. (2008) 'Action learning', in P. Reason and H. Bradbury (eds), *The SAGE Handbook of Action Research* (2nd edn). London: Sage, pp. 319–332.

Pettigrew, P. (2003) 'Power, conflicts and resolutions: A change agent's perspective on conducting action research within a multiorganizational partnership', *Systemic Practice and Action Research*, 16 (6): 375–391.

Pine, G.J. (2008) *Teacher Action Research*. Thousand Oaks, CA: Sage.

Preskill, H. and Torres, R.T. (1999) *Evaluative Inquiry for Learning in Organizations*. Thousand Oaks, CA: Sage.

Punch, M. (1994) 'Politics and ethics in qualitative research', in N.K. Denzin and Y.S. Lincoln (eds), *The Sage Handbook of Qualitative Research*. Thousand Oaks, CA: Sage, pp. 83–97.

Putnam, R. (1991) 'Recipes and reflective learning', in D. Schon (ed.), *The Reflective Turn: Case Studies in and on Educational Practice*. New York: Teachers' College of Columbia Press, pp. 145–163.

Quick, J., Paulus, P., Whittington, J., Larey, T. and Nelson, D. (1996) *Management Development, Well-Being and Health*. Chichester: Wiley.

Raelin, J.A. (2008) *Work-based Learning: Bridging Knowledge and Action in the Workplace* (rev. edn). San Francisco, CA: Jossey-Bass.

Raelin, J.A. (2009) 'Seeking conceptual clarity in the action modalities', *Action Learning Research and Practice*, 6 (1): 17–24.

Rahman, M.A. (2008) 'Some trends in the praxis of participatory action research', in P. Reason and H. Bradbury (eds), *The SAGE Handbook of Action Research*. London: Sage, pp. 49–62.

Ramirez, I. and Bartunek, J.M. (1989) 'The multiple realities and experience of internal organization development consultation in health care', *Journal of Organizational Change Management*, 2 (1): 40–56.

Ravitch, S.M. and Wirth, S. (2007) 'Developing a pedagogy of opportunity for students and their teachers', *Action Research*, 5 (1): 75–91.

Reason, P. (ed.) (1988) *Human Inquiry in Action*. London: Sage.

Reason, P. (1999) 'Integrating action and reflection through cooperative inquiry', *Management Learning*, 30 (2): 207–226.

Reason, P. (2006) 'Choice and quality in action research practice', *Journal of Management Inquiry*, 15 (2): 187–203.

Reason, P. and Bradbury, H. (2008) *The SAGE Handbook of Action Research* (2nd edn). London: Sage.

Reason, P. and Marshall, J. (1987) 'Research as personal process', in D. Boud and V. Griffin (eds), *Appreciating Adult Learning*. London: Kogan Page, pp. 112–126.

Reason, P. and Torbert, W.R. (2001) 'The action turn: Toward a transformational social science', *Concepts and Transformation*, 6 (1): 1–37.

Reed, J. (2007) *Appreciative Inquiry: Research for Change*. Thousand Oaks, CA: Sage.

Revans, R. (1982) *The Origins and Growth of Action Learning*. Bromley: Chartwell-Bratt.

Revans, R. (2008) *ABC of Action Learning*. Farnham: Gower.

Riemer, J. (1977) 'Varieties of opportunistic research', *Urban Life*, 5 (4): 467–477.

Riordan, P. (1995) 'The philosophy of action science', *Journal of Managerial Psychology*, 10 (6): 6–13.

Rogers, C.R. (1958) 'The characteristics of a helping relationship', *Personnel and Guidance Journal*, 37: 6–16.

Ross, R. (1994) 'The ladder of inference', in P. Senge, C. Roberts, R. Ross, B. Smith and A. Kleiner (eds), *The Fifth Discipline Fieldbook*. London: Nicholas Brealey, pp. 242–246.

Ross, R. and Roberts, C. (1994) 'Balancing inquiry and advocacy', in P. Senge, C. Roberts, R. Ross, B. Smith and A. Kleiner (eds), *The Fifth Discipline Fieldbook*. London: Nicholas Brealey, pp. 253–259.

Roth, G. and Bradbury, H. (2008) 'Learning history: An action research in support of actionable learning', in P. Reason and H. Bradbury (eds), *The SAGE Handbook of Action Research* (2nd edn). London: Sage, pp. 350–365.

Roth, G. and Kleiner, A. (1998) 'Developing organizational memory through learning histories', *Organizational Dynamics*, 27 (3): 43–60.

Roth, J., Sandberg, R. and Svensson, C. (2004) 'The dual role of the insider action researcher', in N. Adler, A.B. Shani and A. Styhre, *Collaborative Research in Organizations*. Thousand Oaks, CA: Sage, pp. 117–134.

Roth, J., Shani, A.B. and Leary, M. (2007) 'Facing the challenges of new capability development within a biopharma company', *Action Research*, 5 (1): 41–60.

Rousseau, D. (1985) 'Issues in organizational research: Multi-level and cross-level perspectives', in L.L. Cummings and B.M. Staw (eds), *Research in Organizational Behavior*, Vol. 7. Greenwich, CT: JAI Press, pp. 1–37.

Rowan, J. (2000) 'Research ethics', *International Journal of Psychotherapy*, 5 (2): 103–110.

Sagor, R. (2011) *The Action Research Guidebook* (2nd edn). Thousand Oaks, CA: Corwin.

Savall, H. and Zardet, V. (2011) *The Qualimetrics Approach*. Charlotte, NC: Information Age Publishing.

Scharmer, O. (2001) 'Self-transcending knowledge: Sensing and organizing around emerging opportunities', *Journal of Knowledge Management*, 5 (2): 137–150.

Schein, E.H. (1979) 'Personal change through interpersonal relationships', in W. Bennis, J. Van Maanen, E.H. Schein and F.I. Steele, *Essays in Interpersonal Dynamics*. Homewood, IL: Dorsey Press, pp. 129–162.

Schein, E.H. (1987) *The Clinical Perspective in Fieldwork*. Newbury Park, CA: Sage.

Schein, E.H. (1993) 'On dialogue, culture and organizational learning', *Organizational Dynamics*, 22 (2): 40–51.

Schein, E.H. (1995) 'Process consultation, action research and clinical inquiry: Are they the same?', *Journal of Managerial Psychology*, 10 (6): 14–19.

Schein, E.H. (1997) 'Organizational learning: What is new?', in M.A. Rahim, R.T. Golembiewski and L.E. Pate (eds), *Current Topics in Management*, Vol. 2. Greenwich, CT: JAI Press, pp. 11–25.

Schein, E.H. (1999) *Process Consultation Revisited: Building the Helping Relationship*. Reading, MA: Addison-Wesley.

Schein, E.H. (2003) *DEC is Dead, Long Live DEC*. San Francisco, CA: Berrett-Koehler.

Schein, E.H. (2008) 'Clinical inquiry/research', in P. Reason and H. Bradbury (eds), *The SAGE Handbook of Action Research* (2nd edn). London: Sage, pp. 267–279.

Schein, E.H. (2009) *Helping*. San Francisco, CA: Berrett-Koehler.

Schein, E.H. (2010) *Organizational Culture and Leadership* (4th edn). San Francisco, CA: Jossey-Bass.

Schein, E.H. (2010[1989]) 'Organization development: Science, technology or philosophy', in D. Coghlan and A.B. Shani (eds), *Fundamentals of Organization Development*, Vol. 1. London: Sage, pp. 91–100.

Schein, E.H. (2013) *Humble Inquiry*. San Francisco, CA: Berrett-Koehler.

Schon, D. (1983) *The Reflective Practitioner*. New York: Basic Books.

Schon, D.A. (2004)[1995] 'Knowing-in-action: The new scholarship requires a new epistemology', in B. Cooke and J. Wolfram-Cox (eds) *Fundamentals of Action Research*, (Vol. III, pp. 377–394). Sage: London.

Schutz, W. (1994) *The Human Element*. San Francisco, CA: Jossey-Bass.

Senge, P. (1990) *The Fifth Discipline*. New York: Doubleday.

Senge, P., Roberts, C., Ross, R., Smyth, B. and Kleiner, A. (1994) *The Fifth Discipline Fieldbook*. London: Nicholas Brealey.

Shani, A.B. (Rami) and Docherty, P. (2003) *Learning by Design: Building Sustainable Organizations*. Oxford: Blackwell.

Shani, A.B. (Rami) and Docherty, P. (2008) Learning by design: Key mechanisms in organization development. In T. Cummings, (ed.) *Handbook of Organization Development*, Thousand Oaks, CA: Sage, pp. 499–518.

Shani, A.B. and Pasmore W.A. (2010[1985]) 'Organization inquiry: Towards a new model of the action research process', in D. Coghlan and A.B. Shani (eds), *Fundamentals of Organization Development*, Vol. 1. London: SAGE, pp. 249–260.

Shani, A.B., Coghlan, D. and Cirella, S. (2012) 'Action research and collaborative management research: More than meets the eye?', *International Journal of Action Research*, 8 (1): 45–67.

Shani, A.B., David, A. and Willson, C. (2004) 'Collaborative research: Alternative roadmaps', in N. Adler, A.B. Shani and A. Styhre (eds), *Collaborative Research in Organizations*. Thousand Oaks, CA: Sage, pp. 83–100.

Shani, A.B., Mohrman, S.A., Pasmore, W., Stymne, B. and Adler, N. (eds) (2008) *Handbook of Collaborative Management Research*. Thousand Oaks, CA: Sage.

Shepard, H. (1997) 'Rules of thumb for change agents', in D. Van Eynde, J. Hoy and D.C. Van Eynde (eds), *Organization Development Classics*. San Francisco, CA: Jossey-Bass, pp. 191–190.

Shotter, J. (2003) 'Wittgenstein's philosophy and action research', *Concepts and Transformation*, 8 (1): 295–301.

Shotter, J. (2007) 'With what kind of science should action research be contrasted?', *International Journal of Action Research*, 3 (1+2): 67–92.

Smyth, A. and Holian, R. (2008) 'Critical issues in research from within organisations', in P. Sikes and A. Potts (eds), *Researching Education from the Inside*. Abingdon: Routledge, pp. 33–48.

Soh, K., Davidson, P., Leslie, G. and Rahman, A.B.A. (2011) 'Action research studies in the intensive care setting: A systematic review', *International Journal of Nursing Studies*, 48 (2): 258–268.

Somekh, S. (2006) *Action Research: A Methodology for Change and Development*. Maidenhead: Open University Press.

Stephens, J., Barton, J. and Haslett, T. (2009) 'Action research: Its history and relationship to scientific methodology', *Systemic Practice and Action Research*, 22: 463–474.

Stringer, E.T. (2013) *Action Research: A Handbook for Practitioners* (4th edn). Thousand Oaks, CA: Sage.

Susman, G. and Evered, R. (1978) 'An assessment of the scientific merits of action research', *Administrative Science Quarterly*, 23 (4): 582–603.

Taylor, S., Rudolph, J. and Foldy, E. (2008) 'Teaching reflective practice in the action science/action inquiry tradition: Key stages, concepts and practice', in P. Reason and H. Bradbury (eds), *The SAGE Handbook of Action Research* (2nd edn). London: SAGE, pp. 656–668.

Torbert, W.R. (1991) *The Power of Balance*. Thousand, Oaks, CA: SAGE.

Torbert, W.R. and Associates (2004) *Action Inquiry*. San Francisco, CA: Berrett-Koehler.

Torbert, W.R. and Taylor, S. (2008) 'Action inquiry: Interweaving multiple qualities of attention for timely action', in P. Reason and H. Bradbury (eds), *The SAGE Handbook of Action Research* (2nd edn). London: SAGE, pp. 239–251.

Ury, W. (1991) *Getting Past No*. London: Business Books.

van der Meulen, E. (2011) 'Participatory and action-oriented dissertations: The challenges and importance of community engaged graduate research', *The Qualitative Report*, 16 (5): 1291–1303.

Van Maanen, J. (1979) 'The self, the situation and the rules of interpersonal relations', in W. Bennis, J. Van Maanen, E.H. Schein and F.I. Steele, *Essays in Interpersonal Dynamics*, Homewood, IL: Dorsey Press, pp. 43–101.

Walker, B. and Haslett, T. (2002) 'Action research in management: Ethical dilemmas', *Systemic Practice and Action Research*, 15 (6): 523–533.

Wasserman, I.C. and Kram, K.E. (2009) 'Metaphors of identity and professional practice: Enacting the scholar-practitioner role: An exploration of narratives', *Journal of Applied Behavioral Science*, 45 (1): 12–38.

Weisbord, M.R. (1988) 'Towards a new practice theory of OD: Notes on snapshooting and moviemaking', in W.A. Pasmore and R.W. Woodman (eds), *Research in Organizational Change and Development*, Vol. 2. Greenwich, CT. JAI Press, pp. 59–96.

Weisbord, M.R. (2012) *Productive Workplaces* (4th edn). San Francisco, CA: Jossey-Bass.

Wheelan, S.A. (2012) *Creating Effective Teams* (4th edn). Thousand, Oaks, CA: Sage.

White, L.P. and Wooten, K.C. (1986) *Professional Ethics and Practice in Organization Development*. New York: Praeger.

Wicks, P.G. and Reason, P. (2009) 'Initiating action research: Challenges and paradoxes of opening communicative space', *Action Research*, 7 (3): 243–262.

Williams, B. and Hummelbrunner, R. (2011) *Systems Concepts in Action*. Stanford, CA: Stanford University Press.

Williamson, G. and Bellman, L. (2012) *Action Research in Nursing and Healthcare*. London: Sage.

Williamson, G.R. and Prosser, S. (2002) 'Action research: Politics, ethics and participation', *Journal of Advanced Nursing*, 40 (5): 587–593.

Williander, M. and Styhre, A. (2006) 'Going green from the inside: Insider action research at the Volvo Car Corporation', *Systemic Practice and Action Research*, 19: 239–252.

Winter, R. (1989) *Learning from Experience: Principle and Practice in Action Research*. London: Falmer Press.

Young, M. (1991) *An Inside Job*. Oxford: Clarendon Press.

Zuber-Skerritt, O. and Fletcher, M. (2007) 'The quality of an action research thesis in the social sciences', *Quality Assurance in Education*, 15 (4): 413–436.

Zuber-Skerritt, O. and Perry, C. (2002) 'Action research within organizations and university thesis writing', *The Learning Organization*, 9 (4): 171–179.

Author Index

Subject Index